MAKING BETTER PLACES:
URBAN DESIGN NOW

MAKING BETTER PLACES: URBAN DESIGN NOW

edited by

Richard Hayward

Sue McGlynn

Butterworth Architecture
An imprint of Butterworth-Heinemann Ltd
Linacre House, Jordan Hill, Oxford OX2 8DP

    A member of the Reed Elsevier group

OXFORD   LONDON   BOSTON
MUNICH   NEW DELHI   SINGAPORE   SYDNEY
TOKYO   TORONTO   WELLINGTON

First published 1993

British Library Cataloguing in Publication Data
A catalogue record for this book is available from the British Library

ISBN 0 7506 0536 7

Library of Congress Cataloguing in Publication Data
A catalogue record for this book is available from the Library of Congress

Typeset by Footnote Graphics, Warminster, Wilts
Printed and bound in Great Britain

CONTENTS

Contents

JOINT CENTRE FOR URBAN DESIGN

The Joint Centre for Urban Design this year celebrates 21 active years at the forefront of urban design education.

The JCUD was established by the Oxford Schools of Architecture and Planning and continues to benefit from the daily dialogue between the architects, planners and those from related disciplines who teach at Oxford Brookes University. Students and staff of the Joint Centre have always come from a wide range of ethnic and professional backgrounds, and have gone on to practice and teach across the world.

The JCUD is recognised as a centre of excellence and offers full and part-time Diploma/MA courses, research programmes for MPhil and PhD degrees and short courses for continuing professional development. In addition the Centre offers a range of research and consultancy services.

THE AUTHORS

ALAN ALCOCK one of the authors of *Responsive Environments*, currently co-ordinates the part-time course. Alan has particular interest in issues of aesthetics and representation in architecture and urban design.

IAN BENTLEY is one of the authors of *Responsive Environments*, a graduate of the Joint Centre and is currently Co-Chair. Ian maintains a broad involvement with teaching, research and practice, particularly in the area of urban regeneration.

GEORGIA BUTINA is currently Co-Chair and research co-ordinator of the Joint Centre. Georgia also teaches in the school of Planning and with Ian Bentley leads the Urban Regeneration Unit.

BRIAN GOODEY is a past chair of the Joint Centre and is a leading figure in research and teaching in the JCUD and the School of Planning. Brian has practised and published extensively in the areas of interpretation, tourism and landscape planning.

BARBARA HAMMOND is a graduate of the Joint Centre and after working for the London Docklands Development Corporation now teaches urban design at Cheltenham and Gloucester College of Higher Education.

RICHARD HAYWARD is a past chair of the Joint Centre and is Deputy Head (Academic) of the School of Architecture. Together with Ivor Samuels he is currently developing a programme in Town Centre Management.

JOE HOLYOAK is a graduate of the Joint Centre and is currently an External Examiner for the courses. He teaches at the University of Central England and has a practice in Birmingham.

SUE McGLYNN is a graduate of the Joint Centre. One of the authors of *Responsive Environments* she teaches in the JCUD and the School of Planning and has extensive experience in urban design briefing which she is currently developing in the area of urban coding.

PAUL MURRAIN is a graduate of the Joint Centre and one of the authors of *Responsive Environments*. He recently left David Lock Associates to practice on his own account. In recent years Paul has worked extensively in the UK, USA and Australia.

JOHN PUNTER was until recently an External Examiner at the Joint Centre. He has just moved from teaching at Reading University to take up a chair at the University of Strathclyde. John has published extensively in the area of design guidance, development control and planning and urban design education.

ALAN REEVE is a recent graduate of the Joint Centre and is currently engaged in research into the design of places for leisure consumption and teaching in the School of Planning.

IVOR SAMUELS is a past chair of the Joint Centre and is currently chair of the Built Resource Studies Course. Ivor practices and teaches internationally and is developing the application of urban coding in France.

ROGER SIMMONDS is a past chair of the Joint Centre and teaches in the JCUD and the School of Planning. Roger also teaches and researches regularly in the USA.

GRAHAM SMITH is a graduate of the Joint Centre and one of the authors of *Responsive Environments*. He teaches in the School of Architecture and the JCUD and has been actively developing research into traffic calming which he started ten years ago for his Masters thesis.

ACKNOWLEDGEMENTS

Our particular thanks to: Adrian Bullock for guiding us through the entire design, editorial and production process; Elaine Hermon for turning endless drafts into text, ably supported as ever by Linda New who keeps us all on the right track! The editors thank the authors for their forbearance and good humour, and Alan Alcock and Paul Murrain for their help with the illustrations. We must also thank the staff of Butterworth Heinemann for their enthusiasm for the project, and Mike Ersser of **Footnote Graphics** for bringing it to print.

Our thanks also to all our colleagues (students and staff) at Oxford Brookes University who have kept us going with comments, information, advice and criticism.

In addition, the Joint Centre for Urban Design wishes to thank David Wyatt of Basil Wyatt and Sons Ltd, Oxford for their generous support for this project.

INTRODUCTION

For many years the Joint Centre for Urban Design has worked with the broad intention of making better places — better places than those otherwise produced by the modern development industry — and better places for everybody.

Much of the argument that has sustained this approach has been most clearly articulated in the book *Responsive Environments* (Bentley *et al.*, 1985). Much of this argument is based on the idea that only one specific configuration of urban development provides support for the widest range of activities. This notion of urban form is sustained by a potentially safe public realm which defines clear boundaries with the private realm. At its simplest: gridded streets and perimeter buildings designed to support a wide mix of uses.

Responsive Environments has been a hugely successful book. A lively critique of the broad concepts and the detail of the propositions contained within it has continued both publicly and within the Centre. Much of this has focused on assertion and counter-assertion about how essentially monotonous or rich and exciting such development may be; about how traditional or stultifying the approach may be; about how appropriate the approach is for modern traffic requirements; about how realistically such an approach may satisfy the demands of the market; about how such an approach can be sustained in the face of an international tide of urban dispersal.

Much of this volume *inter alia* answers these challenges. The authors of *Responsive Environments* have naturally developed their own thinking in the intervening years and their colleagues represented here continue to support, challenge and extend these ideas both with their own critique and the focus of their own particular interests. Many colleagues were or are students at the Joint Centre and their investment in the ideas presented here has been substantial.

As urban designers most of us perceive that we have a powerful vested interest in concepts of place, supported by local groups who can find and wield adequate power and resources to keep us in business. By simple extension, we have a similar interest in helping such groups to identify and marshal those powers and resources. In so doing, we subscribe to ideas of local legitimacy. To a greater or lesser extent we challenge other ideas of power and legitimacy — from the priorities of established local democracy to those of central government agencies and the dominant powers of the market economy. So what? At least we should recognise the place in the radical Utopian tradition of what we are doing, and we should avoid complacency with our real achievements as enablers in a context that moves ever more powerfully in other directions.

Urban design at the Joint Centre has long allied itself with democracy and that even more dubious quality of life: pluralism. Where the latter sits in relation to hegemony, and how urban interest groups might create or recreate places to support such living virtues where they have all but withered or been constrained by other interests, is a matter we will have to deal with.

For those able to read the indications, the built environment has always given concrete manifestation to power structures that have driven its development. We commonly refer to simple manifestations: the dominance of the gothic cathedral above the huddle of the temporal city; the radiating militaristic *enfilades* of the baroque city. Yet the reality of most urban environments is naturally a more subtle palimpsest of power built, reformed and re-built. Daunton (1984) and others have shown how the prevailing orthodoxy has ousted unwelcome heterodoxies from urban places: the warrens of the nineteenth century poor, so graphically fictionalised by Disraeli and Dickens which are remotely like the *barriadas* and squatter settlements of the twentieth century developing world, with their sub-culture of the court, alley and street, were soon swept away by the municipal grid-irons of health and social security. The places of the people, whether residential, industrial, commercial, or places of public assembly, have thus ever been controlled for the public good or otherwise, according to the will of the prevailing power hierarchies.

Despite this, communities have long maintained a healthy *entente* with the emissaries of more central power. As described by Weber (1958) and more poignantly for the urban designer, by Jacobs (1961), mixed communities of interest bound by propinquity have put place and the exchanges of the daily and yearly round above mere power legislation.

We hope that the chapters that follow raise as many questions as they answer. Written by those of us who currently have some passing tenure in the Joint Centre, they are offered to all of those with an interest in urban design, but particularly to those who over the last twenty-one years have been here and formed ideas that have gone out across the world to be restated, renegotiated and reformed.

SECTION ONE
PROCESSES AND PRODUCTS: PRACTICES AND THEORIES

The focus of primary urban design intervention and the knowledge and skills required continue to be hotly debated in practice and education. Most urban designers are unashamed pragmatists, although over the years, a substantial body of theory has been marshalled for the cause. McGlynn gives an overview of the emergence of urban design and raises questions about its legitimacy as a practical discipline and the potential gap between its rhetoric and the ability to deliver. John Punter has made earlier significant contributions to challenge us all about what exactly it is we expect to do and how we believe we can achieve it. Here he makes a thoughtful and finely judged case for the necessary skills of urban designers in the role of development controller.

Most of us subscribe in public to the rhetoric of interdisciplinary teamwork and public participation in the urban design process. In two contributions Hayward argues that by structuring unequivocal arguments in the form of 'rationales' we may facilitate involvement of the widest community of interests. The case is then made that similar objectives may be served using existing urban 'tissues' to negotiate new development proposals.

Reeve and Biddulph challenge us and directly confront the issues of meaning and value. It is fitting that Alcock who has tussled with the theoretical and practical issues of aesthetics in urban design should conclude this section with a reasoned plea that we re-socialise aesthetics.

Sue McGlynn

REVIEWING THE RHETORIC

Introduction

After a period of 25 years it seems reasonable to ask, not the usual question, 'what is urban design?', but the more fundamental ones 'can we urban design at all?' and, if so, 'when, where and how can we urban design?' These are difficult questions to answer, and are particularly troublesome for a group of people who do not have the planning profession's legislative or political legitimacy to fall back on, or the clear and financially powerful client base of architecture. In such a short chapter I cannot hope to answer these questions, but instead offer some exploratory thoughts and working propositions to be debated and developed elsewhere.

In addressing these questions, this chapter identifies two gaps: in the first place, the gap between the existing environmental disciplines which was a major impetus for the emergence of urban design; and second, the gap between the rhetoric and practical achievements of urban design which now calls into question the legitimacy of our activities.

The Emergence of Urban Design in Britain

The emergence of urban design in the 1960s coincided with two interconnected developments. First, it had become apparent that as the existing environmental disciplines – particularly architecture and planning – had become professions with increasingly specialised and protected areas of activity, a gap had opened up between their concerns.

Architecture's clear concern was with the design and production of a building or buildings within a defined site. Planning took responsibility for the general disposition of land uses through policy formulation and plan making and for the detailed and necessarily piecemeal regulation of individual building projects through the operation of the development control system. As these professional boundaries hardened and were institutionalised it became clear that the gap was the public realm itself – the void between buildings, the streets and spaces which constitute our everyday experience of urban places.

In addition to the recognition of this gap, the second main impetus for the emergence of urban design as an activity was the crisis of confidence in architecture and planning. As people had lived in and experienced the simplified, fragmented and frequently alienating forms of post-war urban development, they began to challenge the values and assumptions of architects and planners and to distrust their ability to improve upon the spatial and physical forms of pre-modernist urbanism. This challenge came not only from outside the existing professions but also from within them as some designers began to lose confidence in the products of their modernist ideologies. This disaffection with the established disciplines is reflected in the professional backgrounds of urban designers to this day – we are usually architects, planners and landscape architects who have defected.

By the late 1960s a diverse group of people had started to respond to these two perceived gaps and to define an area of activity which gradually came to be called urban design. Although some of the founding texts of urban design had already been published by the early 1960s, with the writings of Jane Jacobs (1961) being the most significant contribution, they tended to be empirical rather than theoretical. This tendency has continued and, in common with most of the other environmental disciplines, urban design has been slow to develop theoretical constructs to underpin its activities. The work of Bill Hillier (1984) and his research team over the past 20 years provides a notable exception to this generalisation. Even as they defected therefore, the new urban designers had to fall back on the working practices of the old disciplines of architecture and planning in particular.

From planning, urban design adopted a concern with the social, economic and political processes of urban development and a commitment to public participation. In practice, in urban design as in planning, this has all too often been interpreted as consultation rather than a genuinely participatory process involving a wide range of user and other interest groups. In terms of techniques, the use of briefing documents to guide future development proposals is the most obvious legacy from planning practice.

The legacy from architecture has perhaps had a more profound effect on the practice of urban design, not least because, as opposed to planning, it is a design-based discipline and many of the early practitioners were architects who saw urban design as big architecture. Jarvis in his article *Urban Environments as Visual Art or as Social Settings* (1980) makes a distinction between 'the artistic tradition in urban design' and 'the social usage' approach to urban design. It is this artistic design tradition, inherited primarily from architecture, which has had such a fundamental effect on the ways urban designers think about, represent and operate in the built environment.

First this tradition is chiefly concerned with 'product' — building form and appearance — rather than spatial configuration or process. The architectural design tradition values individuality and architects gain their professional reputations and peer group status through the originality of their products. Furthermore, urban design has adopted from architecture an almost identical set of representational media; plans, sections, axonometrics, measured perspective drawings and models, although at different scales. Whilst some means of representing design proposals is obviously necessary it is highly debatable whether these conventional methods facilitate the involvement of everyday users in the design process

and may, subconsciously at least, be used to preserve expert knowledge rather than demystify it.

There is a further strand of influence on the working methods of urban designers and this comes from the work of the urban morphologists and urban geographers. The accumulation of empirical work in this field by Hoskins, Conzen, Whitehand and many others in this country alone has provided a systematic means of analysis and exploration of the pattern and process of urban development. Although these techniques are an accepted part of design practice in Europe, they have been far less influential in this country (Samuels, 1990). This is further evidence for the dominance of the 'artistic tradition' which tends to reject rigorous or systematic analysis of urban processes in favour of originality, creativity and prototypical forms.

The Rhetoric of Urban Design

Despite much inspired writing about the social use of space, urban design in practice has done little to develop this approach. In the absence of any strong theoretical frame of reference urban designers have no easy way of translating the empirical evidence from the 'social usage' tradition into operational rules of thumb and have instead relied heavily on the working methods and concerns of the artistic design tradition. What urban design has done instead, and perhaps even to mask the apolitical nature of this tradition, has been to develop a non-expert vocabulary. John Punter's matrix in his article *The Ten Commandments of Architecture and Urban Design* (1990) gives some evidence of the gradual emergence and definition of this vocabulary (*Figure 1*).

Unfortunately, when these same people come to put pen to paper the product often reveals how little common meaning there is behind this widely used and accepted vocabulary. In place of rigorous theoretical and methodological development, it would appear that, instead, a rather sophisticated rhetoric has emerged. I use the word rhetoric in its most literal definition taken from *The Oxford English Dictionary* as the 'art of persuasive or impressive speaking or writing; language designed to persuade or impress (often with the implication of its insincerity, exaggeration, etc.).' This may seem a rather harsh criticism, but any group of people who repeatedly use words such as 'choice', 'empowerment', 'democratic process', 'democratic settings' must demonstrate that they can deliver, or at least be able to identify what must be done and by whom in order to deliver.

As we pointed out in the introduction to *Responsive Environments* (Bentley *et al.*, 1985) social consciences and good intentions are not enough – they have to be translated into physical form. We tried to suggest in the book one way in which this might be possible, but I think the introduction, (not the remainder of the text) does illustrate this very problem. '. . . the built environment should provide its users with an essentially democratic setting, enriching their opportunities by maximising the degree of *choice* available to them' (p. 9).

Choice is, of itself, a quality of dubious virtue. Choice, translated as the freedom to consume, is central to the dogma of capitalism. One of the strongest themes of the urban design literature of the last 30 years is the decline of the public realm. This decline is in large part to do with the operation of the political economy of the capitalist city, which has the imperative of maximising personal choice in order to achieve maximum personal consumption – often at the expense of the collective good.

We live in a culture where those who have economic power can make choices; they can live where they like, work where they like, travel when, where and how they like and play where they like. With this ability to exercise such choice, the desired variety of activities and opportunities can be reached and used and the nature of urban form becomes of little relevance. This is, however, an untenable position for urban design which should seek, with what influence it has, to address issues of social and economic equality through the means it has at its disposal – the configuration of urban places.

I am not making an argument here against individual empowerment in as many areas of life as possible, but I am issuing a warning against the acceptance of 'choice' *per se* as a rationale for urban design practice. The design of a place cannot directly confer choice.

One's ability to take advantage of 'choice' depends on a number of factors, economic power being the most obvious. Other factors within our democratic political system, such as social class and education,

influence how aware one is of the opportunities available and how to get the best out of the system; cultural and sub-cultural factors affect the individual and group perception of the built environment, its meanings and ways in which it can be used. Age, gender and ability affect independence of movement and therefore choice. On top of all these there are the unknowable (in terms of any practical use for urban designers) effects of individual character, personality and perception. The ability to exercise choice is therefore an intricate combination of all of these things.

Urban design must therefore be wary of claiming too much for its activities. The matrix discussed in the next section illustrates the lack of real power of urban design in relation to many of the other actors in the development process. What is more realistic and is more likely to lead to effective urban design is a 'bottom line' approach. That is, urban designers must always try to *avoid the restriction of choice* for the eventual users of a place.

This has at least two dimensions. First, we must be particularly careful to avoid the restriction of choice for those individuals and groups with less power to exercise in the social and economic processes which lead to development. The second dimension is the temporal one. The built environment lasts a long time, particularly at the level of street systems and buildings, and urban design must work to ensure that future options are not compromised by present day developments. This is where the concerns of sustainability mesh so well with those of urban design.

Making a 'Powergram' for Urban Design

When trying to address the question, 'can we urban design at all?' it is necessary to set the role of the urban designer alongside the other actors in the development process. Unfortunately, the crisis of confidence in and within the professions has been polarized into an unproductive apportionment of blame between architects and planners. It is also misleading as it has diverted attention from the roles of the more powerful actors in the process of urban development – the landowners, funders,

	Kevin Lynch 1982	Jane Jacobs 1961	Bentley Alcock McGlynn Murrain Smith 1985	Tibbalds 1988	HRH The Prince of Wales 1989	Holyoak 1985	Urban Design Group 1987	Wates 1988	Buchanan 1988
1.	vitality (include biological and ecological)	appropriate activity before visual order	'responsive environments'	places before buildings	the place		responsive forms	urban environment in broadest sense	place making public realm outdoor rooms
2.	(see sense)		visual appropriateness	respect history	harmony and context	(i) retain the best (ii) respect street line			dialogue with context and history: re-contain street
3.	(see fit)	mixed use mixed age mixed rent concentration	variety	encourage mixed uses		more than one use	mixed uses		
4.	(see vitality)	the street	human scale	scale enclosure	enclosure in scale with context				
5.	access	permeability (short blocks)	permeability	encourage pedestrian permeability			public access		public space and movement systems
6.	control	social mix and consultation	personalisation	social mix and consultation	community	'acceptable' personalisation	consultation	individual responsibility professional enablers local action and control integrating experience optimising resources envt. education	
7.	sense (clarity with which it can be perceived)		legibility	legibility	hierarchy	visual accessibility reflect uses			(i) respect conventions (ii) articulate meanings (iii) connect inside and out
8.	fit (adaptability)	robust spaces	robustness and adaptability						
9.	(see efficiency)	gradual not cataclysmic money		small scale change					
10.		activity richness	richness	visual delight	materials and decoration	'visible' construction integral ornament	stimulating		natural, rich materials good weathering decoration
	two meta criteria efficiency (relative cost) justice (social equity)	automobile attrition surveillance (safety)			signs and lights		protection security comfort shelter		

Figure 1. The vocabulary of urban design. (Punter, 1990)

ACTORS.	SUPPLIERS.		PRODUCERS.					CONSUMERS
ELEMENTS OF THE BUILT ENVIRONMENT.	LAND OWNER	FUNDER	DEVELOPER	LOCAL AUTHORITY		ARCHITECTS	URBAN DESIGNERS	EVERYDAY USERS.
				Planners	Highway Engineers.			
STREET PATTERN	–	–	○	○	●	–	○	○
BLOCKS	–	–	–	–	–	–	○	–
PLOTS - subdivision or Amalgamation.	●	●	●	○ (in U.K.)	–	–	○	–
LAND/BUILDING USE	●	●	●	●	⊕	○	○	○
BUILDING FORM · Height/Mass.	–	●	●	●	–	⊕	○	○
· Orientation to Public space.	–	–	○	⊕	–	–	○	○
· Elevations.	–	○	○	●	–	⊕	○	○
· Elements of construction (details/materials)	–	○	●	⊕	–	⊕	○	○

KEY: ● POWER - either to initiate or control.
⊕ RESPONSIBILITY - legislative or contractual.
○ INTEREST/INFLUENCE - by argument or participation only.
– No obvious interest.

Figure 2. A 'powergram' for urban design. (Drawn by Peter Boyle)

central and local government and development agencies.

The matrix, which I have called a 'powergram', (*Figure 2*), attempts to compress into a single diagram a representation – albeit crude – of the power relations between actors. (Obviously, these power relations are to a large extent determined by the political and economic system within which they operate.) Even more ambitiously, the powergram is then used as a tool for examining the roles and potential effectiveness of urban design in the development process.

Down one side of the matrix are listed the physical components of the built environment which are manipulated, combined, traded and negotiated to produce spatial arrangements and three-dimensional forms. They are essentially the analytical categories used by urban morphologists: streets, blocks, plots, and building forms. I have added building uses to this list as they are, for different reasons, of key concern to many of the actors in the development process, and are critical to the economic performance of urban land.

Along the other axis are set the major actors in the process, subdivided into the 'suppliers' of commodities, such as land and capital; the 'producers', from developers through to local government, the professional groups and urban designers; and lastly the 'consumers', who are the users – that is, all of us, even if we also appear in another category.

The diagram differentiates levels or degrees of power – hence its title – and makes distinctions between actors who can exercise *power* to initiate or control development, actors who have a *responsibility* towards some aspect of development, whether this be legal or contractual, and actors who have *interest or influence* and who therefore can only be effective through argumentation, alliance or participation.

There are obviously all sorts of qualifications which ought to be made for this type of diagram – the inclusion of some actors and the exclusion of others, the rationale for the categories used, and so on. It can undoubtedly be improved upon, but what it does show quite clearly is the huge potential to disadvantage the 'user' group within the development process. As one would expect, the real power in the system lies on the left half of the matrix – with the landowners, funders and developers whether they be private, public or quasi-public. Along with plan-

ners, architects and engineers (landscape architects didn't make it onto the matrix!) urban designers inhabit the rather ambiguous middle ground. They have a strong interest in the development process and some active influence, but much less power to affect the shape of the built environment than many people think – Prince Charles and many professionals included. However, urban designers are in an apparently weaker position than the professional groups who have a formal responsibility which guarantees their representation in the process. In this respect, they are in an even worse position than the user group who usually, at local level, are formally invited to comment on development applications at a range of scales.

Developing the Legitimacy of Urban Design

How, then does the powergram help to define the legitimacy of urban design activity and so go some way towards answering the questions posed at the start of this chapter?

First, the very act of making a matrix such as this places urban design into a political rather than professional frame of reference which forces us to acknowledge the real conflict of values between actors in the development process.

Second, it identifies that urban designers, alone among the 'middle ground' actors, have the widest range of concerns and interests at all scales of urban development. Through its writings and practice over the past 25–30 years urban design has been able to marshal a strong and convincing case for embracing this wide range of elements and scales and demonstrated how their interaction affects the performance of the public realm for everyday users. The need to use this body of knowledge and make it explicit through the form of design rationales is the subject of Hayward's chapter in this section, 'Rationales and the Practice of Everyday Urban Design'. The ability to make clear explanations of design intentions and proposals must be an essential part of urban design practice as argumentation is one of the few means by which we may gain influence in the development process.

Third, the powergram illustrates that urban

designers, of all other actors represented, have the closest congruence of interest with those of the user group. This, at last, gives some basis for the populist rhetoric of urban design. It is clear that it is in this alliance of interest that the legitimacy of urban design practice must rest. However, in order to get beyond the rhetoric of enabling, empowering, etc., urban designers must make more effort to open up the design process to everyday users. One of the most pressing research tasks, therefore, is the development of methods and techniques which will allow a more exploratory and interactive debate about these shared interests to take place before, during and after the development of design proposals. Johan Gerrie's unpublished MA thesis (1988) in the JCUD provides an excellent evaluation of current methods used in participatory exercises and provides evidence from the observation of case studies that very crude, hands-on models, visits to existing places and slide presentations, for instance, are far more effective than the more conventional methods of representation discussed earlier.

Urban designers have gained most public and peer group attention when working with developers on large urban projects. This more traditional alliance is obviously the easiest way of increasing the urban designer's influence in the development process and it is from this source that most of the funding for urban design activity comes. Some good results have been achieved through this power by association, particularly by urban designers who have been able to win over the hearts and minds of developers through argumentation and by making clear and explicit explanations of design aims.

There is clearly a risk that urban designers may increase the potential for disadvantage of user groups by taking on the interests of those who are already powerful rather than the values of those who are not. In order to avoid this urban designers must stress the political significance of their congruence of interest with the user groups in the local development process. Urban designers must also take a proactive role in gaining financial and political support for participatory exercises and design *charrettes* from local and central government and developers themselves.

Presuming that participatory techniques can be improved, there are two commonly expressed scepticisms about their use. The first is that the built environment lasts a long time and that even the best

of participatory exercises in design can only benefit the first-off users of a place. There is also a more fundamental objection to the assumed relationship between process and product, here expressed by Paul Murrain in a paper given at a recent RIBA Colloquium (1993) 'Advancing Urban Design':

. . . a good deal of 'democratic' town form has been designed and/or managed by undemocratic political regimes throughout history. More recently and sadly, very 'undemocratic', isolationist town form has been designed, built and managed by people who would genuinely claim to be interactive and essentially democratic in their own political persuasions'.

To get around this problem in participatory exercises urban designers must encourage the use of tried and tested types and tissues which have proved their worth over time. They must move away from the preference for experiment and prototypical design solutions which are so prevalent in the design tradition. This implies also a refocusing of design effort away from building form and block configuration towards what Bill Hillier (1992) has called 'the architecture of the urban grid'. It is in the making of special places through the design of ordinary things that urban design can escape the attention seeking, award winning set piece mentality which dominates much professional design activity, and find some real legitimacy for its activities.

Conclusions

In the absence of any legal, political, contractual or institutional legitimacy what, then, can urban design achieve? My 'bottom line' working definition would be that urban designers must concern themselves with *the making of the physical world so as not to disadvantage first-off and future users*. Social and political theorists will tell us that this is impossible — the placing of a physical object such as a building implies an allocation of resources which will benefit some at the expense of others. However, within the current framework, which is unlikely to change in the foreseeable future, urban designers can do little about the overall allocation of resources. What they can and must do is to ensure, as far as possible, where finite resources are being allocated, that they work through and evaluate the physical implications of that allocation so as not to disadvantage the less powerful and less influential users.

What this means in practice is a willingness to engage in open, exploratory and interactive design processes; it means promoting tried and tested solutions so that we are least likely to disadvantage unknown future users; and, as we are reminded in Murrain's chapter 'Urban Expansion: Look Back and Learn', it also means challenging urban forms which are promoted by the development industry, but which clearly disadvantage particular groups such as 'the transport poor.' (Ravetz, 1980).

This simple reversal from 'maximising choice' to 'minimising disadvantage' is, I believe, an important reorientation of the focus of urban design practice. It moves away from the rather grandiose claims of much urban design rhetoric and leads more strongly towards an evaluative process. It requires the working through of the implications of location and configuration for the widest possible group of users in the making of better places.

John Punter

DEVELOPING DESIGN SKILLS FOR DEVELOPMENT CONTROLLERS

Introduction

Development control demands many skills. The managerial and communication skills of time management, administrative efficiency, interpersonal communication and negotiation have to be combined with knowledge of the legal and policy context, the techniques of financial appraisal, knowledge of market forces as well as an awareness of urban processes and morphology, environmental and architectural quality. The latter may be encapsulated as design awareness and it is often the area in which planners feel least competent and where their efforts seem least appreciated.

This chapter offers some suggestions as to how planners in practice (and those undergoing training) can develop their design skills and awareness. It suggests that development controllers need to develop visualisation skills; techniques for site and place analysis for development briefing; an ability to analyse and articulate both public and professional values and to interrogate their own preferences; an awareness of architectural heritage, values and different styles of architectural criticism; and an awareness of the value of precedent and principles, the one derived largely from travel, the other from reading. It suggests that controllers need to structure and systematise their learning and experience and to develop a programme of self-education, in the absence of sufficient opportunities for formal training. These ideas are explored against a background of architectural and development industry hostility, central government agnosticism, a declining design skill base in control, limited time, energy and resources in planning departments, and now a property industry,

and especially an architectural profession, in the depths of a recession.

Design Skills – Architects', Planners' and Public Views

Successive leaders of the architectural profession like Lyons, Luder, Manser and Hutchinson have often ridiculed planners' design skills while government circulars have simultaneously insisted that design judgement is largely subjective, and that architects have special competence in this area. Central government advice has constantly warned planners against design control except in environmentally sensitive areas, and it has never wholeheartedly endorsed design guidance although it has gradually become more positive about proactive advice in statutory documents. Even then the implication is that design is largely a matter for the developer and her/his architect/client and the planner should not 'interfere' with details. So while some architects belittle planners' skills and central government discourages their application, most development controllers retain a particular interest in the evolution and quality of their built environment (it is often the reason why they entered the profession in the first place). Furthermore they know that their political masters, local councillors and the public they serve, are deeply interested in development control outcomes and the quality of environment that each produces, because this directly impacts upon their lives. They know that 'design' is intrinsically important but that it often carries much more significance serving as a focus or symbol for a sense of social invasion, economic powerlessness, environmental degradation and unwelcome change. For these reasons, quite apart from a general lack of visual literacy or design awareness amongst laypeople, it is often very difficult to articulate design criticism and advice and to resolve design conflicts, even where planners possess design skills.

The Shortage of Design Skills

There has always been a shortage of design skills in development control in Britain. The Goss Report noted it as long ago as 1965, while recent surveys of the number of architect-planners in planning departments indicate a precipitous fall from 40% in 1965 to 10% in 1986, with less than 3% of those entering the profession today being architects. Restraints on local authority budgets and booming private consultancies led to a haemorrhage of talent in the 1980s, and some of the most able design teams were disbanded in the interests of economy and sometimes politics (e.g. London Borough of Camden). Conservation officers at county, district and national (English Heritage) level have often provided important inputs of design skills, but usually only where conservation areas or listed buildings are affected, although they have often been authors of key design guidance (e.g. Essex Design Guide). However a minority of authorities possess such expertise, while it is rapidly being privatised at county level and reduced within English Heritage itself. Perhaps architect-planner consultancies will become the main source of design expertise for the production of guidance briefs and special studies in the future, but the control function will continue to need a full complement of expertise.

Planning and Design Education

To add to this erosion of skill the teaching of design has been generally down-graded in planning schools. Long hours on the drawing board engaged in site planning are very much a thing of the past in most schools, and many planning graduates have a very limited ability to understand places, assess sites, read plans, visualise forms, and provide positive criticism of development proposals. The ability to analyse succinctly and communicate graphically, the eye and hands skills of the architect-planner which are so necessary to constructive advice, remain the preserve of the few. The Royal Town Planning Institute keeps expanding its core syllabus, and planning courses are continually expanding their range of core and specialism subjects with the result that little time is left to develop design skills and awareness.

Postgraduate urban design courses are meeting some of the needs of practitioners, but funding for the part-time mid career mode is very vulnerable to the endless round of budget cuts. Few 'urban designers' would actively choose a career in development control, even in a recession, because it is perceived wrongly as a negative function with little creativity or sense of achievement. One suspects few urban design schools really encourage such a career path. Most architects share the same prejudice, offering a variant of the time honoured cynical epithet that those who can 'do' and those who cannot do 'teach', or in this case control. There are new courses gradually emerging – the *RTPI Certificate in Development Control Studies* offers modules in Design and Briefing for example – but opportunities for structured part-time learning remain rare. This is one gap that planning and urban design schools might be able to fill.

Visualisation Skills

In an ideal world development controllers would always be able to play a proactive role, able to select sites in need of or ripe for development or redevelopment. They would have time to analyse the site, assess its potential, test various alternatives and outline an optimal or at least a satisfactory design solution. In reality, in the majority of cases, planners are going to find themselves in a reactive situation, facing development proposals that have already been worked up, and trying to find the time and the negotiating power to go back a stage or two in the design process. So visualisation skills, taking two-dimensional drawings and converting them into three-dimensional space, locating and imagining developments in their context and assessing the spatial and environmental experience they will produce is a most important skill. There is a natural tendency to focus upon elevations and to become obsessed with the detail, focusing more on the building envelope than the building's relationship with its surroundings, the spaces it creates, and their utility, and the way in which the building responds to the public realm. It is easy to forget that full elevations are rarely seen, that oblique views are much more typical, and that these will define much of the apparent quality of the building. Artists' impressions, photographs, line drawings and the like can be obtained from the architect on larger schemes, as can models, though without a modelscope or modelscope photographs models can be very misleading. Increasingly computer drawing and graphics will replicate three-dimensional experience and will be able to simulate moving through a development, the effects of light and shade, etc.

Better presented planning applications may help controllers, but they are also a trap for the unwary. Illustrative materials need to be carefully checked for accuracy especially as they are so often prepared by specially commissioned artists without a visit to the site, rather than by the architects themselves. A good design controller may also want to establish a variety of other perspectives in the development and for this may need to produce his/her own sketches, and these can be developed from appropriate prints or slides with practice.

Government circulars warn against dabbling in details but the important thing is to decide which details are significant. Here one needs to establish who will observe the building, from where, and to ensure appropriate levels of richness (see *Responsive Environments*, Chapter 6), particularly in terms of the modelling of the facade, the incidence of shadow, and the use of materials.

Site Analysis and Development Briefing

Analysing the key views of the building requires a thoroughgoing site analysis and full consideration of the proposed development's context. Such an analysis is vital to ensure that the full range of planning considerations are addressed — land form, features worth retaining, context, land use, scale, height, massing, access, car parking, open space provision, landscape, etc. In a proactive planning department such site analysis would not await a detailed planning application but would be conducted as soon as a firm development enquiry was made, or might even be undertaken to promote a development. Design briefing is a critically important skill, but one which has hardly been discussed at all in the planning literature.

Site analysis should reveal the site's potential whether it be existing features worth retention or enhancement, the role of the site in the townscape, its capacity to provide useful facilities or amenities or its ability to create new links in the public realm. Releasing this potential, while fulfilling at least some of the aspirations of the developer or owner, will be the difficult task and one that will require much time for creative design thinking, the generation of different alternatives and the identification of key constraints. It is important for planners to go through the design process so that they understand the real constraints of the site, the repercussions of changing parameters, and the thought processes that the designer/architect has been through, just as it is important for them to understand the costs of changing the design.

The actual approach to development briefing depends upon the site. With small infill sites it may be largely a matter of the elevations and skyline of the scheme, and the problem may be primarily a matter of relating to the architectural context. On larger sites in existing built-up areas the context will not merely be an architectural one but will involve the analysis of vehicle and pedestrian flows into and through the site, the relationship of spaces and buildings, behaviour settings and user requirement, the mix of uses and facilities and how these are juxtaposed, the kind of public realm and landscape created and its safety, comfort, convenience and attractiveness. This will involve significant visual analysis of the townscape variety but the full range of site planning considerations will come into play. On green field sites where there is no obvious context the emphasis should initially be upon the physical/ecological context and the potential for conservation and sustainability in all their forms. Functional efficiency, ecological continuity and how the landscaping will mature may be more important than architecture and building form.

Public Consultation

Observation needs to be supplemented with public consultation. People's perceptions of sites and places, what they notice and what they want to see maintained or changed, are frequently surprising to any systematic or professional observer. There are a variety of ways in which consultation can be undertaken from informal conversation with locals, to interest group consultation on prepared briefs, through to the broadest form of consultation by environmental forums and/or public meetings.

Of course it is often very difficult to get people to articulate what they want to see happen on a particular site, because they lack the confidence and vocabulary to express themselves. Furthermore outside of historic towns and cities or attractive villages it can be difficult to arouse public interest in seemingly 'abstract' design issues. While this might suggest a lack of public interest in design such a view is frequently confounded once development proposals are actually forthcoming. One of the difficulties is that most consultation is undertaken only once an application has been lodged and significant design negotiations have taken place, unless the officer or the authority have the inclination and the energy to consult informally. If key criticisms have not been anticipated significant problems will arise, for the disregard of public comment is likely to lead to councillors intervening late in negotiations, to protests to newspapers, chief executive or politicians, and sometimes to officers' recommendations being overturned. Where this occurs on design grounds the chances of a subsequent loss at appeal, often with costs, rise dramatically.

The new generation of district-wide and unitary development plans will have to address this problem, developing through public (and preferably inter-professional) consultation a set of design policies and a hierarchy of design guidance appropriate to the locality. A sustained dialogue that can isolate the key issues of design control will markedly strengthen the plan's policies and provide a firm foundation for more detailed work in sub-areas or on particular sites. New government advice endorses the inclusion of advice on scale, density, height, layout, landscape and access in development plans and underlines the importance of proper public participation in the setting of these parameters.

It is possible to argue, and some design controllers seem to adopt this perspective, that the main task of control is simply to collate and synthesise public comments into a consensus, and that this is an adequate and appropriate basis on which to proceed. However in important developments there are likely to be significant variations and disagreements between consultees that will require resolution and the exercise of design judgement. The dialectic between professional expertise and public values is one of the most interesting and difficult aspects of design control. The essential conservatism of public taste — a function of the national psyche and disenchantment with the quality of much post-war development — often seriously impedes architectural innovation, although most planners argue (correctly) that the greatest impediment to creativity is a speculative commercial and residential development process and the lack of attention to design of many businesses and householders. While the design controller must express public values and avoid the trap of professional contempt for lay taste (especially evident amongst some architects) she or he needs to see beyond the self-interest that underlies NIMBYism, and the blind prejudice that seeks to prevent any kind of modern design, while being sympathetic to the desire for contextualism in a thoroughgoing functional (land use, movement, activity, public realm, morphology) as well as a visual sense.

Understanding and Articulating One's Own Values

How to develop the necessary design judgement to enable the controller to confidently tackle such issues is the key question. But the place to begin is with the articulation and interrogation of one's own preferences, distilling what it is that is particularly liked or disliked and most importantly why. That requires an introspective but detached analysis of one's own value system, of what has been inherited, learned, and indoctrinated from experience, education or practice. Choice of house, neighbourhood or holiday, in reality and in fantasy, are very revealing as are preferences about where one likes to shop, walk, cycle or drive. A critical perspective on the received wisdoms of planning ideology (containment), of national culture (heritage and the countryside), of design education (townscape) or of personal experience (escapism or perhaps urbanity) will reveal much of the complex and often contradictory interplay between professional values, and the sources of many public aspirations and disaffections.

It is often difficult to articulate criticisms when presented with a planning application because a specialist vocabulary is needed and a wide ranging, commonly shared set of concepts has yet to be generally agreed. A few texts have tried to set out a basic glossary of terms but as yet no one has attempted a comprehensive list though it would be a very useful document for the advancement of design skills. However such a vocabulary would also narrow the response, usually to a set of largely visual characteristics, whereas it is more fundamental issues of urban design that require attention – comfort, safety, cleanliness, health, as well as the differential meanings that people attach to buildings. Most people have little or no confidence in their aesthetic judgement due to lack of any education in the subject and the impression, carefully fostered in many circles, that environmental aesthetics is the preserve of the elite.

Architectural Intentions and Inspirations

As important to the success of design control is understanding the architects' intentions and the nature of the brief they have been given. In many instances the control process actually operates to the benefit of the architect in placing a premium on design quality and giving the architect more scope for creativity than the client would normally allow. Understanding the aspirations of the architect can often be achieved through discussion of previous work, especially recent commissions, and of current inspirations. Architects' study boards, contextual analysis, conceptual designs, sketch drawings, considerations of alternatives can all greatly illuminate the design process and allow opportunities for creative dialogue. In the *Time for Design* exercise in the mid-1980s Winchester experimented with the idea of a design statement where the architect would set out her/his approach to the site explaining the key considerations, and providing both a deeper understanding of the architectural approach and an opportunity to debate the fundamentals of the scheme.

It is of vital importance to foster a positive relationship with the architect and to recognise that the quality of the outcome will depend entirely upon the architect's skill and her/his ability to exercise it. Avoiding a situation where architects take criticism personally is particularly important. Pointing out areas of uncertainty, disquiet or conflict in the proposals and encouraging further thought can still leave the initiative with the architect. Exploring alternatives can often initiate better solutions providing the planner has properly thought through her or his suggestions. Of course the client may constrain the architect in order to achieve what is perceived as 'funder's architecture', or may want to cut costs with standard components or cheaper materials. Increasingly architects are not doing detailed drawings until the project is actually initiated in order to reduce costs, and this makes the task of controllers much more difficult. Similarly many quality architect's drawings are being passed on to design and build companies or developers who will adjust the designs to save money using government advice to prevent local authorities retaining particular design details. These are all current frustrations in the practice of design control.

It is important to understand what the clients' track records and objectives are and what pressures they are operating under. Local architects and developers will have an established reputation, a known way of working, and a readily accessible stock of examples of their work which will be very useful in any design negotiation. If they are non-local they may have portfolios or brochures which will provide much useful information. The experience of other local planning authorities may be useful and in some cases visits to previous buildings may be justified, to fully understand the intended effect.

Understanding Architecture

As part of the dialogue with architects (and to a lesser extent developers) it is important to understand their professional worlds, the contemporary debates, the exemplary buildings and the landmark developments. An essential point of departure is an understanding of architectural history and the relationship between physical forms and social, economic and aesthetic processes, especially the battle of the styles and cyclical revivals that have characterised the last 50 years. Reading the *Architects' Journal* weekly provides a very useful and economical way of keeping up with current developments in architectural thought and imaging, and in professional values. The monthly *Architectural Review* is more esoteric and international, but again it is an important source of architectural ideas, and it is extremely useful to be able to recognise the source of ideas on architects' study boards and to understand to what extent their ideas are carefully worked out, and appropriate to the context under consideration.

Less confident and ambitious practices may derive much of their design inspiration from recently completed schemes in the locality that are perceived to have the blessings of the planners and committee by virtue of having gained a planning permission. This is usually something to be avoided especially if it is essentially the plagiarism of elevations. Like the necessity for understanding the character of the site and its context there is no substitute for knowing one's patch in development control.

The Value of Architectural Criticism

Much architectural criticism is impenetrable and esoteric, but it is often very thought provoking. Where several critics comment upon the same building or development it can be very illuminating, rather like the consultations in the control process, but working at a much higher level. The architectural journals and quality newspapers are important sources of architectural criticism. To make the best use of it one usually needs to understand the point of view of the critic. So much criticism is doctrinal – espousing a particular set of principles be it those of the modernist, the post-modernist, the conservationist or the townscapist. What is interesting is that a group of critics will produce a wide range of comments and reveal a diverse set of criteria and priorities. Any planner who has watched an Architectural Advisory Panel at work will know the extent of difficulties which the Chairman experiences in achieving a coherent consensus, and these are usually much greater than those experienced by a more lay-oriented Conservation Area Advisory Committee. Being able to recognise entrenched value positions is the first step in being able to assess the value of the comments and criticisms. Certainly being versed in contemporary architectural criticism helps planners to converse with architects and gain their respect, as well as preparing them to fight appeals on design grounds.

The Need to Travel and the Value of Precedent

Contemporary journals may provide many examples of interest but ultimately there is no substitute for visiting new (and old) developments to see them in their context and in use rather than through the contrived angles and special filters of the architectural photographer. Travel has always been an integral part of urban design experience – indeed some textbooks read like versions of the nineteenth century Grand Tour – but it is important to try to draw out the key *principles* and *precedents* which each place or development displays. In tackling a major design problem, such as the insertion of a large shopping development into an historic town centre, it is extremely useful to examine good and bad examples especially if they are recent. This is the value of *precedent*, a concept which is widely used, but rarely systematically, in design. Precedent can be organised by factors like context, type of development, morphology/figure ground, by architect, or even by style. One can even abstract scale, density or functional relationships in searching for examples which can help prescribe do's or dont's, or can illuminate the task at hand.

Visiting landmark developments, particularly metropolitan examples is also important because architects and developers are heavily influenced by what they perceive to be best practice or the most innovative designs. Similarly an awareness of what is happening in other towns – the rash of overgrown domestic office buildings, the spread of neo-vernacular, the rash of 'Superstore barns' and other franchise architecture can provide concrete examples of what to expect and what to avoid. Purposeful travel needs to be supplemented by systematic analysis. Photographic records are a quick and convenient way of gathering and storing information, but they are no substitute for careful observation and systematic analysis of the character of a place. For a best practice example look at Kevin Lynch's early notebooks and his systematic recording of how places work.

Reading Design Texts

What can design controllers read that will aid the development of their skills? Are there useful texts that will help them? A number of key texts have already been mentioned as valuable in particular contexts, but there is of course a much wider literature to select from. Much depends on whether one wants to focus on the *process* of the design or the *product*, the *formal* characteristics of developments or the *experiential* response, the *principles* of design or the wide variety of *precedents*. As yet there are no texts on the practice of design control although an international *Design Review: Practice and Control Issues* is about to be published. This book will have the value not only of an international perspective on design control and its methodologies but will also question its most precious assumptions and its social, political, legal and even moral underpinnings. Planners are used to defending themselves against the indignation of architects, but they have never really thought hard about whether they are achieving more than 'putting lipstick on the gorilla' or defusing protest against economic exploitation in their control practice.

Of course each designer will have a preferred text that reflects a particular orthodoxy, but the most useful texts will be those that actually set out some principles for design control. Few texts actually develop principles, *Responsive Environments* being an honourable and most accessible exception. *A Pattern Language* (Alexander *et al.*, 1977) is the ultimate

example of a set of principles, Utopian, contentious and intended to be trans-cultural but exceptionally useful at all scales of planning, while Clare Cooper Marcus's work on *Housing as if People Mattered* and *People Places* offer extremely detailed research-based principles. In the more visual traditions of British design control *Making Townscape* (Tugnutt and Robinson, 1987) provides a basic methodology for contextual design while Brent Brolin's *Architecture in Context* deals only with infill situations. Anne Beer's *Environmental Planning for Site Development* offers a very contemporary environmentally-oriented synthesis of site planning methodology which is of great value to design briefing, while Kevin Lynch's *Site Planning* is still extremely valuable. Francis Tibbalds' *Making People-Friendly Towns* provides an accessible synthesis of key design principles and recommendations for practitioners. Every controller should read at least one text by a female urban design writer, in addition to Jane Jacobs. Recent work on housing design and women's use of town centres provides important correctives to the predominantly male world of urban design (Bowlby, 1990). As more and more women work in design control it is to be hoped that their particular perspective on the urban environment will come more to the fore. Finally urban design now needs to embrace the broader urban environmental agenda and arguments for sustainable development, ecologically based planning, urban greening and landscape conservation. Stephen Owen's *Planning Settlements Naturally* and Michael Hough's *City Form and Natural Process* are useful primers.

Learning from Experiences

In the end most controllers will rely upon experience as the source of their skills. While this can be construed as a way of avoiding continuing professional development or active pursuit of design expertise it is undoubtedly the best way to learn. Over the years controllers will of course not only develop the ability to read and visualise drawings quickly and effectively but also to understand the social process of design and what can be achieved. There will be major mistakes made – typically elevations will be misread, tank rooms forgotten, spaces will appear smaller than they did on the plan, and amenities will be dingier than anticipated – but there will also be successes, instances where layout, elevations or materials were changed for the better.

It is worthwhile considering how experience might be nurtured and systematised by careful examination of completed developments, by seeking comment from a variety of respondents, including, perhaps most importantly, the users/inhabitants of the scheme. Planners very rarely evaluate the results of their work, not least because they seldom have the time, but evaluation is a particularly important function in a contentious arena like design and when one is trying to accelerate learning. Design awards provide one avenue for positive evaluation. Local architects, the Advisory Panel or Civic Society, or local residents' groups should also be able to give feedback on what they consider the successes and failures of design control to be. Councillors too can be encouraged to review the new developments they have approved, since their ears are closest to the people who have to live with the designs. The relationship between design and commercial viability is particularly interesting and can be explored through agents and the like, and this can become a powerful weapon in the planners' argumentation. Last but not least discussions about what is being sought and what is being achieved by the control team are essential to promote consistency, quality and professionalism. The Audit Commission's recent study (1992) emphasises the importance of monitoring and feedback, of frequent internal quality audits and appraisals, and offers a number of ideas for further development in the design arena.

Evaluations of design change over time. They change as the 'shock of the new' gives way to familiarity, as landscaping matures or materials weather, and as the whole climate of taste shifts. All development controllers should be aware of the shifts in fashion which have taken place in the design of office buildings, shops or housing over the last twenty years, of how consistent these are across the country, and how novelty can quickly become uniformity. While there is a general consensus that design quality has improved planners need to be aware of the dangers of following preset formulae or styles, of creating uniformity and discouraging innovation, just as they need to resist the lowest common denominator product that is so often proposed by speculative developers regardless of local character.

Conclusions — The Need for Self-Education in Design

A paucity of design skills is likely to be a permanent feature of development control, particularly as it is slimmed down to minimal staffing levels. If development controllers are to acquire skills most will have to teach themselves, supplementing their learning by experience through their own casework, through short courses, or through office practice and advice from senior staff. In many localities achieving design quality may be regarded as an indefinable and elusive quality and accorded low priority, and the climate for design may be very negative particularly if central government advice is narrowly interpreted. Successive government circulars have discouraged design intervention except in 'environmentally sensitive' areas, which have generally been narrowly defined. The new design advice in Planning Policy Guidance Note 1 does not fundamentally change that view, though it does encourage the production of design advice in development plans. So the pursuit of design skills may have to be a lonely and unsupported vigil, but that makes their acquisition more rather than less important.

The prescriptions contained in this chapter may seem simultaneously Utopian, intimidating and naive. The ideas for professional development are certainly not intended to denigrate formal education in urban design or to deny the need for more architect-planners or experts in conservation and historic buildings. Similarly it must be recognised that development controllers are under constant pressure of throughput targets and deadlines, that design is only one of the multiplicity of factors that they have to deal with in each application, and that their leisure time cannot always be busman's holidays!

Some of the most highly prized skills in urban design, particularly the ability to illustrate ideas by sketching or correcting drawings, and the ability to visualise in three dimensions, are only likely to be fully developed through intensive training. However there are advantages to a lay approach in developing a focus upon everyday experience, upon pedestrian experience rather than elevations, upon urban spaces rather than design details, upon comfort and safety rather than surface treatment. The development of urbanistic rather than architectural approaches to design control and briefing offer important advantages and circumvent much of the professional antagonism of architects. However all development controllers must aspire to a visual literacy capable of identifying the design potential of a site, the key qualities of a place, and capable of clearly articulating lay tastes and comprehending architectural, landscape and urban design values. For professional design control is a key to ensuring the quality of new development and, as Lewis Keeble argued back in the 1960s, planning's success and standing is largely judged by the quality of development which receives planning permission.

I wish to acknowledge the helpful comments of Lesley Punter and Alan Rowley on the first draft of this chapter.

Richard Hayward

RATIONALES AND THE PRACTICE OF EVERYDAY URBAN DESIGN

Essential to the practice of urban design as advocated in Oxford, is the premise that environments should be transformed or created to provide the most opportunities for the largest possible range of users. Most of us clearly recognise that we will always be making trade-offs privileging one group over another. But we have a confidence in our basic preoccupations with well surveilled, clearly comprehensible public space, clear definition between public and private, fronts and backs and robust building typologies, to believe that we go as far as we can in using physical form to support and enhance democratic social and economic frameworks.

To promote the most democratic development, or at least, development which enables the widest range of current interest groups, requires dialogue with all these groups, and their contribution to and support for the proposals.

Now academics, architects and planners are noted for their convoluted and esoteric forms of communication (Gerrie, 1988). So part of our work at the Joint Centre has been to develop a tool for communication and dialogue with the widest range of actors concerned with the development of the built environment. We call this the 'rationale'.

There are a number of ideas fundamental to the thinking behind the rationale. First, comes the belief that we need every idea we can get from the widest community to make a good piece of town. Second, that to elicit the best contributions to a developing proposal, you need to explicitly integrate ideas about WHAT you intend to do, WHY you believe it to be a good plan, and HOW you are going to achieve it. Third, that proposals have to be made with strength, to elicit strong responses. Fourth, that words and images of explanation need to be unequivocally closely

related, without mystery – or the need to excuse early sketches, or the prescriptive nature of developed proposals. Fifth, that a clear argument for a piece of development needs to be restricted to no more than about eight or nine points, if people are to maintain a grasp of most aspects of the proposal.

Rationales are usually prepared in such a way that they may be presented in a variety of different formats. Most commonly, the basic rationale comprises a series of illustrated points somewhat less than A4 portrait size, mounted on an A1 board (*Plate 1*). Prints of each numbered point may then easily be bound full-size in an A3 or A4 report, and transparencies for overhead projection or colour slides for projection may be made. Frequently, where overhead, or slide projection is employed for a presentation, adjunct illustrative material using the same medium may be used to expand points in the argument.

Despite the popularity of parlour tricks with ink-blot images, most architects seem to believe that the drawings which they put before people will convey to the viewer what they intend. Indeed, many, if not most architects, dislike annotations on presentation or design development drawings. Urban designers also take some convincing of this point. Images from Wittgenstein (1953) are used to persuade them. But by far the most effective image used is one redrawn after M.L.J. Abercrombie (1969), not reproduced here, so that only those with the energy to chase the reference will spoil their chances of being surprised by a live test.

Using this image, the audience is asked not to communicate with each other during the period of the experiment. They are told that an image will be projected and that after an interval information will be given in a sequence. They are to raise their hands when they recognise the image, and keep it raised until the end of the experiment. The image is then projected; in most cases, in groups of between twenty and eighty, nobody immediately recognises the image. A very generalised verbal characterisation is then given (such as 'most people see this as the face of Dame Edna Everage'), at this point, commonly up to about one-third of the group gradually recognise the image. The next information given is more explicit; it describes the image by area and points out details ('Dame Edna's mouth is in the centre of the picture and in shadow, at the top of the image her spectacle tips merge with her hair . . .'); again, about a further third or more recognise the image. Finally, the presenter takes a pointer and moves it to the salient features whilst describing them. At this point, usually all but one or two rapidly see the image. For the remainder, a more explicit version of this easily recognisable image is projected.

The scientific basis of the experiment is clearly illustrated by another diagram, also after Abercrombie (*Figure 3*). For a while after taking part in this experiment, most students will provide images with arrows to the salient points connecting them with clear annotations.

Polanyi describes the manner in which the mathematician 'works his (sic) way towards discovery, by shifting his confidence from intuition to computation and back again from computation to intuition, while never releasing his hold on either of the two, (which) represents in miniature the whole range of operations by which articulation disciplines and expands the reasoning powers of man.' (Polanyi, 1958, p. 131), and he describes the technique used to manipulate the material thus: '(1) set out the problem in suitable symbols and continuously reorganise its representation with a view to eliciting some new suggestive aspects of it, and concurrently (2) ransack our memory for any similar problem of which the solution is known.' (Polanyi, p. 128).

Most urban designers recognise that problem solving in urban design veers from the marshalling of explicit requirements to the black box of intuitive leaps, promoted by healthy obsession. Yet sadly, there is often a reluctance to progress and map the progress of a developing proposal by constructing and reconstructing the rationale. If we really wish to empower everyone that we can, in the development of *our* designs, then the failure to update the rationale

in step with the design is fundamental. For our ephemeral explanations will generally lack the contrived complexity of argument of the rationale point as well as the evidence of our struggle to articulate it and are likely to be comparatively opaque.

Accessible images and explicit captioned arguments tend to help every individual reach for a pencil, or state a position, and these are the contributions we need, as we assemble a better design and the accumulative goodwill of those that have a personal stake in the design. For though we can satisfy our craving for peer-group recognition whenever we wish, by pointing to our urban design achievements, we can also encourage, reward and flatter those who have helped us by highlighting their design contribution, when this may promote and progress what we believe to be a good urban design scheme.

This raises the spectre of unhealthy manipulation. However, in most cases, the currency of a rationale ensures that it represents at least a reasonably open and consensual negotiated position. For, whilst the rationale may be a powerful tool, it is unwise to try to produce different rationales for different audiences. The most useful response to a presentation is the request by a member of the audience to borrow the rationale panel, or to take a copy of it in the report. This means in most cases, that not only is someone prepared to put in thinking time on our proposal for nothing, but the chances are that they will show it to others who, directly or indirectly, will make a contribution. If one were to carefully pitch a rationale for one audience, the chances are that it would be of limited utility and it would be impossible to give it a free distribution, when others who would see it might be antagonised by its biased presentation of the argument.

In all of this, 'argument' is the key word. For more than anything else, the urban designer constructs and develops the argument for development.

The rationale is thus used for presentation and the development of an urban design proposal. But more than anything else it is a taskmaster for the urban designer. The rationale forces us to articulate verbal and graphic synthesis, it says, without pretension, 'this is my best current shot at a statement of the what, why and how of a proposal.' In this respect, the rationale is part and parcel of an approach to problem solving which is incremental rather than rational comprehensive.

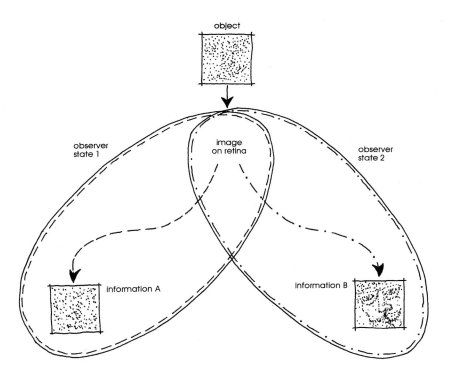

object

observer
state 1

image
on retina

observer
state 2

Information A

Information B

Figure 3. Observer state and information received, after Abercrombie, 1969.

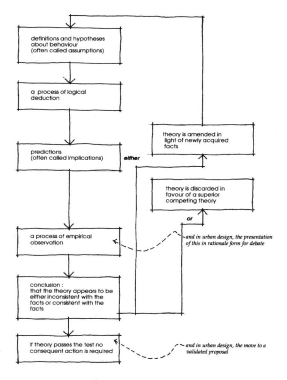

definitions and hypotheses
about behaviour
(often called assumptions)

a process of logical
deduction

predictions
(often called implications)

either

theory is amended in
light of newly acquired
facts

theory is discarded in
favour of a superior
competing theory

or

a process of empirical
observation

*and in urban design, the presentation
of this in rationale form for debate*

conclusion :
that the theory appears to be
either inconsistent with the
facts or consistent with the
facts

if theory passes the test no
consequent action is required

*and in urban design, the move to a
validated proposal*

Figure 4. Diagram after Hollis, 1985.

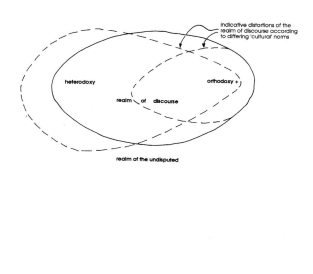

indicative distortions of the
realm of discourse according
to differing 'cultural' norms

heterodoxy

orthodoxy +

realm of discourse

realm of the undisputed

Figure 5. The realms of discourse and 'the undiscussed'
after Bourdieu, 1977.

The concept of analysis paralysis is one with currency across the globe. The so-called rational problem solver seeks to first gather all the data, before moving to comprehensive analysis of the problem and thence smoothly to a solution. Few problems admit neatly of this process, and indeed the very approach is logically flawed, for even if we could gather all the data for a split second, in no time more data would have arisen, and then more, as the world turns. Yet this approach, and its architectural equivalent of the SAD approach (Survey, Analysis, Design), permeates most educational systems. It can be easily seen that this approach also tends to appropriate the decision making process for the designer alone.

The use of the rationale is much closer to a rapid fire version of the most respectable approaches to research, a combination of deduction and empirical testing leading to firmer design hypotheses (*Figure 4*). From our understanding of urban design theory and practice we deduce a working hypothesis, which we present to the world in the most explicit form we can muster. We then test this hypothesis against views of the particular world in which we are to operate. We then revise our hypothesis, and so on, until the point when we have sufficient supporting evidence and arguments to put forward our proposal as a new theory of appropriate design.

This approach is very much contrary to that which Popper dismisses as the 'bucket theory' of the mind (1972), and has the added advantage that our own striving for transparency may also extend the field of thinking of others who have to confront the situation. Bourdieu (1977) has a diagram – in the book which de Certeau (1984) rightly says provides 'a fund of material that can be indefinitely cited in marvellous fragments' (p. 50) – which has the elegance of a universal truth (*Figure 5*). It suggests the reality of the way different groups see and interpret the world that they inhabit. Conservative, homogenous and orthodox groups prefer that the realm of discourse should be relatively limited and it is effectively defined by a realm of the undisputed (what one knows, and holds in common, but need never discuss); genuinely radical or heterogeneous, heterodox groups tend to put much more up for discourse and can count on common assumptions much less. Having an eye to relative power, it is diverting to draw a version of Bourdieu's diagram for, say, Franco's Spain, or Stalin's Russia, against modern Denmark or the United States; or again, for members of the architectural or surveying profession, or development control planners, or housing developers. Stereotyping yes, but one doesn't have to do more than recognise that seeing past the fence between discourse and unspoken assumptions is difficult for us all, and that we usually need a challenge to our covert assumptions or a leg up to see over the fence to do it. And those in power, would generally prefer that we did not do it; that we did not move the discourse beyond their defined limits.

I think also, that the problem-solving, hypothesis enriching, argument making, use of the rationale is close to what de Certeau describes as '. . . a know how (savoir-faire) by means of discourse. The frontier thus no longer separates two hierarchized bodies of knowledge, the one speculative, the other linked to particulars, the one concerned with reading the order of the world and the other coming to terms with the details of things within the framework set up for it by the first; rather it sets off practices articulated by discourse from those that are not (yet) articulated by it.' (1984, p. 65).

In practice, rationales prepared from working design development material are cut and pasted together with comic book captions and word-processed sub-text, to form an evolutionary story board for progressing proposals. They help a team to articulate the arguments and to order and pace a presentation. They suggest the integrative nature of the material being employed to explore the way forward, and help to provide an agenda for the production of other necessary material.

Do rationales really work? Those that use them believe that they do, and will ascribe the winning of jobs or smooth progress through difficult development stages to them. But most people find them difficult to produce, and many conventionally educated designers find the crude conjunction of intentions with the 'current best attempt' at a solution especially problematic. They would prefer a set of objectives and an evocative sketch.

In recent years there has been considerable debate in urban design circles about the potential for the 'professionalisation' of the field. Whilst most of those who call themselves urban designers have another 'profession', the branching out into the relatively unorthodox field of urban design, has, I believe, generally been a liberation and an education. This should in particular act as the basis for an ongoing individual and collective critique of the dangers of narrow professionalism and the way that this can effect an unhelpful power relationship between all of those with a stake in making better places. The rationale is an explicit mechanism for keeping us in an uncomfortable role as brokers and enablers. The rationale helps to keep us in a position where others will continue to question our legitimacy, appropriate knowledge and skills, and power base; all to the benefit of a more collective approach to urban design.

Richard Hayward

TALKING TISSUES

For almost a decade staff and students in the JCUD have been using urban tissue plans in the production and evaluation of site development appraisals and design proposals. Essentially a tissue is a scale graphic representation, usually a plan, of a piece of urban development.

In common with the practice of colleagues in planning, architecture and urban design, a number of staff at the Joint Centre had for many years previously employed a variety of plan 'precedent', morphological and typological studies in site appraisal exercises. The crystallisation of these disparate approaches into the present tissue method was prompted by a series of articles by Stephen Kendall, John Carp and others in *Open House International* (1984). Our approach owes much to Kendall's, but has been adapted for specific urban design purposes and extended in its intentions, most significantly as a tool for dialogue in the urban design process.

The simple technique and its theoretical position is fully explained by Hayward in Urban Design Quarterly (Dec. 1987) but here in summary are the basic operations.

Essential tissue information comprises the layout, usually at 1:1250 or 1:500 scales, but workable from 1:5000 to 1:200. This is the primary tool, which must be supplemented with as much typological information as possible — house types and so on, usually at 1:50 or 1:100. Patently, a 1:1250 Ordnance Sheet often provides the best tissue and will lead one to investigate and gather typological information.

A rigid operational framework for carrying out the exercise has been established to ensure, as far as possible, that time is taken to consider carefully the relationships between tissue and site, rather than running on rapidly to some new design, simply using the tissue as prompt or inspiration.

First, the tissue is laid over a plan of the site and manipulated to achieve the best fit. The group should have regard to existing linkages and established or potential routes across the site. Once the best fit is established, the tissue is trimmed with scissors and glued in place, ignoring minor misfits and remaining entire and unmodified. The group then 'interrogate' the result by debating the consequences of this superimposition in terms both of the tissue and the site and as many notes as possible concerning the outcomes to these discussions are added to the plan.

Second, taking a new base plan and another copy of the tissue, a further version is made. This time the tissue is modified as little as possible to achieve a workable plan; that is, a plan that could be developed practically on the site, retaining as much of the integrity of the original tissue as possible. Again the plan is discussed and annotated.

Finally, the most dangerous stage, the group take a further base plan and tissue and following a recapitulation of all the known development and site requirements, modify the tissue to achieve a transformation and 'design' which most closely meets the group's aspirations. Where dimensional and morphological relationships are thus significantly adjusted, this should be noted on the plan, and before the new arrangements are confirmed they should be checked for workability to the best of the group's expertise. Where unknowns remain, they should be stated as such for further investigation.

Urban design has grown and flourished in the vacuum left by the planners unable to give form to their intentions and architects unable or unwilling to give user groups confidence in the functioning outcomes of what are all too commonly 'black box' creative leaps to prototypical solutions. In addition, architects tend to overestimate the need for specialness, both in the generality and the building specifics of their urban design proposals.

The use of tissues in the preparation of design proposals can help all the actors in the urban design process to establish the development potential of an area and move from the initial broad intentions to a detailed urban framework which identifies where flexible commonplace development solutions are appropriate and where non-thematic specialness is called for. The approach may be further extended to indicate the location of desirable building types, and with the appropriate technical support, even building design solutions. In every case, the concrete nature of tissue explorations enables the preparation of a range of cost and feasibility studies to be carried out.

Wherever tissues are used beyond the educational process, a number of guidelines are important. All of the tissues employed should have a clear purpose; some tissues from the vicinity of the study/ development area should be employed; as many of the tissues as possible should be familiar in their reality to as many of the urban design participants as possible.

In an educational setting we have found it useful to include some apparently inappropriate or unlikely tissues, in particular to draw out a debate about the particular tissue type, and its transformation in relation to the location and needs of the site. Frequently it is difficult to persuade students of the utility of this approach, even in a setting specifically set up for research and inquiry. The adverse reaction is even more marked with proactive development groups. This impatience is understandable, but I will return to the point in order to try to demonstrate that such diversions are both intellectually and practically useful as part of the process of using tissues in design.

In our first experiments with tissues, we restricted their use primarily to residential development. This went very much against the grain of the Centre's commitment to mixed-use development, but was simply a product of the early work of Roger Simmonds with planning students and my own with architecture students, and the fact that funding, standards and guidance make the pathology of residential tissues easy to read and compare with the physical results.

The benefits of the technique in urban design became rapidly apparent – particularly as a focus for cross-cultural debate and learning. Almost from the start nineteenth century by-law tissues were included. These, of course, demonstrate the ability of close-grained perimeter development to accommodate a wide range and mix of uses, from the odd corner shop, or pub, or church, through to substantial retail, commercial, industrial and public uses combined with housing. Subsequently, we have worked from the other direction by identifying tissues which are primarily made up of non-residential uses. As ever, the two primary concerns are to look beyond the type or the footprint, specifically at the morphological and simple dimensional relationships between like elements and unalike elements.

As a result of incremental course development, the use of tissues has come to have a key underpinning role for the introductory urban layout project, providing students with a common vocabulary of physical development approaches. The dangers remain that students will neither interrogate the tissue adequately to establish the reasons behind its form and its potential and limitations in current practice, nor will they sufficiently investigate what the tissue actually represents in built form.

The latter problem has been partially tackled by having students make their own tissues from observation during the first field study visit. These visits are held at the very beginning of the course. They are generally based in large cities with a history of mixed local economy – in recent years, Manchester, Liverpool and Bristol. Students are directed to investigate particular parts of the city which between them include the widest range of urban uses from predominantly residential through to almost exclusively commercial or industrial. Each sub-group must describe and explain both the physical characteristics and a group view of the relative success of the tissue. A record of this information has to be provided in the form of a dimensioned annotated tissue and commentary, which is then bound in with all the others to provide a first tissue book of shared experience for the entire cohort. (*Figure 6*)

Beyond the educational setting, a common characteristic of groups embarking on projects promoting user participation in design, is the tour of comparative developments. Enablers and groups establish the core of a common vocabulary which recurs in design discussion with references '. . . like the housing we

Figure 6. Examples of student tissue analysis.

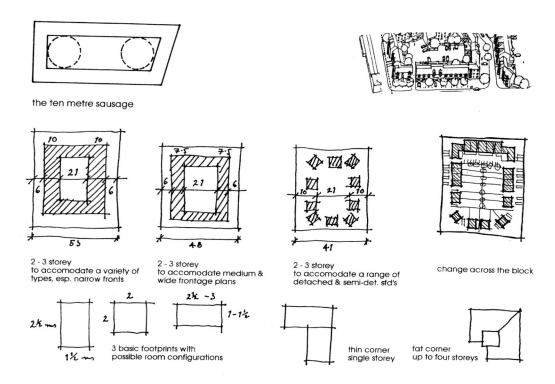

the ten metre sausage

2 - 3 storey
to accomodate a variety of
types, esp. narrow fronts

2 - 3 storey
to accomodate medium &
wide frontage plans

2 - 3 storey
to accomodate a range of
detached & semi-det. sfd's

change across the block

3 basic footprints with
possible room configurations

thin corner
single storey

fat corner
up to four storeys

Figure 7. A simple band of 'building' for layout purposes: 'the ten metre sausage.'

saw at Milton Keynes'. The use of tissues enables groups to go a stage further in using what they have seen and admired. The approach also helps to keep the enabler on tap, rather than on top, as the group recognises from life the potential and limitations of paper plan relationships. Users are both empowered in terms of positive understanding of manipulating known tissues and against the introduction of prototypical solutions that are not related directly to existing tissues by sensible, demonstrable incremental development.

Perhaps even more interesting in the context of urban design is the potential for the use of tissues in interprofessional negotiation and group working. For almost as long as we have employed the technique within the Joint Centre, we have been using it with professional groups outside. Initially most work was done with teams of local authority planners who were looking for mechanisms to permit them to negotiate with developers and their architects in a more informed way about the development potential and value of land within their areas.

Even if planning offices can muster high levels of design expertise, which is rare, they are generally in a position where all but the most important sites cannot sustain any but the smallest resource investment beyond normal delegated procedures. The adept use of tissues and a simple feasibility software package provides them with a significantly improved basis for negotiation than simply challenging the developer to verify the basis for proposals.

This raises the issue of tissues as 'expert system'. The delight of tissues in an academic or design participatory setting are that they promote dialogue, debate and understanding; they arguably enrich design intention and solutions; and they empower students in relation to teachers and users in relation to enablers. However, within the approach are obvious commercial benefits rooted in aspects other than those of transparency and empowerment.

Tissuing can enable a development consultant to explore alternative feasibilities for site development very rapidly. It must be also readily apparent that tissues may very easily be reduced to development types — not simply in the statistical way suggested overtly by many common analyses — that is in terms of density yield, plot ratios and car parking per hectare, but also in terms of a physical shorthand, a design template that contains only the

yield information and basic spatial relationships but irons out the accessible richness and reality of naked tissue!

In the essays which accompanied that of Kendall in *Open House International*, was one on 'Conjoint Measurement' (Velduisen *et al.*, 1984). In the tradition of the work of John Habraken and his group, this study examines the dimensional characteristics of a highly complex plan support matrix to provide the potential for alternative dwelling layouts within an overall expert system. Almost inevitably, given the imperatives of practice one is bound to seek to reduce some of the information of tissues to a similar rational system for exploiting the benefits of certain development patterns on potential sites.

In the past practice of Bentley Hayward Murrain Samuels and the continuing work of the Joint Centre, this has led to the use of simple graphic forms, primarily based for housing on the elegantly named 'ten metre sausage' (*Figure 7*), which is accompanied by a set of front to front and back to back rules for various building heights and performance characteristics in terms of, say, numbers of habitable rooms per metre run. The system is largely opaque in terms of the qualitative potential of the information it embodies or the reasons for the rules it adheres to; it is simply an expert shorthand.

A rather more transparent system, which is only expert in as much as it is dependent on significant resourcing and a degree of technical expertise, is the use of tissues on computer. A number of graduates of the Joint Centre have built tissue collections on computer, which they can simply manipulate over site projections. Undoubtedly this development is inevitable and powerful (and used in a variety of versions by commercial developers beyond our transitory sphere of influence).

Two recent experiments with tissues have been particularly interesting. The Australian example is discussed elsewhere, as the cross-cultural aspect is the more interesting. The second concerns work which has been carried out with the City of Leicester and other consultants, referred to as The Leicester Housing Study.

The study has focused issues of future housing standards on a particular large landholding to the north of the city. An early decision was made to use the site as a way of concretising principles that the City would promote for future housing development, regardless of any intention or opportunity to actually carry them through on the particular site.

The study team comprised a broad range of professionals including planners, urban designers, architects, landscape architects, ecologists and energy consultants. Briefing materials for the site assembled over a number of years were impressive and the preoccupations of the many experts fiercely held. In addition, the team, working on a limited budget danced the dance of a new *ad hoc* group, sensitive concerning the role relationships of professional to professional, academic to practitioner and public sector to private sector. Tissues broke the ice.

The team was divided into two mixed professional groups, and over a day, two schemes were produced at 1:1250 scale, briefly presented by each sub-group and debated by the whole group. Copies were made and the team took them off to their specialist offices for further scrutiny, debate and comparison with standards, rules, developing ideas regarding sustainability, traffic and issues arising from the site.

Over a period of months layers of modification were applied to the plan, some of which led to the substitution of tissues. Finally, a time was reached when the rationale for the proposals had to be presented to a wider audience, when it was decided that a masterplan should be prepared which was essentially less specific and apparently prescriptive than the modified tissue plan. The urban designers then reduced the proposal to a masterplan which indicated linkages, a hierarchy of routes and development parcels together with other key landscape and infrastructure elements — linear managed open space networks, tree belts, balancing ponds, reed beds, and local power stations.

The reaction from some members of the team was particularly interesting. Not only did they find the masterplan relatively mute and opaque in terms of its overall intentions, but they deeply regretted the loss of richness that was present in the tissue-based original.

Now all good planners and urban designers are concerned about the dangers of prescriptive briefing or design guidance, and with some justification. But what was apparent here was that even experienced professionals found it difficult to maintain a broad and satisfactory agreement and enthusiasm for 70 hectares of development when, rather than showing how it might be, it was stripped to its planning essentials.

The story is not yet finished. But in the meantime, the urban designers have embellished the master plan with a more limited range of building footprints within the structure than the tissues generated, but nevertheless, enough to indicate a density gradient and typological change from an urban spine to different sorts of suburban rural edge. This has satisfied the plannerly concern to avoid prescription whilst giving some indication of the richness of thinking developed across the site by the use of tissues.

However, it does bring me back to the issue related to the use of 'bad' tissues. In all our work with tissues we have observed that rapid operations usually produce relatively poor results. We have developed the use of tissues primarily as a technique for collective interrogation of both specific examples of physical development and actual sites, the transformations suggested by one or the other and the likely consequences of those transformations. In our experience, when a group moves to a rapid resolution, it tends to do so at the loss of the truly informing debate and negotiation; it tends to have perceived the tissue simply as a 'type' which repays no further scrutiny, and therefore fails to note the detailed potential, particularity and richness.

Not surprisingly, perhaps, by-law tissues often elicit this response from architects. They 'know' what they are, and they 'know' the key shorthand characteristics of the form; they find it boring. It is not perhaps surprising that one frequently has to draw the attention of students to the simple perimeter development structure of Bath, Edinburgh, Prague or Paris with their notably boring urban presences!

But this brings us back to the key issue of representation, transparency and perception. Whatever techniques are used to represent the progression of architectural or urban design, the commonest element in dialogue between student and tutor or designer and user or patron is the recourse to analogy: 'Is it like . . .?' (Hayward, in Bines and Watson, 1992). By using tissues, design variation, progression or transformation can be explicitly considered within reliable limits of negotiated common perception, without recourse to expert language or systems which tend to misappropriate the transformation and production of the build environment from the user.

What tissues do not do, of course, is to provide any element of user evaluation of their performance.

Ideally, 'tissue files' should incorporate evidence of post-occupancy evaluation, press cuttings, interview notes and building studies, to give the best background information. But the real value of tissues lies in the tendency for them not only to yield comparative design approaches, but to generate fierce debate about the qualities of the alternatives thus generated.

In his seductive book *Invisible Cities*, Italo Calvino (1979, p. 104) tells of one conversation between Marco Polo and Kublai Khan. Polo speaks of the wooden chessboard between them: ' . . . "The square on which your enlightened gaze is fixed was cut from the ring of a trunk that grew in a year of drought: you see how its fibres are arranged? Here a barely hinted knot can be made out: a bud tried to burgeon on a premature spring day, but the night's frost forced it to desist . . . here is a thicker pore: perhaps it was a larvum's nest . . . This edge was scored by the wood-carver with his gouge so that it would adhere to the next square, more protruding . . ."

The quantity of things that could be read in a little piece of smooth and empty wood overwhelmed Kublai; Polo was already talking about ebony forests, about rafts laden with logs that come down the rivers, of docks, of women at the windows . . .'

Alan Reeve

THE ONTOLOGY OF THE BUILT ENVIRONMENT: THE PRODUCTION OF PLACES AND BUILDINGS IN A CULTURE OF HISTORICAL AMNESIA

'They had taken out such a good insurance policy that when their house in the country burnt down, they were able to build another one, older than the first'.

Baudrillard (in Gane, 1991)

It has become a commonplace of recent continental philosophy and, more broadly, cultural theory, that under post-modernism (as a condition) there has arisen a new structure of feeling in relation to artefacts and time. Since the built environment is an artefact, of a particular sort, the implication might be that a similar restructuring of feeling or consciousness has occurred here. I want to examine this contention under the caveat, however, that for the built environment this shift in feeling is by no means total; if it were we would find it difficult and probably impossible to recognise. Whilst it is the case that both urban form and architecture are increasingly produced which deliberately conflate past and present within a general culture of amnesia, neither that amnesia nor that conflation are total. This is primarily because of the complexity of the built environment historically and existentially. It is also because, arguably, planners, architects and developers — that is producers — are not simply fictively committed to an indifference to distinctions between past and present. Not everything is a simulacrum or experienced as such — yet; the hyperbolic generalisations of writers such as Baudrillard often imply that the process of forgetting is both ineluctable and complete, and this implication needs to be questioned.

The built environment exists as a lost presence to the extent that as a phenomenological reality its exist-ence depends entirely on the actions and intentions of individuals at moments already gone. However, the meaning of the built environment (even that it has been created in the past) is contained in the present, by virtue of the fictive wish of individuals as they experience it. To that extent — to the extent that all meaning has its foundation only in its being willed or chosen contingently — all meaning is magical, potentially free floating and beyond guarantee. This temporal and absolute disjunction between the values and intentions of producers and the perceptions of users or consumers lies at the heart of the ontological condition of the built environment as a phenomenon. Jean Baudrillard's (ironic) tale, and it can be read as a kind of contradictory narrative, at least alludes to this ontological fracture: the built environment exists from the past, but that past is no guarantee of any present meaning.

One might ask, if this has always been the case, if it is a necessary condition of the being of all artefacts (including the built environment), that their meaning is given at every moment from the present, then what is new in Baudrillard's fable?. The answer would have to be that for him, for example, it is the immediacy of the illusion of temporality. There is a new (and for some frighteningly so) transparency to the fiction that the intentions of individuals who have gone before us can faithfully be reproduced in our present day experience. The illusion of a teleological movement, or at least coherence, with a decipherable 'narrative' content presses on us, according to Baudrillard, so that all we can believe is that there is simply a sequence of disconnected presents.

The cultural and historical reasons why the (real) experience of illusion has displaced the (illusory) experience of reality have been well rehearsed by not only Baudrillard (1983) but, amongst others, Adorno (in Bernstein, 1991), Debord (1972), Jameson (1983), and Ewen (1988). Each of these writers broadly identifies the rise of mass consumer culture, along with the predominance of the reproduced image over the original in the mass media, as the primary cause of this sense of illusion at the heart of the everyday experience of most people. The argument at the cultural/psychological level is that inhabiting a world dominated by vicarious worlds and vicarious experience, all worlds and all experience become equally valued or equally valueless. Jameson (1983) in particular, argues that under the intense pressure of ubiquitous representation and reproduction of the real in the media, we have lost the wish to make what he calls (after Jaques Lacan) 'syntactical' connection between past, present and future.

At the level of economics and politics, the argument is that the built environment – along with all artefacts – is now seen as a commodity, in which any symbolic value the original may have had and which they resemble, has become absorbed into the commodity as a resource and transformed into an exchange value. The illusion of symbolic value (ethnic difference, vernacular specificity) in any object is promoted under capitalism in order to provide a (arbitrary) reason for consumption. Places are, for instance, 'themed', in order to produce a return on financial investment, and in that commodification have their differences from other places highlighted or abstracted so that their original symbolic meaning is displaced by an instrumental one. (Ashworth and Voogd, 1990 give a number of interesting strategies for such theming).

What I have attempted to do above is to indicate one fashionable view of the current ontological condition of the built environment: the view that all places, whether new or old, private or public (and, arguably, whether manufactured or 'natural') are experienced and lived differently today, in the sense that the meaning of the built environment is no longer given by a belief in the past as being the

foundation in some way of the present, but of the present containing that foundation as an illusion. That is, that postmodernism can be defined here as a cultural condition which holds that all previous epistemological faiths have dissolved and all valued differences between things are fully felt to be arbitrary and contingent.

If there has been this shift in the ontological condition in which the built environment is experienced and if this has in part determined a new condition in its production, it ought to be open to some sort of empirical investigation. The intention of the rest of this analysis is therefore to define how this ontological shift may be seen to be revealed in a particular instance of the production of the built environment, and how it can be qualified; and second to raise the question whether there are particular built forms which arise as a consequence of this shift.

The Richmond Riverside development, designed by Quinlan Terry and built between 1984–1988, may be regarded as an appropriate case for investigation. (The observations given here are based on a recent unpublished study of the development by the author.) It is appropriate because it appears to play with the notion of architectural tradition and precedent-based place making, and because it occupies an important site and has been the subject of much critical debate (*Building Design* 1984, Gardiner, 1988, Scruton, 1988).

The production of the scheme, as a brief, as drawings, in its promotion and in its final built form, reveals a number of interesting features and relations relevant to this discussion. For example, it is clear that the institutional development process – capitalist in terms of the investment of money towards the accumulation of capital, on the one hand, and cultural/bureaucratic, in terms of the sanctioning of broad design decisions through a political planning system, acting with its own agenda and 'democratic' imperatives, on the other – remains relatively static; but, within this, the exercise of design power between individuals can be regarded as dynamic. That is, although the structure of capitalist production and consumption and of planning control with its exercise of accountable authority as a structure has remained the same in general outline over the last few decades, the values and intentions of actors within it have also remained the foundation of particular decisions. Therefore, I want to argue that, at least in

31

the present constant structural condition, the shift in values and thus design decision, must be traced in the intentions and relations of actors and in the changes in relative power of individuals as circumscribed by their professional/bureaucratic/investor roles in the given structure. It is here that the shift in the ontological condition occurs and is registered.

This being the case, the question is how would the shift in the structure of feeling and the application of particular values (of historical continuity, for example) actually make some difference to what comes to be built, or to the experience of decisions taken. The answer, suggested by the Richmond case at least, is through the expressed ideological allegiances of individual controllers and producers. This is because without ideological commitments, individual actors have neither voice nor authority since all social values (and all values are social) require agreement between individuals within a group. In the Richmond case, it is evident that the different ideologies of different actors have a specific relationship to the ontological shift described. It is not simply that particular ideologically defined groups either tend to resist or to help that shift, since that would be to imply that it was a movement somehow external to the relations between different groups. It is rather that certain groups (or sets of values identified with those groups) can be described as creating or 'proposing' this new tendency, whilst others come to define themselves in opposition to this and thereby dialectically give it being. It is clear for example that the ideology of Quinlan Terry, as designer, whilst in an important sense in sympathy with that of the developers and planners (both of whom wanted a traditional development) was in another sense in opposition to their values. For instance, Terry's knowledge of classical and neo-classical detailing was of no interest to either planners or developers except in so far as that knowledge could be used to legitimate the particular design chosen. They valued, the architect's professional knowledge because it could be presented at meetings with the press and public to give symbolic authority to the design. For Terry, the style of the building could have been no other way, and thus was for him symbolically given, whereas for the planners its necessity arose out of the absence of any acceptable alternative falling within a loose set of criteria. This is to say no more than that the architect's values in this case can be defined as arising

from a continuing faith in 'syntactical coherence', and that the architect could exercise authority because of the degree to which architects still have a symbolic power recognised by capital as producing an exchange value. And it is to say no more than that the planners' ideologies have a more ambiguous relationship to that 'syntactical coherence' — ambiguous because structurally open to democratic shifts in taste.

The ideologies of the producers — the funding institutions, letting agent and developer — in this case happened to want the project designed by Terry, and in part explicitly because of a notion of tradition; but this idea of the present's relationship to the past must here be recognised as instrumental rather than symbolic, precisely because of the requirements of capitalism placed upon producers. And it is a short step from recognising the imperative of capital accumulation and commodity production given to producers by capitalism, to a recognition that the primary function of the commodity for them is to induce consumption: to present the object as having a greater exchange value (at heart) than its competitors. What provides the competitive edge to new goods does not come from the goods themselves as a use value, but from the values perceived by producers in the market.

It becomes a matter of necessity to promote through new goods a sense of the 'good life', and a principal strategy today of this is the dramatisation of the idea of the 'good life' metonymically or conventionally — in goods. In terms of the Richmond scheme, the idea of the 'good life' (or quality) has been promoted through a style which (because of such contingencies as the perceived status of Terry, of classicism and of an abstracted idea of the past) conveniently suited the market, the planning authority and the architect. But, the idea of the 'good life' is indifferent to the good life itself (whatever that may be), and must be understood as an instrumental strategy for selling which at once denies the thing it promotes.

What is hopefully revealed in the foregoing analysis is that within the development and production process of any new scheme, it is possible first to define the relationship of particular actors to the tendency towards the breakdown of syntactical coherence, or the ontological shift; second to tentatively argue that interests closer to the capitalist imperative will be more closely allied to this shift in terms of helping to define environments which are primarily concerned with image; and third to suggest, beyond indicating such general conditions, that it is possible (as writers such as Baudrillard do) to say that all individuals and groups potentially share the same sense of schizophrenia — to use Lacan's analogy.

The second issue, of whether certain built forms necessarily follow from this differential shift in the ontological condition, can now be addressed. There are perhaps two responses to this question: the one based on the evidence of what has recently tended to be built under late capitalism, and the other based on an understanding of the changing structure of power between producers and controllers of the built environment.

It seems, from the rise of what Demetry Porphyrios (1982) calls Modern Eclecticism, that over the last twenty years or more there has been, amongst producers, a break with previous notions of architectural tradition: that all architectural styles have become available as a resource with which to give new buildings a conscious reference (metonymically) to some idea of quality. This of course can be seen as arising both out of a general cultural apostasy and as reinforcing that break with a faith in cultural coherence, represented in such cultural apostasy. Each new project, borrowing from the past, effectively brings the past into the present and helps create the condition of temporal amnesia. One of the consequences of this is that buildings or built projects which attempt the new (say, any scheme by Richard Rogers) will be experienced by those, at least, whose sense of the past has become a commodity of the present as only novel rather than radical.

In terms of urban form, it is possible to detect a preference by those who control capital — funding institutions — particularly in commercial developments for particular controllable forms. The atria, or enlarged shopping mall (Meadowhall, Sheffield and the Metro-centre Gateshead, are obvious examples) in which the abandonment of syntactical coherence can be most completely effected. Within a closed and controlled 'public' environment it becomes much easier to maintain an illusion compared with what is possible in the traditional high street where the present, in the weather or spontaneous human action, constantly threatens to intrude upon any constructed mythical ambience.

The predominance, as it seems, in the 1980s of the 'post-modern' style, which works precisely by bringing the past into the present and aestheticising empirical reality, suggests that either the power over design decision has shifted from architects to those closer to the imperatives of capital, or that design ideology itself has changed.

This brings us onto the second response to the issue of what urban form becomes possible because of the general ontological shift, the shift of consciousness and its structuring of reality. If it is the case that power has moved from designers to developers in controlling the form of things at the design stage, and in which the controlling imperative is to create the novel by the use of such devices as metonymy and stylistic metaphor and pastiche, then one would expect a resistance of some sort from designers. This would be in the shape of an avant-garde, perhaps, defining itself in opposition to the commodification and commercialisation of design. That opposition would arise out of a desire to retain symbolic power through a strategy of manufacturing the genuinely new. In this case the built environment would have the opportunity at least of resisting, or giving new direction to, the ontological shift described above — for those identifying with its resistance.

But if it is the case that the ideology of designers has changed and now defines itself in terms of the values of investors and other producers, then there is no source within the realm of production for resistance to the inevitable move to a design ethos which is predicated on what Debord (1972) called spectacle — the loss of syntactical coherence and the manufacture of spectacular and fantastic form.

Both positions — the resistance of the avant-garde and the absorbtion of a distinctive architectural ideology into a more purely capitalist ideology — hold contemporaneously. Designers who see themselves in opposition to the dominant and reifying trend will be increasingly marginalised, except in so far as their work provides novel styles to be commodified and neutralised in turn by the dominant trend.

I want to conclude this interrogation by, first, reiterating the caveat with which I began: given the complexity of the built environment as a phenomenon and as a location of individual experience, it is at least contestable whether the ontological restructuring which Baudrillard ironically celebrates (in the energy of his prose as much as in the poetic manner of his thinking) has occurred in any significant sense.

And second, by suggesting that the question:

what ought designers to do at the scale of individual buildings as much as at that of the city, remains. It is not answered by the implication that since under the capitalist imperative and the creation of an illusory and instrumental reality by this imperative, then everything is actually the same as everything else and that therefore designers need only concern themselves with satisfying the demands of capital by producing the superficially new. What designers ought to do is actually given in opposition to this view: however logically untenable might be the argument for the foundation of difference in the built environment, symbolic differences are none the less experienced by individuals aligning themselves with particular social values. Those allegiances can be addressed in the built environment without pastiche and without turning those allegiances into the mode of consumption which would result (to borrow from the language of semiotics) from turning the signifier of built form into a commodity.

Michael Biddulph

CONSUMING THE SIGN VALUE OF URBAN FORM

. . . What is real? Because increasingly we are bombarded with pseudo-realities manufactured by very sophisticated people . . . I do not distrust their motives; I distrust their power.'

. . . in Disneyland there are fake birds worked by electric motors which emit caws and shrieks as you pass them by. Suppose some night all of us sneaked into the park with real birds and substituted them for the artificial ones. Imagine the horror the Disneyland officials would feel when they discovered the cruel hoax. Real birds!

Dick (1985)

Introduction

Urban design theory is frequently naive with regard to the influence of the mode of production under late capitalism on the generation of what will be termed 'late industrial' urban form. Theorists who only have regard for the product of development, i.e. the physical, ignore at their peril the determining factors that shape the product. A designer, with an incomplete knowledge of the social and economic characteristics manifest in particular forms, can also therefore be naive as to the implications of their design.

This chapter aims to provide an abstract perspective that regards built form as a (theatre) set of signs. This provides a mechanism for explaining the commodification of urban space under late capitalism. The commodification of the public realm, manifest within the fashion of exchanging sign value in an abstract social space, offers a seduction to the public that alienates more fundamental social development. It is argued that such a trend serves the interests of capitalists, whilst drawing a veil over more fundamental material inequalities that exist between people.

Such an approach to thinking about the city provides a critique of the high ideals manifest in the 'urban design principle'. Common principles such as 'mixed-use', 'legible', or 'robust' (Bentley et al., 1985, Tibbalds, 1992) will be ineffectual without closer regard to the reasons for actual trends away from such ideals. It is held that the reasons are not manifest in the 'physical' but in the process for which the 'physical' is the outcome. To focus on the language of the principle is to move no further than the concept or the drawing, and to continue to regard the product of development (in this case the public realm) as an apolitical, pseudo-objective outcome, when in fact at every stage of design and development power is exerted so that vested interests are secured. Analysis of sign value and its manipulation within the public realm serves to expose some of the relationships that exist between the product, and the objectives inherent in the process of its creation.

Urban Form and the Appropriation and Exchange of Sign Value

Charles Levin, in his introduction to the translation of Baudrillard's *Towards a Critique of the Political Economy of the Sign* (1981) suggests that consumption has become a kind of labour, and that the motivation for such a labour is the desire to organise our existence with consumed forms of some signification relative to social space. Firth (1975) concludes that: 'Man does not live by symbols alone, but man orders and interprets his reality by his symbols, and even reconstructs it.'

Built form is a commodity into which symbolic meaning becomes manifest (Baudrillard, 1981)). Upon consumption, therefore, the sign value is appropriated and exchanged in a spatial discourse of social posturing. This 'symbolic exchange value' reflects the social relation between people that Marx (1957) described as manifest in the fetishism of commodities:

. . . the existence of things qua commodities and the value-relation between the products of labour which stamps them as commodities, have absolutely no connection with their physical properties and with the material relations arising therefrom. There it is a definite social relation between men, that assumes, in their eyes, the fantastic form of a relation between things.

Urban space is the ' . . . social space of encounter, assembly and simultaneity . . .' (Lefebvre, 1991). Urban space is also a manifestation of the spatial demands of the dominant mode of production. The spaces of urban form are an exemplary arena of production and consumption. Within this spatial and temporal domain the relations of society are manifest, and the appropriation of sign value provides a form of justification for labour, as well as a positioning device that transparently justifies the relations of power manifest within society. Harvey (1988) suggests that space in the city of late capitalism serves an ideological purpose and that '. . . in part it reflects the prevailing ideology of the ruling groups and institutions in society.' Furthermore it is the meanings associated with the signifying qualities of the forms that '. . . fashion our sensibilities, extract our sense of wants and needs, and locate our aspirations with respect to a geographical environment that is in large part created.'

The Illusory Qualities of the Sign

The sign can create what Ewen (1990) regards as being an ' . . . illusory transcendence of class.' The

polished surface of the product and its advertisement creates the fetishised space of the false consciousness. (*Figure* 8) To Lefebvre (1991) the world of images and signs is a ' . . . tombstone of the world . . .'. Within this realm the deception of signs ' . . . exercises a fascination, skirts or submerges problems, and diverts attention from the "real" – i.e. from the possible . . . Differences are replaced by differential signs.'

The scenario of a transcendent consciousness played out in the closing minutes of films such as Gilliam's 'Brazil' or Verhoeven's 'Total Recall' is the possibility of a virtual urban reality, where the power to shape the evolving 'fraud' within social space becomes the dictate of those who control and seek expansion by nurturing surplus value. Within this sphere lies the opportunity to manufacture the potential to appropriate distinction, and reaffirm the distance Bourdieu (1984) identifies as being a necessary (even if illusory) reaffirmation of rank. The rank for which the 'lowest' reference point is a working class aesthetic. The desire to manufacture demand and manipulate an image of obsolescence (fashion) establishes new wants.

The Los Angeles riots offer a stark, even if extreme metaphor of the priorities of a radical and violent response to material and racial oppression. A personal lasting vision of news coverage is the theft of consumables made possible by the chaos. The looting of shops offer a medium for venting anger. The appropriation of consumer goods could be for some the short term goal of confrontation and resistance to the structures that maintain more fundamental inequalities.

Creating the Market for the Exchange of Sign Value

The 'symbolic exchange value' of the commodity positions the possessor within a class where the consensual meaning associated with the object finds manifestation. What the object signifies (its sign value) is more important in social terms than what the object does (its utility value).

The appropriation of signifying signs associated with the properties of a manufactured object provides the connection with the hierarchy of a social order.

Figure 8. The polished surface of the product and its advertisement creates the fetishised space of the false consciousness. (Photos: Nick Plews)

Society therefore manufactures the potential for social prestation. This mechanism of discrimination and prestige shapes our tastes and therefore our patterns of consumption. In simple terms, therefore, it is not only the product that we consume, but the idea of the product, and what the product will allow us to become.

According to Marx and Engel's theory of historical materialism capitalism is reliant upon the qualitative characteristics of ideologies which ratify society's institutions. As an attribute of the superstructure ideology also, therefore, serves to sanction the status quo. Freedom to consume the broad range of products that capitalism offers has a democratic charm. The power to choose the image that sanctions a place within social space is equated with freedom in society. Tomlinson (1990) links such a consciousness or ideology with the need to accumulate capital:

Our personal identity is created out of elements created by others and marketed aggressively and seductively . . . based upon an individualised sense of selfhood and well-being and the notion of free choice. But if we think we are free when our choices have in fact been consciously constructed for us, then this is a dangerous illusion of freedom.

Dangerous or not the strong sense of affiliation to the idea of production that can enhance individuality supports the idea of a pluralistic society and the ability to instigate, even if not fundamental change in society, then a change in self relative to the social space of images. To put it in more simple terms, it is possible to instigate a change in lifestyle.

Zukin (1988) charts the interest of capital in establishing a 'loft lifestyle', and promoting the idea of living in the spaces of disused industrial buildings in New York. The ability to nurture the image of authenticity and the sense of the Bohemian in converting spaces that were previously used as artists' studios was motivated by purely commercial objectives. Modern American artists during the 1960s attracted increased public attention due to the escalating value of their work. As a result the space that they inhabited became in demand: 'From housing for artists "living poor" outside the mainstream of society to luxury housing for an urbane, "artistic" bourgeoisie, living lofts reflect an interesting ex-

pansion of middle class culture.' (Zukin, 1988)

Such developments reflect an interest in accumulating what Bourdieu (1977, 1986) termed 'symbolic capital' — the consumption of goods that through their signifiers associate the owner with distinction and respectability.

Style, Culture and the Creation of Sign Value

Harvey (1989) argues that architecture and urban design are complicit in this process of creating symbolic capital because the market for particular forms and images is a response to '. . . differential taste and aesthetic preferences . . .' that the patron and/or consumer of developments can dictate. The evolution of the 'high tech style' attests to such a process. From the drawing board of Richard Rogers as a scheme for the cultural centre of Pompidou, to the industrial sheds of business parks everywhere, the 'high tech' aesthetic is legitimised via the process of association. (*Figure 9*) This fetishism has prompted what Risbero (1992) regards as '. . . an arid aesthetic debate . . .' where arguments regarding the legitimacy of competing architectural styles illuminate the discourse, if not the content, of an essentially conservative postmodern culture.

Prestation and fetishism therefore explain why Jameson (1991) could suggest that in postmodern culture, '. . . culture has become a product in its own right . . .' or that '. . . postmodernism is the consumption of sheer commodification as a process.' An 'arid aesthetic debate' suggests that the hot air expelled over a concern for legitimising styles is an extension of the conditions of postmodernism, and its stranglehold over consciousness.

What is on offer is the freedom to explore a stage of 'cultural schizophrenia' where the set is made up of artifacts and society is the acting body. Raban (1975) notes: 'Techniques of mass production, mass communication and rapid movement from one part of the city to another have made it very easy for us to drift into being dandies and gangsters . . . it sometimes seems as if one might flip over the edge into a deliriously fragmented confusion of posture and roles.'

Signs Manifest within the Characteristics of 'Late Industrial' Urban Form

The 'shopping experience' of Meadowhall, Sheffield represents a clear manifestation of the process. The themed retail setting is no less than a stage of consumption, a virtual reality when juxtaposed to the industrial dereliction of its exterior context. Here the desire to control externalities has resulted in a truly self-contained and controlled environment that is increasingly reflected in the morphology of office developments (for example Broadgate, London), business parks (for example Wavertree, Liverpool or Stockley Park, Bristol) or speculative housing developments throughout the country. Thomas (1990) defined the form as the outcome of a desire to manufacture '. . . glittering islands in a polluted sea . . .'. This essentially 'late industrial' urban form addresses four distinct issues: (*Figure 10*)

1 **Security**: manifest within the orientation of buildings away from public routes reinforced by secure boundaries; the dominance of focused, hierarchical route patterns; the importance of entrance features and building clusters; and policies that employ aggressive spatial policing such as the ideas manifest within the 'secured by design' initiative of the employment of private security to physically and visually police public spaces.

2 **Image**: manifest within the symbolic reference intrinsic to built form; in the currency of styles used (reflecting a balance between what might be considered traditional [i.e. certain] and progressive and 'modern' [i.e. forward looking']; the extent to which schemes isolate themselves from their surroundings; the use of cultural artifacts and works of art; the capacity to show off other cultural items, for example in housing areas the family car; or the extent to which marketing and promotion nurtures a particular image.

3 **Management**: aimed at maintaining the image and ensuring security with the overall intention of securing the investment in fixed capital and more transient cultural capital against fluctuations in demand. Examples would include business park site managers or city centre managers whose primary objectives should be considered the nurturing of commercial compatibility of uses and activities.

4 **Secondary consumption**: in line with evolving patterns of consumption, spatial relations and built forms reflect the state of the art in living and working. The low density edge of town developments rely, for their feasibility, on the availability, consumption and continued developments in: transportation (cars and fuel, etc); household durables (refrigerators, washing machines, etc.); information technology (computers, faxes, telephones, etc.) and fast food and entertainment (the drive-in McDonalds, or the suburban 'traditional' pub, etc.). To fully participate in the urban form of late capitalism requires access to the products that the mode of production itself creates.

These characteristics of 'late industrial' urban form and its management are considered to be mechanisms that provide a response to inherent contradictions thrown up by, and the transitory characteristics of, the production process under capitalism (Berman, 1983). Such a process involves what Marx and Engels (1985) allude to as the '. . . constant revolutionizing of production, uninterrupted disturbance of all social relations, [and] everlasting uncertainty and agitation . . .'. Characteristics that distinguish, Berman argues, this age of modernity.

Urban Design and the Commodification of the Public Realm

The implication of such tendencies for the public realm is its commodification. The built form becomes purely a commodity in itself and people must consume the products of capitalism in order to find meaning within the built forms created. The public realm of the city is increasingly the arena for the consumption of signs, be they the signs implicit in the transparent stage set of built forms, or the consumed items that litter the stage. The actors within society create themselves and their identities through what they consume, and through the act of consumption.

But to view the products of late capitalism as purely signs is to succumb to the veneer of the fetish. The products of labour '. . . embody and conceal

Figure 9. Above and above right: high-tech. associations. (Photos: author/Nick Plews)

Figure 10. Above and right: characteristics of late industrial urban form: security, image and secondary consumption. (Photos: Nick Plews)

Figure 11. Above and right: freedom and democracy; the sign value of multi-national capital.

social relations . . .' (Lefebvre, 1991). The built form of the city is such a product. The city also has a social life that relies in part on its design (Sennett, 1990) and that social life should not be dictated by the vagaries of a commodification which codifies the material distinctions manifest between classes.

The desire to understand and contribute to the discipline of urban design should require an understanding of such processes, for it is in contributing to and challenging the assumptions or values inherent in particular designs (products) that the urban designer has effect.

Responsive Environments (Bentley *et al.*, 1985) and *Making People Friendly Towns* (Tibbalds, 1992) are populist texts that really fail to address contemporary built form as a spatial and temporal morphology resulting from the processes of accumulation intrinsic to late capitalism. As such the content of the books naively scratches the surface of designer consciousness, but fails to confront the vagaries and details of the development process, development finance or the potential alienation inherent within the physical realm and the abstract space of the mind. The idea that the built environment '. . . should provide its users with an essentially democratic setting . . .', and to regard the city as '. . . a political system in its own right' (Bentley *et al.*, 1985) ignores two concerns. First the extent to which current forms do provide evidence of quantitative, material discrimination between groups within society. Second the effects of the powers manifest within the process of production that shape and manipulate the product in the primary interests of producers and clients. Such an understanding would provide the beginnings of an explanation of why built form, as it currently exists, is not the physical manifestation of the free, democratic society that we assume we live in.

Beyond Sign Value: Developing Social Life in Urban Public Space

To regard the city's buildings and public spaces as signifiers of manufactured meaning is to regard the city as a metaphor. Lefebvre (1991) regarded the world of images and signs as a '. . . tombstone of the world'. Such a metaphor would appear to be appropriate for our city. Urban design needs to move towards understanding and challenging (or manipulating) the forces that attempt to impose such meanings with the intention of exposing them for what they are. The sign inherent in space submerges the more real problems by creating environments of perceived security, exclusivity and therefore distinction. The sign also has the potential to defer recognition of built forms that nurture spatial discrimination at the expense of a more exposed, free public realm of confrontation and learning, as well as built forms that reduce the material opportunities of groups within society.

Sennett (1990) regards an exposed, and I suggest non-commodified public realm in the physical city as important for nurturing an individual's true identity relative to a society that is known and understood:

The borders in fiction show what is lost in urban planning of open space by treating borders as though they are walls. People who live in sealed communities are diminished in their development. The wounds of past experience, the stereotypes which have become rooted in memory, are not confronted. Recognition scenes that might occur at borders are the only chance people have to confront fixed, sociological pictures routinized in time. It is only in crossing a boundary when people can see others as if for the first time. This experience of displacement and resistance we have in art and lack in urban design

The sign value of the commodified public realm is a wall to be crossed. A public realm dominated by the sign offers a domain, not for a 'city society', but for the false consciousness of multi-national capital which offers the illusion of freedom and democracy via consumption of the commodities that late capitalism itself creates (*Figure 11*). To design the exclusive and distinctive is to ignore the implication. The implication is a decline in emphasis on 'public' and the beginnings of a denial in the existence of any urban crisis.

The crisis of forms that deny opportunity for sections of society, and the cultural schizophrenia of the commodified city should be a truly public affair. If urban space has a political dimension, then the urban designer needs to have regard for the structures of power and influence in the development process, and of course society in general, if urban design wants to instigate any significant change in spatial trends. The logic of the recognition of the political dimensions of urban form is that the design of urban form becomes a political act.

Alan Alcock

AESTHETICS AND URBAN DESIGN

Introduction

Aesthetic is a difficult word. It first appeared in English in the nineteenth century and derives from Alexander Baumgarten's attempt, in the mid-eighteenth century, to outline a 'science of sensory cognition' (Beardsley, 1975). According to Raymond Williams (1976), the 'adjective aesthetic, apart from its specialised uses in discussion of art and literature, is now in common use to refer to questions of "visual appearance and effect"'. That is how the word will be used here, at least initially since the purpose is to discuss the topic reasonably clearly.

The products of urban design are inevitably experienced, they have the potential to engage our feelings, so some part of urban experience is aesthetic experience. It follows that urban designers must have some understanding of aesthetics. Clearly it is beyond the scope of this paper to comprehend fully what Scruton has called 'this continuing intellectual disaster' (Scruton, 1979). The purpose here is to discuss the relation between aesthetic theory and current approaches to urban design, and to outline how urban designers might more effectively take these matters into account. As there is some controversy about the extent to which aesthetic concerns should be taken into account in urban design, particularly between planners and architects, since these are the main professions from which urban design has evolved in the UK at any rate, it seems appropriate to start with this issue.

The Extent of Aesthetic Concerns in Urban Design

If we look back at the history of aesthetic control in the UK we find that architects took the initiative to try to impose these controls and were subsequently involved as panel members in putting them into effect. This system began to break down when architect panel members found themselves in conflict with other architects who were submitting designs for approval. Subsequently development control has largely been undertaken by the planning profession and so these conflicts of aesthetic value have been translated into conflicts between the two professions (Punter, 1984). Despite this history a recent Royal Fine Art Commission study *Planning for Beauty* (Hillman, 1990) continues to argue for an essentially similar system on the basis that 'plenty of people should be able to judge whether or not a design is good, apt, different and/or exciting of its kind, even if they might flinch on being asked about its aesthetics'. Well, whatever word we use it is certainly a continuing problem in practice. The idea that these aesthetic concerns might conflict with social concerns is implicit in Jarvis (1980) *Urban Environments as Visual Art or as Social Settings*. He is careful to be even-handed but the purpose of his review is 'not to deny the importance of visual matters in urban design although it does demonstrate their dominance in urban design philosophy and method to the virtual exclusion of any other approach to urban environments'. He contrasts 'the artistic tradition in urban design' with 'the social usage approach to urban design' and concludes that 'the traditional pictorial approach to design tends towards an esoteric and specialised view of environmental quality — the environment as fine art, to be appreciated'.

Jane Jacobs (1961) is more forthright. 'When we deal with cities we are dealing with life at its most complex and intense. Because this is so, there is a basic aesthetic limitation on what can be done with cities: *a city cannot be a work of art*'. She goes on to

42

say that this is to make the mistake of substituting art for life. However, she does put forward 'various tactics for capturing city visual order' from bits and pieces in the city. If Jane Jacobs is forthright, Robert Goodman (1972, p. 153) is simply outraged by the aesthetic attitude:

The more architecture can be described in the morally neutral currency of aesthetics, devoid of political content for the people affected, the more elite and the more removed from the political review of ordinary people become the experts who use this currency. Meanwhile, as those who practise architecture, criticize architecture, those who teach architecture and those who learn about and appreciate architecture continue to see it in aesthetic rather than political terms, the more useful this aesthetic becomes to those who rule. For the rulers are no longer repressing people with their highways and urban-renewal projects; they are supposedly bringing them progress and culture.

This critique of the aesthetic attitude is developed by Barbara Rubin (1979, p. 361) who argues that aesthetic ideologies are perpetuated by professionals as a means of resolving class tensions over control of urban space:

the merchandising of 'good taste' in urbanising America long ago coalesced as an aesthetic ideology which has permeated public policy and public programs. Urban "ugliness" and urban "blight" variously defined, have been employed as rhetorical gambits in propaganda campaigns to control the use of appreciating urban space . . . Aesthetic ideology remains a potent vehicle for the perpetuation of urban, economic and social inequalities, and serves as reinforcement for another oppressive ideology: that our economy is based upon the maintenance of efficiencies through free enterprise.

So at one extreme we have an apparently innocent but problematic desire for 'good design' while at the other aesthetics is branded as a sinister weapon in ideological struggle. Given this wide spectrum of views on what the extent of aesthetic concerns in urban design ought to be, let us now turn our attention to what the aesthetic approaches of urban designers are.

Aesthetic Approaches to Urban Design

There seem to be three reasonably distinct approaches each aiming to achieve aesthetic quality, although in practice, designers may combine them. The first approach envisages an urban viewer who will respond appropriately when presented with tableau of high aesthetic quality. Just as there are good pictures and bad, so there are good and bad townscapes, indeed this is the term used to describe the most recent variant of this approach which includes the possibility that the viewer is mobile and can thus experience 'serial vision' (Cullen, 1971).

This approach has its origin in eighteenth century landscape concerns known as the picturesque. It also underlies the studies of old towns by Camillo Sitte (Collins, 1986) in the late nineteenth century which put forward a series of rules mainly about how to group buildings around public squares and streets for aesthetic effect, and the tradition continues through the work of Raymond Unwin (1909). The influence of this approach is now widespread and underlies many recent prescriptions and guidelines. It is also the basis for Peter Smith's (1987) work although he tries to relate it to such earlier concerns of classical aesthetics as harmonic proportions. Essentially this first approach relies on choosing from existing successful towns those ingredients or principles which appear to contribute to their aesthetic quality and using them elsewhere. (*Figure 12*)

Smith's concern with divine proportions and Sitte's focus on plan geometry both overlap with the second main approach which one might call the aesthetics of the plan. A basic distinction between the first and second approaches is that the second is a more abstract version of the first. However in addition it relies on the notion that certain geometries or forms have aesthetic qualities of a universal kind. These essentially mathematical ordering characteristics are claimed to arise in nature and to be responsible for the aesthetic quality of for example, a flower. Although the underlying theory dates back at least to Pythagoras and thus appears to underlie classical urban design and its derivatives, it has been codified in relation to architecture rather than to urban design (e.g. Wittkower 1988). Nevertheless it is the basis for guidance such as height — width ratios and, in practice, is clearly the ordering principle of many urban plan patterns and geometries. Like the first approach then it is supported by an interpretation of existing cities, in this case classical cities, and these in turn are given authority not only from tradition but from a proto-scientific interpretation of nature.

(Cullen, 1971)

Visual qualities are given a relation to plan form . . .

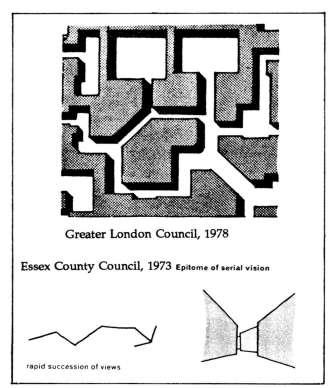

Greater London Council, 1978

Essex County Council, 1973 Epitome of serial vision

rapid succession of views

. . . then it is assumed that visual qualities depend on maze-like plan forms . . .

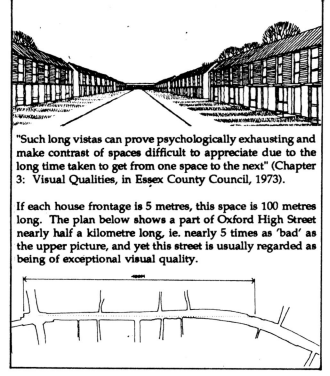

"Such long vistas can prove psychologically exhausting and make contrast of spaces difficult to appreciate due to the long time taken to get from one space to the next" (Chapter 3: Visual Qualities, in Essex County Council, 1973).

If each house frontage is 5 metres, this space is 100 metres long. The plan below shows a part of Oxford High Street nearly half a kilometre long, ie. nearly 5 times as 'bad' as the upper picture, and yet this street is usually regarded as being of exceptional visual quality.

. . . but plan forms do not determine visual qualities

Figure 12.

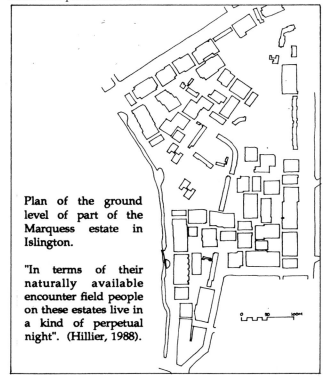

Plan of the ground level of part of the Marquess estate in Islington.

"In terms of their naturally available encounter field people on these estates live in a kind of perpetual night". (Hillier, 1988).

. . . while maze-like plan forms can have unfortunate social consequences.

A concern with axes and vistas links it to the visual concerns of the first approach but the achievement of aesthetic quality rests on claims of universal validity, rather than judgements of taste.

A third approach, which abstracts even further in relation to the real city, has parallels with the concerns of some modern painting. The analogy between plans and abstract painting has been noted by Summerson (1949) in the work of Le Corbusier, but as an aesthetic approach to urban design it is more connected to notions of the expression of ideas and philosophical ideals which, it is claimed, distinguish satisfactory city designs throughout history (Wilford 1984). The approach is exemplified by Bacon's *Design of Cities* (1975) which oscillates between interpretations of plans of cities of high aesthetic value like Rome, Florence, Venice and commentaries by painters, particularly Paul Klee. A concluding passage entitled 'Moving through three dimensions' (p. 321) gives an indication of the approach:

We end as we began with the participator. But we see him through the eyes of Paul Klee, linked to his environment in a way that is very different from the relationships imposed by Euclidean geometry or Newtonian physics. The space he is in and the infinity he seeks are a far cry from those evoked by the stable 'lina del Centro' of the Renaissance diagram on the title page of this book, and are more closely related to those suggested by the elusive 'far point' of Paul Klee shown above. Here are expressed a great new range of awareness, an interaction of emotion and perception, a total involvement that we have only begun to sense. Thus we are able to develop a feeling of what lies ahead, far transcending what we already know.

In as much as this approach is concerned with aesthetic experience then, it appears to envision a lone occupant experiencing something closely resembling sensory deprivation, but this is put forward as an ideal. So the city is here seen as an aesthetic medium comparable to a painting or a piece of music and thus it may be a legitimate consequence that disturbing aesthetic experiences are induced.

Problems With These Approaches

The first approach corresponds to a subjective theory of aesthetics but involves individual subjects having similar aesthetic experiences if it is to have any practical value. Aesthetic philosophers grappled with this question in the eighteenth century in the face of growing evidence that aesthetic experience varies from one individual to another. Perhaps the most well known expression of this dilemma is that of David Hume (1974) who proposed that 'Beauty is in the eye of the beholder' but went on to put forward the notion of a 'qualified observer' to distinguish good taste from bad. The relation of this strategem to the class structure of eighteenth century England is clear in Humphrey Repton's comment: (Forty 1990): 'a knowledge of what is good, what is bad, and what is indifferent whether in actions, in manners, in language, in arts, or sciences, constitutes the basis of good taste and marks the distinction between the higher ranks of polished society and the inferior orders'. So the aesthetic theory underlying this approach has its origins in an aristocratic theory of society which is particularly at odds with modern notions of egalitarian democracy.

These problems give rise to practical difficulties since the good examples on which the approach is based necessarily involve taste judgements in the first place. These may be wrong. Furthermore the selection of characteristics from these good examples involves a further judgement about which characteristics account for the earlier judgement. The characteristics selected may be the wrong ones, they may only 'work' as a complete ensemble or they may not be transferable. An illustration of the confusions that can occur is given by Rothenburg, used as a good example by both Sitte and Unwin, and from which it was deduced that complex spatial form was the basis of its charm: an idea which is now fairly pervasive in urban design guidance.

The accompanying illustration suggests that the spatial structure of Rothenburg (*Figure 13*) has been misinterpreted as intricate. In fact like many medieval towns it has quite straight routes leading from the gates to important public spaces near the centre surrounded by a deformed grid. If anything accounts for its charm it is the profusion of building forms and their elaborate details. Of course, to emulate these is too close to copying for modern appetites used to originality as an automatic virtue. Paradoxically, since this approach expanded in response to the perceived monotony of modern planning, its major criticism in practice is its monotony (Hillman, 1990).

Rothenburg: Germany (Drawing: Olga Samuels)

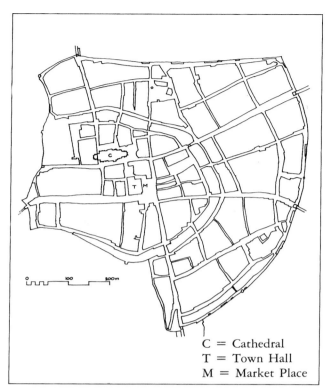

C = Cathedral
T = Town Hall
M = Market Place

Rothenburg: public space map (based on map of 1884 in Unwin, 1909.)

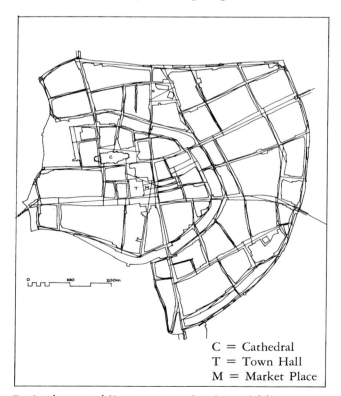

C = Cathedral
T = Town Hall
M = Market Place

Rothenburg: public space map showing axial lines

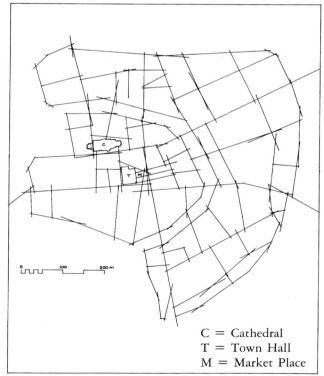

C = Cathedral
T = Town Hall
M = Market Place

Rothenburg: axial map

Figure 13.

The second approach corresponds to an objective theory of aesthetics. As we have seen above in discussing the selection of objective characteristics to account for subjective aesthetic responses, these two theories are complementary. But a further claim is made that certain characteristics have universal aesthetic value. This theory has its origins in Plato's theory of Forms supported by Pythagoras's discovery of relations between whole numbers and musical harmonies which appeared to relate mathematical properties of objects to qualities of experience and led, for example, to mathematical theories of proportion. By the end of the eighteenth century these theories were discredited, nevertheless in practice they have survived (Beardsley, 1975 p.p. 204–5). However there is no evidence that they are effective in terms of achieving aesthetic value and plenty of evidence that they are not.

Arguments for the continued use of this approach in urban design are based on references to good models; usually classical, where plan geometry and the proportions are perceived to account for their success. So, as in the first approach there is the problem of whether these chosen characteristics are correct. The use of these particular geometries and proportions in itself cannot guarantee success even, apparently, when adopted by highly regarded designers. When James Stirling's project for housing at Runcorn was published in the Architectural Review (Nov. 1976) the architects stated:

The height of terraces relative to the size of a typical square (300 ft by 300 ft) is of similar proportion to eighteenth-century squares in Bath, Edinburgh, etc. In the case of the Georgian square all terraces front onto the square with public roads intervening between terrace and the garden square on each of its four sides. At Runcorn the organisation is an L-shaped arrangement with two fronts and two backs facing over the garden square.

So the geometry and the proportions of height to width of good examples were selected whereas the spatial relationships between public garden space and private housing fronts and backs were reversed for half of each square. As we now know the estate, known locally as Legoland, was so plagued by social problems that it was demolished some twenty years later. At least one architectural journalist (Pawley, 1989) implied that the occupants had the 'wrong' aesthetic values: 'If you want architectural precedents for "Legoland" you have to find them in the eigh-teenth century squares of Bath and Edinburgh, where the same suppression of individual identity to grand geometry occurs. But the sort of people who appreciate that sort of thing don't live in Runcorn and never did'. Thus a problem with the universal validity of the theory is nimbly transposed into a failure of taste. A large proportion of modern architecture and urbanism has been based on this kind of approach with results in terms of aesthetic value which are generally considered to be rather worse than might have arisen by chance.

The third approach corresponds to theories where aesthetics is synonymous with art in its modern sense. Since no satisfactory theory of art has been proposed, indeed it has been argued that it is insuperable (Tilghman 1987), this approach is problematic at the outset. In particular the approach corresponds to a theory of expression which aims to express ideas and ideals through the medium of urban design. Now clearly the expressive possibilities of the city are not the same as those of literature, painting, sculpture or music. Nor do we experience them in the same way. Art is an autonomous realm and to try to include the city in it is really a category mistake. There is a further problem which can be illustrated by one of the earliest examples of this approach, – Antonio Sant Elia's Città Nuova. According to Giedeon (1954) his artistic intentions were to express 'mobility and change'. Now with the benefit of hindsight one can see that these artistic intentions closely correspond with two of the most powerful determinants of modern city form, namely the interests of traffic engineers and commercial developers. These interests are given a powerful boost by eliding them with artistic intentions which simultaneously conceal and legitimate them. A similar point is made by Rick Poynor (1989) in *Nigel Coates: City in Motion*, when he notes that the economic necessity of the idea of the disposable building because of land value inflation is now being celebrated as the 'fluidity' of the contemporary city.

This approach then is really about mapping the interests of designers onto the dominant interests in the city in a manner which appears to resolve aesthetic concerns but which results in aesthetic consequences which may or may not coincide with the values of the citizens – for this is not a primary concern.

In summary then we find that the first two approaches set out to achieve cities of high aesthetic value but are ineffective, whereas the third tries, and fails, to oblige us to accept its aesthetic consequences by a kind of confidence trick. If we accept that urban design should result in aesthetically satisfying cities then there seems to be no guarantee that designers using these approaches can achieve this although it is in their interests strongly to deny it and the reason is that this kind of aesthetic satisfaction depends on aesthetic values which in modern societies are both varied and volatile.

Aesthetic Values

The history of aesthetic theory shows an evolutionary development closely related to more general social developments suggesting a close relation between these theories and other contemporary ideas whether magical, metaphysical, religious or, more recently, moral ideas (Beardsley, 1975). Recent work seeks to explain these relations, including the renegotiation of aesthetic values over time and the co-presence of competing aesthetic values, as social facts (Mukarovsky, 1979). These can in turn be shown to relate to the class structure of modern society (Bourdieu, 1984). Since those with most power are more able to impose their aesthetic values on the production of the city, the practical outcome in urban design is the reproduction of dominant aesthetic values. Often these values are incompatible with those of occupants at the outset (Prak, 1984). In any case it is difficult to see how in a class society where a range of competing aesthetic values co-exists, it would be possible for urban designers to treat them all equally as required by egalitarian ideals. It would seem that we are faced with two alternatives: one is to accept the impossibility of the situation and in effect to ignore it, the other is to pretend that these problems do not exist and to continue with approaches which are demonstrably ineffectual. Needless to say this corresponds to the spectrum of positions which were outlined at the beginning.

Aesthetics and Urban Design as Problematic

We seem to have come to a dead end, which suggests that we may have set off in the wrong direction, since it was clear at the outset that the relation between aesthetics and urban design is inescapable. So let us summarise the argument so far. First we saw that the study of aesthetics arose at the moment in history when it became problematic and the meaning of the term has both changed and remained elusive. In terms of visual appearance we found a spectrum of opinion about the emphasis that should be placed on it in urban design. We noted that this spectrum of views closely corresponds to a range of aesthetic approaches used by urban designers which in turn closely corresponds to a range of aesthetic theories, themselves corresponding to historical circumstances, but none of these theories relate directly to urban design. When we try to relate them to urban design we find an apparently insoluble conflict between the variety of aesthetic values and our notions of equality which cannot be resolved in the physical design of the city. It seems likely then that our problem arises from a mismatch between paradigms for aesthetic theory, particularly those developed in the era of industrial capitalism in relation to autonomous arts such as painting, music, sculpture, literature, etc., and our aesthetic experience of the city. What characterises these arts is that the aesthetic intentions of a painter, a composer, a sculptor, an author or poet are interpreted and experienced by other individuals looking, listening, or reading albeit at a particular place and time and embedded in a social tradition. Each of these arts is a medium for relating individual to individual in terms of notions such as universals or absolutes. Now our experience of the city is not this kind of thing at all; it relates the individual to the collective; it is the experience of our relation to everyone else. In so far as these are aesthetic experiences, in the sense that we feel them, it seems appropriate to call them socio-aesthetic to distinguish them from the other kinds.

Socio-Aesthetics

In the absence of theory some fragments will have to serve as illustrations. First there is the question of how encounters arise from spatial arrangements in the city. The work of Hillier *et al.*, (1992) has shown how spatial relationships powerfully influence the way we encounter others. They demonstrate that our experience of being alone in space, of being crowded or being in a comfortable relation with others arises from the relation of each space to all the others. To put this in aesthetic terms, it is difficult to see how our experience of others in the city can begin to feel good unless the spatial relationships are conducive to a comfortable relation with everyone else, and this must precede any other physical attributes having any effect on us.

Second, there is what we might call social distance i.e., the sizes of space or the distances between buildings which constrain the distances between the occupants of space and the occupants of buildings. This seems to relate to visual acuity, in the same way for example, that the distance between an actor and the furthest member of an audience (about 18 m) depends on the ability to see the actor's eye expressions. Again this relates to how we experience others; beyond this distance it is a remote relation — others become increasingly object-like — within this distance relations become increasingly intimate. We should note that this applies to the relation between occupants of upper floors and occupants of public space on the ground as well as just horizontal distances. Also this notion should be distinguished from those arising from earlier paradigms which imply that certain sizes of spatial enclosure are mysteriously 'better' than others (Arnheim, 1977).

A third example arises from our experience of the behaviour of other people. Now it is obvious that urban design does not cause behaviour, nevertheless it can constrain it to a greater or less extent and it can allow more or less visibility of activity in or around buildings adjoining public space particularly at ground floor level. Similarly one of the arguments for mixed-use is to try to increase this experience of others' activities in public space at all times of the day or week. (Bentley, *et al.*, 1985)

A final example relates to the detailed design of both buildings and public spaces. Much attention has recently been devoted to semiological studies of the city, often ignoring the conflict between contemporary concerns for innovation and the need for conventionality if signs or symbols are to have shared meanings. However in socio-aesthetic terms what is far more important is the idea of the index i.e. something which indicates something else without the need to know codes or conventions, in particular, things which indicate that the public realm is valued, that we value each other and each others' experience. What this implies is that the things we see in and from public space should indicate that care and effort have been invested in them. The word elaboration begins to capture this idea that effort (labour) has been invested in our experience.

These then are some illustrations of how a modified view of aesthetics might more particularly and more directly relate to urban design to replace approaches borrowed from elsewhere which will not work or are in conflict with more direct urban aesthetic concerns.

Conclusion

I have argued that urban designers cannot escape some level of aesthetic concern since their designs are experienced in a variety of ways including aesthetic. I have tried to show that the approaches currently employed are ineffectual because they do not relate directly to the concerns of urban design and indeed are often in conflict with those concerns. It is thus important to develop what I have called socio-aesthetics so that these concerns are given their proper priority. It may be that all that is required is a shift of paradigm from one which aestheticises politics to one which re-socialises aesthetics. I am encouraged in this view by a series of articles which have appeared in a comparatively new magazine called *Architecture Today* in which each month the last page has been written by various architects, artists and designers under the title 'My Kind of Town'. On reading these articles it is interesting to note that a majority of the experiences described to account for the choices of town are closely related to the concerns advocated here, although, as practising designers, they are likely still to advocate and pursue the earlier design approaches.

SECTION TWO

ISSUES OF URBAN CHANGE IN ESTABLISHED CENTRES

For many of us, urban design is concerned first and foremost with established urban centres. Goodey returns to ask clear questions about the demands to be met in the city of the twenty-first century, along the way challenging our perceptions of our own power and skills for making positive changes. Holyoak gives us a personal review of urban dwelling since the 1960s and reaffirms a confidence in vibrant urban living. In contrast, Butina Watson takes a *fin de siècle* eclectic view of the pressures and products of late capitalism.

Coming home, as it were, Bentley concludes this section by showing how urban designers can act as enablers to a group of urban tenants, helping them to remake their place and presence in the city.

Brian Goodey

URBAN DESIGN OF CENTRAL AREAS AND BEYOND

Approaching the end of the present century, it is possible – even preferable – to allow nostalgia to take over, and to contrast the contained city-state of the industrial revolution and before, with the sprawling scatter of the post-industrial city, often judged as out of control by its detractors.

In reality the focused city-state provided opportunity for the few, whilst offering constraining repression for the majority. The car-oriented, post-industrial city has been generated and sustained by the individual decisions of the majority. It reflects the energy of a new type of urbanism, one which may be difficult to come to terms with for those, like myself, who value the function, image and social symbolism of the tightly woven, centred, urban place.

Make no mistake, if the majority had shared my belief in, and desire for a functioning urban heart, it should be retained, unthreatened. Punitive road costing, fuel rationing, or prescribed sustainability in design could change attitudes fast, but thus far technological and social change have precipitated a steady sequence of political, economic and individual decisions that fundamentally alter the nature of city centres and generate new landscapes (Goodey, 1992).

Even prior to Second World War destruction, Garden Cities and healthful workers' suburbs began to remove central area populations. In the post-war period, cities extended beyond their bounds as more private road traffic replaced public transport, and rapidly heavy industry was forced from centres and the inner ring because of air pollution and traffic generation. New suburbs drew with them office and industrial employment and, since the 1976 breakthrough in Britain, retail opportunities and public and private, space-extensive, leisure facilities.

The diffusion of activity and investment patterns has led to an increasing desertion of traditional town and city centres. The mix of activities which generated twenty-four hour life has gone, and buildings and spaces regarded as significant and worthy of conservation, are isolated in space and time. This process is likely to continue. Ward (1992) citing the 1992 NOP Regional Lifestyles survey:

More than 13 million people living in cities yearn for a more tranquil existence in a small town or in the country side . . . only economic realities prevent them from moving . . . More than half (54%) of those questioned cited dirt and noise as the main reasons why they were fed up with city life. 45% desired the open spaces of the countryside.

With much day to day activity circulating around the periphery of the city, the role of the centre was and still is – in question. Few policies prohibitive of development elsewhere have ensured its survival, although positive policies for spatial stability but market re-positioning of the city core, seem to have been judged as more successful.

The Success of Urban Quarters

The policy for demarcating and marketing urban quarters owes its origin to pre-industrial cities. Religious pilgrimage sites have survived to provide focus to some of our best-established 'quarters' of today. Their definition and content owe much to the enduring townscape values of the pre-industrial city – even where no pre-industrial city existed! The successful quarter may, or may not be based on a traditional craft or residential area, but if it has evolved from such it will now be designed and manufactured to fit a promotional, rather than a merely functional, image.

The typical contemporary quarter will share some, or all, of the following characteristics, emphasised to ensure its visibility from, rather than its integration with, its surroundings:

1 Conservation, enhancement, reconstruction or invention of a 'typical' street and building *morphology*. This will be so maintained and amended as to provide optimum pedestrian interest and access to retail or commercial facades, and may emphasise path sequences and landmark-capturing views.

2 Retrieval or generation of a historical image. Presentation of *historic buildings*, building groups or even street furniture as artifacts often with visitor uses appropriate to their origins.

3 Concern for the *pedestrian environment*, reflected in soft and hard landscaping, and in the presence of gathering and events spaces focused on historic buildings or features.

4 Reinforcement of the quarter status with *signing* and use of carefully selected names and logos.

5 Exclusion of the car, but provision of *parking* and clearly directed walkways in the very close vicinity.

6 Management of advertising, *events*, and the user population to attract and maintain the required visitor mix.

7 Attraction of specialist *retailers* who endorse and benefit from the quarter's image.

8 Emphasis on *environmental quality*, and especially on litter control, through high street management strategies.

9 Regular re-statement of the historic significance of the quarter through *local, national and international advertising*.

10 Use of the quarter as a symbol for the extended city, providing a focus for *civic events*, including visits by potential investors.

Central heritage districts, newly regenerated arts foci (as in Macclesfield and Birmingham) and former inner city commercial districts, such as Birmingham's Jewellery Quarter, Bradford's Little Germany, and Glasgow's Merchant City (Patrick, 1991) are indicative of these developments in the UK.

To achieve these characteristics it is necessary to define the area, and to co-ordinate application of planning and management policies. The degree to which these involve consultation with, or the active participation, of residents, retailers, occupiers and users will depend on the local political culture and the agents involved. URBED, one of the key British consultancies involved, maintains a high level of community contribution; in the French context, Vighetti (1986) sees it as essential, but often the community has departed.

In the majority of cases indigenous residents are few (and getting fewer) and users, especially visitors, are seen as participating through the market mechanism alone.

Many towns and cities, at all scales and in several cultural contexts, have reflected on the success of the quarter approach in retaining, or rebuilding, retail activity in the city centre, in supporting conservation initiatives, and, not the least, in providing a renewed context for the existing investment in public infrastructure. From being stranded in a declining heart, many city halls now find themselves adjacent to attractive tourist quarters (Goodey, 1992).

Who Wins and Who Loses?

City authorities are not the only winners in this establishment of urban quarters. The whole community may be expected to recognise the benefit of enhanced historic buildings or provision of a new skyline, together with the revival of public spaces, and increased provision of cultural facilities (Karski, 1990, identifies specific profits and losses in this regard).

Whilst retail activity continues to pass to the periphery, with car access and parking available the major determinants, the city centre becomes a very particular type of retail attraction (Parkin *et al.*, 1989). It is a place for traditional window-shopping, for non-essential goods, and for retrieving the vitality of street events. For over a decade, British planning authorities such as Durham have sought to enhance the character of such areas through development control and guidance.

Now, however, there is the suggestion from the United States that out-of-town malls are dropping from their peak of appeal, and that events and activity programmes there cannot retain the users. (Herbert, 1992). To the mobile population that has now experienced the comfort and convenience of the peripheral mall for a generation, the city centre quarter may offer a safe and comfortable alternative. But clearly there have been major losers in the increasing similarity in the functions of city quarter and out of town centre. Both are essentially car-borne, themed, environments where visible security and formalised events programmes suggest a managed extension of private retail areas. Whilst the theming of malls is contained and media-oriented, quarter theming presents an uncluttered image of the past. The town centre quarter has become just another type of out-of-town mall, but without night-time containment — Rogers (1992) on Carmarthen

Now the centre is a thing apart from the rest of the town; it belongs to Etam and to Freeman, Hardy and Willis. You can do anything there, for it is nobody's responsibility. It is just a trading post surrounded by car parks, and could be anywhere — even the middle of a moor — except that it happens to be where it is.

With the first wave of peripheral shopping malls in the UK, one commercial assessment suggested that these would eventually serve 70% of the population (the exact percentage of Americans currently making a weekly journey to the shopping mall) with the remaining 30% having to rely on a declining urban core.

It is not difficult to identify the 30% — for they are the very groups which have always relied on the vitality of public space for their survival — teenagers and the elderly validating their existence, the poor and disabled, the newcomer and the marginalised (Goodey, 1979). These were excluded from enclosed shopping malls through lack of car access, security, or spending power but are now being excluded from the tidy urban quarters for the same reasons.

The Beaubourg in Paris, the first of the *grands projets*, has been widely hailed as a positive regenerative force for its quarter, attracting street life and new investment but, as Vaizey (1987) noted, at some cost:

. . . visitor profiles show that the deprived, the ill educated, the poor, hardly ever appear at the Beaubourg — for all the crowds, it isn't Trafalgar Square on New Year's Eve, or even Times Square on any night. It is Yuppieville. Self-flushing lavatories and all. The whole is culture as spectacle.

Five years later Trafalgar Square is a secure shadow (Goodey, 1993). Lacking spending power, traditional users are replaced in the city centre by visitors and tourists who, nevertheless, can provide a source of income via soliciting or crime. (Retailers accept such criminalisation by budgeting for 'shrinkage' [Worpole, 1987]). More important, the absence of local people in city centres reduces the opportunity for the young and old to validate their lives through confrontation with or observation of, others. Few of the characteristics which identify quarters are likely to be significant priorities for the 30%. More often the new pedestrian surface, exotic planting, or building conservation exercise is an indication of the direction of public funds towards visitors.

Whilst there is some evidence that tourism and cultural activities retain, or revive, the economic fortunes of the city centre, there is less evidence that such spending transfers to investment in training or job creation, and certainly not to community integration or welfare provision. With the increase in quarter land values and property costs, it is more likely that residual welfare activities are physically marginalised to the inner city ring — the charity shop zone — or to the suburbs. Youth disaffection in suburban areas is likely to grow and, as the elderly come to dominate our societies, may be joined by new forms of social protest from that source.

Design in the Evolving Urban System

In the face of these rapid and permanent changes, urban design solutions have rested far too firmly on a set of principles which are outdated when applied to the majority of the urban space. Traditional concepts of central city space use and design have been re-emphasised and endorsed to the neglect of both the urban periphery, and the zone between.

Characteristics of the urban quarter which have been lovingly detailed and promoted have, in many cases, led to the expansion and debasement of heritage as an acceptable pastiche and its unwitting reproduction through standard materials and details. But as Moulden (1992, p. 109) notes, 'heritage has a tendency to glamorise the past above the present. Rather than inspiring people to perform greater deeds than their ancestors it encourages them to treat the past as a zenith of human achievement'. There is now a very real danger that this patterned commodification of central area design will bore the visitor who, seeing it as a consumable environment, will seek attractions elsewhere. 'There should be limits to the British obsession with heritage,' notes Glancy (1992), 'When functional workday objects such as traffic lights, bus shelters and No Entry signs have to be dressed up in Regency fancy dress to keep us Quality-Street-sweet, heritage has given way to idiocy. This is what has happened to Regent Street, London.'

My particular concern is that the fundamental interplay of urban design factors — space and circulation use, facade design, landmark making, edge definition and furnishing — has failed to develop a new language in keeping with future, rather than promoted traditional demands. This generalisation does, however, blur some exceptions where functional postmodern languages have been used to express the potential of the city centre (most strikingly in Barcelona and in Oscar Niemayer's concrete museum park in Sao Paulo, Brazil), but the tired retreat to a medieval-cum-nineteenth century pseudo-vernacular is much more common.

In the current decade we must develop a new language for detailing the context of contemporary urban activity. Regardless of 'green' proposals and the potential of public transport, the city is now spread — with the majority of residents and users dependent on personal car travel. Although pricing and crowding mechanisms, together with greatly enhanced transport interchanges, may do something to regain the central area, the majority of activity will circulate within, and between, wider urban systems. Yet in most cultures there remains a fundamental divide between highway engineers and urban designers, the latter retracting from any response to the fragmented environment of the periphery where roads generate the edges, retailers the landmarks, and developers the communities. Where, at worst, the urban designer is limited to providing an urban memory in the odd plaza.

Highly regarded urban design values (Punter, 1990) seem largely based on pedestrian use of space, which is difficult to reconcile with the fact that most able pedestrians are only willing to walk a quarter of a mile from their car. Walking, and the environmental enjoyment which it brings, are now leisure activities to be undertaken in heavily managed green spaces.

Urban design as a discipline has shown little willingness to accept the increase in scale implied by a car-dominated society. Even the fundamental ingredients of landmark, edge and node are now viewed from the car, and imply a super-structuring within which a range of car-accessible and highly differentiated functional zones are developed.

The order to be established in our city systems is not that of the old central city. Its differentiation is achieved through the road access hierarchy, and through the orientation of zones, intervisible, but offering very different experiences. The existence of three scales of public city perception has been identified for Brasilia by Hurtado et al., (1988) and such American-generated concepts as 'framework design' may offer an effective method of working within such systems (see Lynch, 1976 and Peterson, 1990). The out of town mall is one key element, but even it has received little urban design attention. Residential zones turn their backs on road access, leisure and recreation areas are hidden from road view, and industrial or office sites are either strung along routes, or set back as country estates.

There is a strange confrontation between popular and professional value systems which has led to a stand-off which benefits neither. The expanding city — sprawling, scattered, confused — is the functional city which we have all designed by use. To claim that it is a city incapable of enhancement represents a failure by urban designers.

Urban design is, after all, a practical process of three-dimensional place making, and not just a specific method of making particular types of place (Moudon, 1989), although the graphic joys of Cullen and Tibbalds (1992) and the various 'commandment' lists (Punter, 1990 after HRH Prince of Wales, 1989) might suggest otherwise. In this context, there are three areas where we must move with a sense of urgency and with new tools fitted to the contemporary task.

Temporal and Spatial Management of Visitors

The identification and promotion of urban quarters and suburban malls as visitor and tourist destinations brings an initial flush of financial success which often encourages further investment. The attraction, for that is what it now is, must be sustained in a tourist, rather than an urban, market and its purpose therefore becomes largely touristic – removing it from the local urban system. Such areas may provide increasing financial benefit with a consequent loss of social benefit, alienating visitors from residents, and excluding the latter on a seasonal basis.

The urban designers' task in such contexts focuses much more on space/time management than in the past, with sign systems, space programming and flexible visitor management as essential tools of the urban design strategy (see Page, 1992 on Canterbury's current strategies).

With the massive tourist flows to key centres – between 5 and 6 million to Venice per annum, for example – the concept of carrying capacity is again being explored with some interest, but it must embrace the considerable findings from psychological and customer care research (Williams and Gill, 1991, Jansen-Verbeke, 1992).

It seems inevitable that the urban designer will have to invest in the role of the high street manager, but a manager whose brief fits within, rather than departs from, the management of the whole urban system.

Sharing Public Spaces

We have reached a stage where public space design presumes very little of the user, save to sit, to walk and to be young. Public space design has become patterned around our expectations of standard figures in the environment, it is a deterministic response which takes little advantage of our increasing knowledge of individual and group needs. (*Plate 2*)

There is no doubt that a broader perspective on public space design could meet the needs and interests of a much wider range of urban residents and users. (Comedia, 1991). Teenagers, for example, require sitting and talking space, in full view of public movement but with little of the delicate detailing so beloved of designers. Their spaces are robust, easily cleaned and essential to personal growth within, rather than alienated from, the urban context. The elderly, on the other hand, require protected and well detailed spaces which are secluded but secure. Teenage spaces are not the same as elderly spaces!

The Barcelona experience is instructive here not because it has revealed a sensitivity towards the design for various age or interest groups, but because it has generated such contemporary public space diversity that there are lessons for all. Rather than see visitors and residents in confrontation; there are methods by which the two groups can be brought into casual intimacy, sharing the qualities of the space around.

Why do we not recognise that space provision for all age levels needs the same degree of attention given to the needs of children?

Suburban and Peripheral Quarters

The most significant area for attention, and again one suggested in Barcelona is the development and design of intermediate quarters between the urban core and the periphery. Here neither the traditional methods of the urban core, nor the new methods of car-directed 'edge city' are appropriate. But neither, perhaps, is the lapse into a misplaced belief in the potential of the 'community' to direct its own design and development.

If the city is to continue to benefit from the spending power of visitors, and if both the tourist quarter and the peripheral malls are full to overflowing, then here is the investment energy which can breathe new life into the structure of nineteenth and twentieth century suburban areas. Typically such areas are losing their retail facilities, but retain a range of interesting industrial and recreational features which can provide the focus for visitor attractions, and a new basis for retail development. This approach has been advocated by the author in a proposal for visitor planning in the London Borough of Islington (Touche Ross Management Consultants and Goodey, 1992, p. 3):

It is difficult to escape from a preliminary conclusion that Islington's interpretive plan will draw heavily on the concept of 'pearls on a string', i.e. a movement sequence punctuated by nodes of attractions or character districts. This pattern, once established, can be reinforced through the full range of interpretive media . . . The essence of Islington is the anticipation in 'turning the next corner' and visitor spend should be applied to community facilities . . . we are, therefore, minded to reject a more traditional interpretive approach which might focus upon one or two buildings and geographical locations.

What we lack is the language by which to express the potential of such areas, together with the poor image which they enjoy. The resource of such districts is their human, rather than built-form character, encouraging the development of urban design character which is people, rather than building, based. We are already seeing the emergence of such ethnic districts in the inner ring of some cities, and here the urban structuring is expressed in a totally new language, emphasising gateways, sound and colour, rather than European medieval traditions. Similarly there is unrealised potential for 'green' quarters which explore variety and contact with natural and semi-natural environments as is suggested by Leicester's Environment City programmes (Goodey, 1992)

Key urban design principles must, however, survive in this diversification of district foci — visual differentiation, comfort, safety, flexibility and internal variety generated through the manipulation of space and time are as applicable here as in the heritage-inspired centre.

The Multi-Image/Multi-Centre Urban Space

In his classic urban design study, Kevin Lynch discussed *The Image of the City* (1960) but, in fact, expressed the *images* of the city. Thirty years on, another Lynch-generated study, *The View from the Road* (Appleyard, Lynch and Myer, 1964) seems a

much more appropriate basis for our discussion of urban design at the close of the century.

To retain a positive concept of the city beyond the year 2000, we must admit that the post industrial era has disposed of the mono-centric urban place, and has replaced it by a form which, whilst negotiated and created by city users, remains largely rejected by urban designers. (Banham, 1971, Goodey, 1989). The long-standing planning investment in the Dutch Randstadt concept is a notable exception (van Beetz, 1989) It is, however, the reality and a retreat to tradition will only serve to divert too many good minds to the reproduction of false facades which reflect past, rather than contemporary values.

In the past, urban design has developed from an understanding of architecture, the evolution of urban form, and a flirtation with selected aspects of human, not to say humane, behaviour. To my mind, the future of urban design, indeed the future of a rewarding urban experience, is in the hands of a consortium of traffic engineers, landscape planners and cultural managers. The fact that I do not see this type of alignment emerging in any European country is a matter of considerable concern.

Urban design training and practice are getting further and further away from the enhancement of a popular experience of urban places. Competition, and especially retail competition between and within towns and cities has been their generative force, but also the source of decline. In approaching the year 2000 we must ask whether the urban designer should — or indeed, can — exert any significant impact on the fortunes of our cities and whether this impact recognises economic and human motives behind city extension, or tries, instead, an imposed doctrinaire solution.

Joe Holyoak

THE SUBURBANISATION AND RE-URBANISATION OF THE RESIDENTIAL INNER CITY

. . . a jumble of mean streets, huddled terraces and dark, insanitary and badly ventilated courts. In its layout there was hardly any sign of intelligent planning, but everywhere evidence of a haphazard development. (Bourneville Village Trust, 1941).

Women return from the shops to be blown about amid the appalling dinginess of rough-shuttered concrete; children of all ages run wild in the undefined wastes known to the faithful as pilotis. (Taylor, 1967).

Vast, monolithic tracts of private land have simply been converted into a crude patchwork of smaller, but equally private plots, each a little protected dream-world, each conforming to a pre-processed image which has more to do with the simplified, suburban culture of television advertising than with the rich tradition of the European city.

(Davies 1987).

We have been busily making and remaking the inner city in various images, but still we seem dissatisfied with the result. Can we make it better?

The 21st birthday of the Joint Centre for Urban Design is also the 25th anniversary of my graduation from architecture school. During the mid-1960s I received an orthodox architectural education in system building, rationalised production and urban re-structuring, while outside the window all these things were happening in great quantities. My first job was working for the Birmingham City Architect Alan Maudsley. The years 1967—69 were the peak of housing production in the city — 24,300 municipal dwellings built. I was asked to help on an exhibition which juxtaposed recent photographs of rundown inner city streets in Balsall Heath and elsewhere with drawings of the brave new world which was to replace them. I was so struck by the revelation that the exhibition was back to front — what was going to be demolished was a better environment than that which was to replace it — that I was moved to write my first piece of architectural journalism. It would

surely have cost me my job had the *Architects' Journal* published it (it didn't, but paid me four guineas all the same).

What was happening out there was the suburbanisation of the inner city. The dense complexes of working class houses, factories and workshops, corner shops and pubs, unrelieved by green spaces built on loose grids of streets, pierced by canals and railways, were being comprehensively swept away. They were being replaced by a pattern which had elements both of Le Corbusier's geometric, high-rise Ville Radieuse and of Parker and Unwin's curvi-linear, low-rise Garden Suburb. These two models had different tendencies, but shared common roots in an anti-urban tradition emanating from William Morris and Ebenezer Howard.

Corb's rhetoric — 'We have allotted the entire ground surface of the city to the pedestrian. The earth itself will be occupied by lawns, trees, sports and playgrounds.' (Le Corbusier, 1967) — was echoed by Birmingham's redevelopment policy of providing public open spaces at four acres per 1000 people, and integrating it into 'a continuous parkway system of over 200 acres.' (McMorran, 1973). But despite the Corbusian influence in the high-rise towers, inner city redevelopment was characterised by a huge reduction in population density in Birmingham's five inner city redevelopment areas, with only 56% of dwellings being replaced. There was an exodus of 49,000 people to the outer suburbs and to overspill towns.

Documents like *When We Build Again* (Bourneville Village Trust, 1941) make clear the motivations behind this process. The movement of population from the inner city to the middle ring (by-law streets), and from the middle ring to the outer suburbs, was seen not only as conventional physical planning policy but also as reflecting working class aspirations. Although a careful distinction was made between high density (people per acre) and overcrowding (people per dwelling), it was taken for granted that an improvement in environmental quality depended upon a reduction in density. In the comprehensive redevelopment of the inner areas this took the form of a reduction in net residential densities from about 120 people per acre to about 60.

There is plenty of evidence that the rehoused residents of the newly redeveloped inner areas were at first very pleased with their new conditions. They had modern homes with kitchens, bathrooms and central heating, modern schools for their children to attend, and grass and trees about them. But the losses were also being documented, in books such as *Family and Kinship in East London* (Young and Willmott, 1957), and *The Forgotten People* by the Vicar of Ladywood (Power, 1965), who described the changes taking place around his church. Of course, there was simply the sudden, traumatic disappearance of a familiar landscape. But there was also the break-up of complex kinship structures; the emergence of single-class areas; the inconvenience caused by the zoning of land uses, which eliminated such things as corner shops; and above all, the fragmentation of the community's collective sense of its own identity. (*Figure 14*)

Distance lends enchantment, and we should examine the feelings of painful loss which we now experience when we look at photographs of vanished streets of terraced houses with children playing football in the street and women chatting on the doorstep. We must not forget the impoverishment which

that environment also represented. Yet what we respond to positively in these pictures, taken as recently as the 1960s yet showing a lost world, is the quality of immediacy. This we might define as the close juxtaposition of the private and the public realms, with the private shaping the public, the concentration of people together to produce a social intimacy, and the close relationship of those various places which form aspects of the same life — house, shops, pub, school, church and work. (*Figure 15*)

While all of these elements of immediacy can be carried to excess to produce a pathological environment, as they did in many slum areas, it is their almost total absence in our replanned inner areas which has brought about much of the social alienation which all too often characterises them. A thinly spread population, with a poorly defined public realm, and with functional land uses zoned apart, will inevitably find it difficult to sustain a rich collective life when that population is also impoverished by lack of resources and a high rate of unemployment, as it typically is today.

Despite their suburban densities, the redeveloped inner areas built by local authorities in the 1950s, 1960s and early 1970s looked nothing like outer suburbia in their morphological patterns and building types. Indeed, the architectural and urban design philosophies which generated them were ideologically opposed to the qualities of suburbia, whose merits only later became intellectually respectable (Oliver, Davis and Bentley, 1981). But with the rundown of local authority housebuilding in the 1970s and after the energy crisis of 1974, which made inner urban areas more attractive for the middle class, the suburbanisation of the inner cities grew with the arrival in large numbers of the private developer.

With the activity of the Barratts and the Wimpeys, either developing land released by industrial decline or obsolescence, or buying hard-to-let 1960s housing from the local authority to radically improve it, suburbanisation became more explicit. Unlike the council architects' departments, developers had no commitment to the modern movement — indeed on the contrary, had a marketing commitment to populist forms — and in any case already had a stock of suburban house-type designs that they were used to building and selling. (*Figure 16*)

This, combined with the country's growing conservatism, and the emphasis by the Thatcher

Figure 14. Figure/ground maps of Ladywood before and after redevelopment.

Figure 17. New development (1992); Moseley and District Churches Housing Association, Balsall Heath, Birmingham. Architects: Databuild Ltd.

Figure 16.
Private development in Duddeston, Birmingham; suburban environment next to 1950s tower blocks.

Figure 15. Birmingham: Highgate (right) and Lee Bank (left) showing nineteenth century inner city housing before redevelopment — 'the terraced street' — and 1960s comprehensive redevelopment 'towers in the park.'

government on placing private and family interests above the collective, led to inner urban areas coming to look more like slightly compressed versions of the suburbs; rows of neovernacular two storey houses, each with a small front garden with a car parking space, but little in the way of communal resources – house production rather than city building. With few exceptions, the products of housing associations in the same period were of much the same character.

Another development contemporary with this was the growth of concern about community safety, and its consequences for urban design. Does alienating estate design cause crime and the fear of crime, or are they caused more by changing social factors such as working-class poverty and unemployment? It is in the nature of the argument about environmental determinism that conclusive arguments cannot be found, and the disputes between the determinists and the anti-determinists remain unresolved (Coleman, 1985). Which side one is on probably depends mostly on one's political and ideological commitment.

But the determinists, while not winning all the arguments, have succeeded in having a big effect upon the design of housing estates. Both through the influence of Alice Coleman's work for various local authorities, and through the influence of the police's 'Secure by Design' programme, the making of public areas that are safe has moved high on the political agenda. This in itself is entirely reasonable, and so is the discrediting of the worst kinds of multi-storey housing built in the 1960s as being not only unpleasant and unsociable, but also unsafe.

But unfortunately, the community safety programme has had reactionary effects, emphasising traditional (i.e. suburban) models in its desire to specify norms for a safe and secure environment. This is not due only to authorities who have not actually read *Utopia on Trial* or police officers who misuse the term 'defensible space'. Coleman herself, using her own special brand of logic, claims that; 'The best blocks of flats are those that are most like houses, and so it is logical to deduce that the most effective way of preventing the various kinds of social malaise would be to build houses and not flats in future.' (Coleman, 1985).

At its most extreme, the fear of strangers becomes pathological, and creates not only estates made of multiple, unconnected culs-de-sac, but also housing

in privatised compounds firmly secured from the rest of the city. This paranoid form of urbanism has nothing in common with the varied, lively and permeable urban quarters described by the woman who started the concern for community safety in 1961, to whom strangers on the street represent a valuable element in the street's safety (Jacobs, 1961).

So for 30 years, the inner cities have been becoming more like the suburbs. Does this matter? The inner city is, after all, a nineteenth century invention, reflecting a particular stage in the industrial revolution in terms of economy, employment, class and family structure, and mobility. These conditions no longer exist, and in fact the neat tripartite built form and class structure described in *When We Build Again* — central area (back-to-backs), middle ring (by-law terraces) and outer suburbs (semi-detached houses) — had already ceased to fit reality.

There are two things, I suggest, that do matter. First, that a certain threshold density (probably around 100–120 people per acre) is necessary in order for an urban quarter to be able to sustain a range of facilities and services, and a quality of vitality, which are appropriate to an urban way of life. Cities like Los Angeles are frequently cited in argument against this claim. But Los Angeles is not all suburbia – it also has mixed-use inner city areas, and in fact because it is so big it has multiple centres. But its dependency upon the motor car for mobility, and the growing dependency of the smaller British cities which are being affected by similar forces, is a powerful argument against dispersal, in terms of economy, equity, convenience and ecology.

Second, that a mixed economy is necessary to sustain conviviality in inner urban areas. The use of compulsory purchase orders to bring about comprehensive redevelopment 30 years ago brought about a monoculture. The middle classes, professionals such as doctors and teachers, and small businesses were all driven out of the inner areas, increasing the cultural poverty of these districts. Local authority monopoly cannot bring about a lively urban quarter, but neither can its Thatcherite equivalent of the 1980s, the free workings of 'the market'. That it could was for many an attractive myth, but the Isle of Dogs illustrates what a futile idea it was.

Today's complex economy needs a judicious mixture of local planning and development stimuli. A Castle Vale or a Barratts estate are both unrealistically simple in their concept of what an urban area is, and cannot produce a sustainable environment. There are currently encouraging signs that the suburbanisation of the inner city is being countered on both these fronts – on density and on the mixed economy. The cycle of learning from the past, the downturn in the economy and the anti-local authority doctrine of the present government .all play a part.

The sheer functional and economic sense of putting different uses, including most critically residential use, together at a reasonably dense concentration, is now increasingly realised, in the contribution it makes to convenience, mobility and sociability. Mixed-use is no longer a case of a special exception to land use regulations, but often a standard condition insisted upon by planning authorities. The 'Living Over The Shop' programme is one particular expression of this emphasis on rediversification (Petherick and Fraser, 1990). Hand in hand with this is a return to the traditional formal typologies of the urban block and the street, and the contained urban square. These are the forms that give coherence to a mixture of uses, and legibility to the urban plan. Comprehensive redevelopment dispensed with them with disastrous consequences. A landmark in this return to coherent urban form was the 1987 Internationale Bauausstellung (IBA) in Berlin (*Architectural Review*, April 1987). The various housing schemes in the inner city area of Kreuzberg crystalised many current tendencies in reaction against disaggregated modernist forms.

It is also arguable that a time when the economy is in recession is an appropriate time to appreciate once again the traditional urban virtues. Both the 1960s, when local authorities restructured large parts of British cities in the name of one doctrine, and the 1980s, when private developers and development corporations did the same in the name of another, were periods of overheated development when minds became overheated also. We are currently experiencing more convergence of thought towards sensible policies of urban renewal. Schemes such as Estate Action are turning unattractive estates into more livable environments; not only improving the often inadequate fabric of the houses and flats, but modifying the spaces around them to bring them nearer to older models of urban space that we know work well. The growing empowerment of residents in the process is an important element in this.

The government's City Challenge programme, whose very future is uncertain as I write, for all its doctrinaire elements has a potential for countering the suburban inner city. In Birmingham's City Challenge area of Newton and South Aston, an appalling legacy of the comprehensive redevelopment policies of the 1960s, the programme includes the building of 800 new dwellings. This represents an increase in density of about 16% without any demolition, just built on space left over after planning. Of course, these houses and flats will not be built by the Housing Department, but by housing associations and private developers, as part of the government's diversification of tenure policy. Despite residents' reservations, this is probably a good move, both in terms of increasing the ability of the local population to support local services such as schools and shops, and of bringing variety to the present impoverished monoculture. (*Figure 17*)

This degree of amelioration of the suburban inner city is probably all that it is realistically possible to do in the foreseeable future. More radical reshaping will have to await a different economy and a different culture, unless we can afford an IBA or two instead of garden festivals. But the vision of a civilised life for ordinary people in the inner city remains. Mark Girouard sketches some of its mundane but vital features from his second floor living room (Girouard, 1985):

I can see, at various times, lovers, roller skaters, policemen, the local busybody, the local lavatory attendant, who exercises neighbourhood dogs for a moderate fee, and the local cripple, processing slowly past in his electric chair, waving to people on the pavement. Twice a year a religious procession goes past, once a year the steel bands and dancers of the Notting Hill carnival. I am within two to ten minutes walk of a street market, at least six churches and chapels, four cinemas, four good restaurants and many bad ones, and at least twenty pubs. I am twenty-five minutes from Piccadilly Circus. The area has its disadvantages, but it does me well enough.

Georgia Butina Watson

THE ART OF BUILDING CITIES: URBAN STRUCTURING AND RESTRUCTURING

Cities are an immense laboratory of trial and error, failure and success. . .
(Jacobs, 1961)

As we approach another *fin de siècle* we try to take stock of many of our urban design failures and successes. The art of building cities is forever high on the agenda of many conferences, symposia and community group meetings searching for methods and urban design concepts that could lead to better and more equitable cities. But these concerns are not unique to our present decade.

Throughout history many attempts have been made to create places that would fulfil a variety of societal requirements and at the same time be aesthetically pleasing to their everyday users and to generations to come. For centuries, visitors to Prague, Florence and many other cities have experienced unforgettable journeys of discovering breathtaking panoramic views and picturesque townscape images whereby each new sequence proved to be even more dramatic than the previous set of images.

These cities have undergone many small and large scale transformation processes whereby both planned and incremental growth patterns have left a variety of morphological patterns that reflect the social, political, economic and cultural richness of the societies that have produced them. These centuries old historic towns acquired their physical and spatial structure components through a variety of factors: natural topographic and landscape features; the availability of building materials; construction techniques; the mode of economic production; the socio-political factors and the design approaches of the period.

From time to time efforts are made to unify and co-ordinate different urban tissues and to provide urban design frameworks that would enable future territorial expansions and urban transformation processes. At the small scale of intervention we have the case of Sienna where building regulations were issued in 1292 to unify individual building components of Campo del Santo. Equally radical was the decision made by the Siennese City Fathers to open up new views towards the Cathedral's *Campanile* in order to reinforce the town's unique morphological structure and therefore promote a sense of orientation.

Far more comprehensive were urban design ideas put forward by Camillo Sitte for the city of Vienna at the turn of the last century. In his proposal Sitte placed great value upon the existing historic townscapes and morphological patterns as 'powerful providers of sensory experience of cities' (Butina, 1991), important for achieving a sense of historic continuity and local identity. At the same time he allowed the city to expand, accommodating all the necessary functions that a modern city should have. Sitte therefore juxtaposed shortcut views of historic townscape sequences with modern, broad, tree planted avenues. Whilst the shortcut views were introduced to support the visual experience at the pedestrian level of movement, the radial, concentric and broad avenues were designed to cater for faster moving traffic and to unify different urban tissues. In adopting this framework a number of Central and Eastern European cities solved the eternal problem of linking old and newly expanding urban areas.

By the beginning of the twentieth century the spirit of industrial growth prompted the search for

64

new city planning and architectural ideas. 'City Beautiful', 'Garden City' and the 'Radiant City' planning and urban design philosophies were seen at the time as radical solutions to some of the most critical problems that the industrial cities began to display.

Within a span of three decades both urban and rural landscapes were greatly transformed. The growth of the car industry brought about new motorways; the motorways and new rail links generated suburbia and new settlements. At the same time plans were prepared by the urban professionals to restructure many historic city centres to reflect new progressive city planning and architectural beliefs. Instead of maintaining and improving the old variety of functions and urban form patterns that were vital for supporting life at the local neighbourhood level these new proposals re-zoned many cities into areas of segregated, distinct uses with a view to clean up many undesirable functions and the chaotic 'slum like' imagery.

In Britain, the Second World War put a halt to the implementation of many of the earlier formulated planning and urban design principles only to be reinstated in the post-war reconstruction period with far greater commitment, vigour and zeal than any other prior urban intervention. Planning legislation was introduced to direct local authorities into the next phase of urban development, receiving much political and financial backing from central government. Instead of a piecemeal, largely localised building tradition, new types of built form production came into operation. Many historically formed areas were designated as unfit for living and comprehensive slum clearance programmes and 'cleansweep planning' approaches were introduced (Ravetz, 1986). Bulldozers moved in, people moved out, and many cities were radically transformed into contemporary urban landscapes dominated by high-rise office buildings, large scale mass housing schemes, shopping malls and other types of large retail outlets (Relph, 1987). Similar initiatives took place elsewhere, especially in North America. By the 1960s it became apparent that modern urban forms which replaced traditional street and block patterns could not support the same vitality and diversity of life that older areas could. Some saw it as 'the death' of our cities (Jacobs, 1961) and proposed alternative ideas, largely relying upon pre-modernist city planning principles.

In spite of the efforts made by urban designers, architects and planners to create urban areas that would be visually pleasing whilst supporting community life at all levels, both small and large scale restructuring of cities continued throughout the 1970s and especially the 1980s. Much of this large scale restructuring was the result of the demands placed by the provision of large corporate office developments, but equally destructive were many new shopping centres and leisure complexes. Some critics (Castells, 1992) see these transformation processes as part of the broader political, economic and technological changes.

Political changes are most obvious in the way that the built environment has been produced and managed, relying to a great extent upon private capital to induce growth. In this development model, planners, architects and urban designers are hired to provide professional advice and to co-ordinate various local level initiatives. Their aim is to satisfy the various actors involved in the production and consumption of the built environment. Each development proposal is judged on its own merit without necessarily conforming to a pre-established set of rules. Various tax and other forms of development incentives can be granted by the central government to attract further investments.

The second major change of the 1980s was the globalisation of economy, where money is managed as any other commodity, being channelled internally to fund the most viable and profitable developments. Resources are often pulled together to finance mega schemes such as Canary Wharf and other similar large scale projects. Since the clients who lease or buy buildings produced by financial consortia also cross international boundaries, they generally seek office typologies that display an international corporate identity. Inevitably, the schemes designed, financed and produced by such systems all look alike. Some critics have accused such developments as failing to take into consideration the existing context and the unique qualities that many historically formed cities possess (HRH The Prince of Wales, 1989).

The third major change has been a technological one. Since the mid-1970s there has been a revolution in the field of information technology required to support complex operations of shareholders' and others' markets. At the local built form level these requirements are translated into special building typologies and different urban morphologies.

Buildings now need to accommodate a broader typology of office space, ranging from smaller cellular units to large dealing floor plates. Where there is no need for large trading floors, smaller open plan or cellular offices are organised around lush and glazed atria, designed to provide both exclusivity and security.

In order to service such new operations and cater for computer cabling, artificial lighting and air conditioning, buildings are constructed with higher floor to floor ratios, on average 5 metres high. Since many older buildings cannot support such requirements, new office typologies, popularly called 'groundscrapers' came on the market. They were first introduced in North America and then transplanted across the globe. In order to develop these bigger and 'squatter' buildings larger plot sizes are required, quite often encompassing several traditional block systems.

Locational preferences of such developments are to stay close to similar working organisations which has brought about large scale restructuring of many historic parts of cities where such businesses tend to be located. Not only have we lost a large number of historic buildings but whole urban tissues were radically transformed during the 1980s development boom. Many publicly relevant buildings and open spaces came into private ownership reducing in the process the old variety of uses and thus weakening the sense of vitality of many parts of cities. Such developments, or 'hybrid cities' (ADPSR, 1992) as some refer to them, have generated highly controlled environments under camera surveillance. Public entrances into such developments are reduced to an absolute minimum for security reasons, acting like medieval walls or citadels, keeping out those who have no business to be there.

London, as the country's financial, political and cultural capital has also undergone many transformation processes. Its unique morphology and skyline are the result of many centuries of urban shaping and re-shaping. Especially significant in this context is the City of London which has always played an important role. The City's geographic location was defined during Roman times, but many of its close-knit morphological tissues are associated with its medieval and later periods of development.

The post-1666 reconstruction was initially carried out respecting the framework of the earlier morpho-logical patterns with the gradual incorporation of Georgian building typologies and new street and public open space layouts. It was the Victorians who brought about more radical transformation patterns. They introduced the first speculative offices usually built upon amalgamated medieval plots. They also aligned existing medieval streets and provided new road and rail infrastructure to cater for the capital's buoyant growth. But even this large scale restructuring was still within the context of earlier developments, being controlled by Building Acts of 1888 and 1894.

The post-war reconstruction of London saw further changes. Bombed sites required repair and at the time it was seen as the great planning, urban design and architectural challenge. Both the Barbican and Paternoster Square still stand as solemn reminders of Utopian visions gone wrong. Many other historic parts of London fell victim to comprehensive re-developments and in the space of fifteen years, between the 1960s and 1970s the historic skyline was irrevocably altered by what HRH the Prince of Wales has termed, 'a jostling scrum of skyscrapers all competing of attention' (1988). Much of the urban character was destroyed but failed to transform London into an efficient city (Marmot and Worthington, 1987).

During the 1980s a great deal of energy and investment was channelled into re-cycling old buildings and regenerating large derelict sites. Backed by various government tax incentives, the establishment of Enterprise Zones and Simplified Planning Zones, London's skyline continued its dramatic change at an enormous speed. In order to provide appropriate office space at the scale attractive to international developers, and to avoid lengthy and complex negotiations required for developing in the City itself, the sites that lie just outside the City boundaries came into great demand.

One such large site that occupies the former Broad Street Station and parts of Liverpool Street Station is the Broadgate development. It lies partly in the City and partly in the Borough of Hackney. It is a third of a mile away from the Bank of England and half a mile from the river Thames. Initial development negotiations started in 1975 when British Rail began to consolidate some of their operations and by March 1979 outline permission for development of 1.2 million sq.ft. of offices; 30,000 sq.ft. of retail space and a new bus interchange was granted to British Rail. The planning conditions attached were that any new development on this site should have a public open space to form a focus of the site and be surrounded by a number of shops, pubs and restaurants and have a public right of way (Williamson, 1989). In 1982 British Rail invited Rosehaugh PLC and Stanhope Properties to develop the site and the developers commissioned Peter Foggo and Arup Associates to design the first four phases. By the time the remaining land was acquired a number of complex factors came into play, determining the final outcome of their 29 acre site.

With the deregulation of the stock exchange market, the so-called 'Big Bang' of October 1986, international banks were allowed to deal directly on the United Kingdom securities market without an intermediary. Due to this deregulation and the fact that London enjoys an excellent geographic location, between the time zones of New York and Tokyo, the City of London and its fringes became the most desirable office location in Europe. Its most direct rival was Canary Wharf which started to pose a threat to the City's future economic vitality. The City's response to this threat was in the form of new planning frameworks formulated through the new City of London Local Plan. By the time this plan came into effect it reflected a completely different development attitude to the earlier more conservative philosophy. Although the City Corporation still aimed 'to achieve a high standard of urban design for all forms of development so that they are successfully integrated into the City townscape' (Corporation of London 1989 p. 124) the City increased its permitted development plot ratio from 3:1 to 5:1. This decision was made to meet a growing demand of a particular type of office space, as explained earlier.

The shift in local planning attitude has significantly influenced the final outcome of the Broadgate scheme. With its 3.5 million sq.ft net of office space; 25,000 jobs; and 90,000 sq ft of retail and other uses it became a symbol of the 1980s development boom (Rosehaugh Stanhope Developments, 1991). So, what are the key urban design principles and the impact on its surrounding areas? In its overall urban design concept, Broadgate reflects two distinct philosophies. The first, Arup's approach (Phases 1–4) makes a successful morphological and contextual urban design reference but at the same time it allows new building types into the scheme, catering for much needed office space. The second, Skidmore Owings & Merrill (SOM) concept (Phases 5–14) is very much embedded in the American school of thought. What ties these two concepts together is the linkage system of publicly accessible routes through the site and the sequence of open spaces, as specified by the planners in the conditions attached for granting the original planning permission.

The most successful in this system of spaces is the Arup designed Broadgate Arena. It sits along an important axis linking Liverpool Street Station and Finsbury Avenue. Its typology echoes great Georgian Squares, in this case the nearby Finsbury Circus. (*Figure 18*) The central, 65 m diameter space is defined by arcades and terraces of predominantly eight storey office buildings made of granite, both polished and flamed, enclosed by glass surfaces. (*Figure 19*) Because of their set-backs at fifth storey level, the office blocks blend well with their immediate neighbours. Lush vegetation provides a pleasing backdrop and softens up large office blocks in the background.

The central Arena forms the focus for many events. In winter, it is an ice rink, popularly referred to by the children of Hackney as 'our rink', whilst in spring, summer and autumn many theatrical performances take place to the delight of both casual and 'official' passers-by (Butina, 1992). The central Arena is surrounded by shops, restaurants and bars that add even more to the impression of the space being busy, active and adding vitality to the whole scheme. (*Figure 20*)

When questioned, the users of the scheme answered positively regarding many aspects of the first four phases of development. Scoring high was the permeability through the site, the district and local legibility, the variety of shops both along the Arena and in the octagon leading to Liverpool Street Station. Most memorable are various events taking place at the Arena, though somewhat 'staged', as some casual passers-by noted. But in spite its very busy atmosphere during the daytime the scheme becomes deserted at night, unless various organised events or ice skating take place in the Arena. The contextual reference is somewhat broken in the treatment of the external edge of the development, its lack of publicly relevant uses, its wide pavements and its lack of permanent residents, which depart

Figure 18. Broadgate, London and its morphological context.

Figure 20. Right, Broadgate Arena during summer months and figure 21, left, SOM, Bishopsgate.

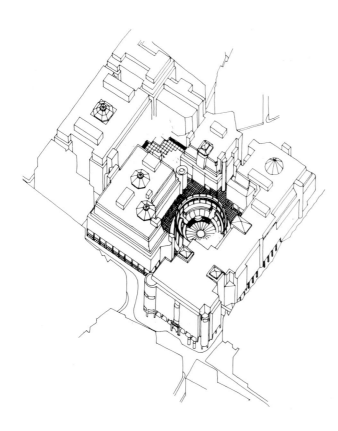

Figure 19. Broadgate, Arup designed phases I–IV. (Drawn by S. Thompson)

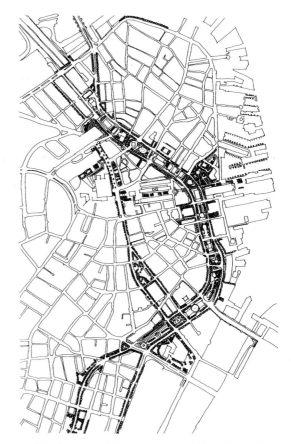

Figure 22. Boston, Massachusetts: The Central Artery redevelopment proposal. (Drawn by Steve Thorne)

from the traditional neighbourhood and street concepts.

The success of the SOM (Phases 5–14) is undoubtedly more debatable. Technical problems of building over the station sheds were more difficult to overcome, hence the existence of the large Exchange Square. It looks deserted most of the time, except during sunny lunch hour breaks. The lack of an active edge is apparent and the space evokes the emptiness and nostalgia of de Chirico's metaphysical paintings. Due to the presence of the three open spaces which were taken into plot ratio calculations and an overall increase in development plot ratios and air rights, the SOM buildings dominate both in height and bulk. Especially critical is the edge along Bishopsgate, where Phases 6 to 8 meet the older Victorian and Edwardian building typologies. The thirteen storey high (66 m) groundscraper, designed in Post Modernist, Chicago-styled Beaux Arts tradition (Spring, 1988) makes a stark contrast to its modest five storey brick neighbours. Its combined floor plates, required to accommodate large dealing floors, are three times the average historic block sizes. Morphologically and typologically this part of the scheme breaks up the area's homogeneity and departs from its contextual congruence. The most positive side to this block is its ground floor retail variety, that makes a useful contribution to Bishopsgate's street and business vitality. (*Figure 21*)

Many critics and everyday users identify Broadgate as a new business quarter (Williamson, 1989), having its own identity and having supplied much needed new types of office spaces. The overall outcome is both positive and negative. First, some of the positive aspects are highlighted. The Broadgate development has revitalised parts of the redundant railway lands and in a way has re-directed some of the 1980s development pressure from the nearby, historically sensitive areas. It has paid for the refurbishment of Liverpool Street Station and subsidised various other improvements in Hackney. The scheme ensures public access via the system of pedestrian routes and open spaces, but the management and surveillance of these spaces are catered for by private money and access to many of the schemes' attractions are highly controlled. The scheme also introduces variety in the retail and leisure sectors of the economy, but fails to cater for residential and other types of socially relevant uses.

Probably the biggest drawbacks are the size, scale and bulk of several office buildings which depart so drastically from their nearby context. By sitting partly in the City and partly in Hackney this development has extended the artificial City boundary. This is likely to push up the land values, gentrify some of its surrounding areas and as a consequence reduce the social and economic richness so important for local neighbourhood vitality.

With its successes and failures Broadgate epitomises all the facets of the development attitudes, politics and finance of the 1980s. It is absolutely clear that planning and urban design frameworks need to be re-assessed. First, development plot ratios, as applied and calculated in the Broadgate development, do not work. Second, in addition to site briefing, development and urban design guidelines we need to adopt more strategic, visionary and more directive urban design approaches. We should strive to create places that would support richness, variety, diversity and congruence at all scales of development. One such approach comes from the other side of the Atlantic, from Boston.

In contrast to schemes such as Broadgate or Canary Wharf where large scale restructuring implies concentration and amalgamation of sites catering primarily for single use functions, Boston demonstrates 'a reversal of fortune' attitude to both large scale and small scale urban design interventions. The area of Boston under consideration is its central downtown artery that runs through a number of business and local neighbourhoods. When implemented some forty years ago the artery was greeted with much professional support whilst being condemned by local people who lost their jobs and homes as a result of this intervention. Accompanied at the time by other large scale improvement and slum clearance programmes this part of Boston dramatically changed its identity and its historic pride. The words of Jane Jacobs still echo in our minds and take us back to re-read her book *The Death and Life of Great American Cities* (1961) where she is particularly concerned with Boston's North End destiny. Declared at the time by the city planners as the 'civic shame' it was in effect, Jacobs describes, a neighbourhood full of little shops, working places, residences and children's play areas. It was a healthy community of social mix, diversity and variety doomed to die and to be transformed into monotonous, sterile and vulgar urban areas. Like its

West End neighbour, North End managed to survive, though heavily marred, undergoing a drastic decline of its population from 35,000 recorded in 1920 to a mere 9,000 accounted for in the 1980s (Boston Redevelopment Authority – BRA, 1990).

The ill fate of North End and other adjoining neighbourhoods started to change in 1984 under the new administration of Mayor Flynn (Schmidt, 1991). The dominant city planning strategy was to channel the rapid economic growth of the 1980s into local neighbourhoods through quality urban design. The key to this enterprise is the proposal to reconstruct, or one may say deconstruct the Central Artery, by placing it into an underground tunnel. Together with the Third Harbour Tunnel project this urban intervention is anticipated to be one of the biggest engineering, planning, urban design, management and above all financial tasks in Massachusetts' history.

The vision for Boston 2000 (BRA, 1990), developed jointly by urban professionals and local community groups, is based on three main long term goals:

1 economic success as a place of work
2 ecological and sustainable city
3 socially, politically and culturally bound local communities (BRA, 1990; p. 2)

'Such goals include encouraging the location of new commercial development away from the heavily developed financial district; preserving and restoring historically significant streets, buildings and neighbourhoods; and promoting downtown housing development' (BRA, 1990; p. 4). These long term goals are further translated into a number of urban design strategies. The key strategy is the reconstruction of the down-town artery and its replacement by a linear system of parks, public open spaces and green avenues, reclaiming some 50 acres of derelict land. (*Figure 22*)

This linear open space system is bordered by two boulevards that run the length of the artery level, acting as a 'ribbon which ties neighbourhoods together' (BRA, 1990; p. 9). The restoration of an east–west historic street system will unify the neighbourhoods that lie on the opposite side of the artery and promote social, economic and cultural re-integration of these historically important areas.

Whilst the north–south system of parks, boulevards and open spaces is designed to promote Boston's new district identity and reinforce the sense of place and legibility at the larger scale of urban design, each section of the plan is conceived to promote distinct local neighbourhood character. This reinforcement is to be achieved not only through physical design but also in terms of the social, cultural and economic vitality of these areas.

Special considerations are given to the revitalisation of Boston's down-town neighbourhoods. North End, one of the city's most densely populated areas, is to benefit from the provision of new housing catering for a wide sector of social and age groups. A new community hall is to provide support for local community participation and various other activities that the project designers in charge, Boston Redevelopment Authority and other supporters see as a 'hallmark of and source of pride to the North End' (Boston, 1990; p. 22). The new provision of parks and other public open spaces is to cater for children's play areas, so much needed in this neighbourhood.

Equally significant is the regeneration of the downtown waterfront zone, so essential for the business and tourist industries. Experiencing a serious decline since 1990 it now promises new vitality through the creation of pedestrian zones, hotels, cultural centres and a number of leisure facilities.

Boston's financial district is not forgotten either. It will benefit from the provision of new open spaces and the establishment of direct pedestrian links to the waterfront. An urban botanical garden will give the city a valuable asset and it will be used for both leisure and educational purposes.

Boston's Chinatown is also to benefit from this project. Despite its considerable territorial losses over the past four decades it is still a lively community rich in small businesses, schools and cultural facilities. The new Asian Garden is planned to reinforce this area's cultural identity and be a symbol of the local community efforts to reclaim land lost in the original artery construction.

The overall project is to be supported by a system of urban design guidelines established to promote district-wide legibility whilst supporting diversity, complexity and richness of individual neighbourhoods. Co-ordinated by BRA, it is to be financed by public, private (for profit) and non-profit organisations. By involving some sixty community groups and many urban professionals this project promises to be a true partnership between all actors concerned.

Boston 2000 is on its way to achieving a more responsive urban design at all levels of intervention.

At the large scale of intervention Boston's revitalisation of the Central Artery shows a long term visionary attitude of those in power to strategically integrate many disparate parts of the city. There are already glimpses of the new city identity, of this new 'view from the road' that will offer healthier, greener and richer experiences to its many uses.

At the local neighbourhood level there is also a constant search for improving the life of those who live and work there. In that sense we ought to thank Jane Jacobs and many other urban designers who followed her ideas and made certain that our cities are planned, designed and managed in such a way as to ensure rich and diverse urban patterns.

The ideas explored in this chapter illustrate the dynamics of urbanism and the perpetual structuring and restructuring of our cities. It is also apparent from the discussion that cities are more than just an amalgamation of their individual parts. Each time we intervene in the urban fabric, as seen in the case of Broadgate or Boston's Central Artery proposal, we affect both the large scale and small scale elements in cities. Urban designers therefore ought to consider both scales of intervention and translate these interventions into long term and short term strategies.

At the long term, large scale of urban design we need to develop frameworks that will give our cities a clearer and more explicit spatial structure, supporting the users' sense of orientation. Sitte's proposals for Vienna or Boston's Artery redevelopment project are only a couple of such examples that demonstrate the methods employed by urban designers to promote large scale legibility and reinforce the identity of places. In each case reference is given to historically important and unique elements in the city, whilst opening up opportunities for future urban growth. By linking the historic and the progressive systems together, we are likely to promote complexity and diversity at all scales of urban design.

At the smaller scale of urban design we ought to cater for different user groups and offer choice through the provision of buildings, building complexes and open spaces. In this provision we need the support of both private and public sector finance to ensure well balanced social and economic diversity in all parts of our cities. We also need clearer and more visionary planning frameworks that would allow creative urban design concepts and local community ideas to interact directly in the design of our sustainable futures.

Ian Bentley

COMMUNITY DEVELOPMENT AND URBAN DESIGN

One of the most important characteristics of urban areas which are already developed, with existing building stock, is that they are often already inhabited. It is therefore possible for urban designers working on the regeneration of these areas to identify real people who can be involved in the process of design. In practice, this potential is often not taken up. In part, this is because the involvement of ordinary users in the design process is not a mainstream part of urban design practice. This is unfortunate because user-involvement has the potential to revive urban design culture from its present rather introverted state. This chapter is about that potential, and ways of realising it in practice.

In so far as it relates to physical design, urban design culture in the capitalist context has evolved largely through market forces. Urban design professionals set out their stalls with ideas for urban places, which they offer for sale in exchange for material or symbolic rewards; so as to accumulate economic and cultural capital. The potential buyers in this marketplace are not ordinary users: rather, they are development agencies operating in the public or (usually) private sector, or agencies of the local or national state. Pursuing their own interest, these various agencies buy some urban designers' products, but reject others. Word gets around, through the design media, that some urban design ideas are bankable, whilst others are not. In the capitalist context, the disciplines of unemployment and bankruptcy ensure that bankable ideas are quickly replicated by other designers, whilst non-bankable ones are ignored. Eventually the bankable ideas, and *only* these, come into the mainstream of urban design culture. In the dynamic operation of this market, urban design culture can therefore only be affected by

those agencies which have the resources to hire urban designers. For the most part, ordinary users cannot afford this.

According to capitalist theory, however, this does not mean that only powerful developers and state agencies can influence urban forms. Because most buildings are themselves produced as commodities for sale, in what amounts to a retail market for urban form, market signals will ensure that only the ones which appeal to potential purchasers will make sufficient profits to be replicated by developers, eventually to form part of mainstream design culture. There are, however, many flaws in this argument. First, it is perfectly obvious that most users are not involved in the purchase of all the buildings they use in the course of their everyday lives. Even people who own their own homes, for example, adapt their lives to space bought by others, in all the sorts of buildings they use for work and leisure pursuits. Second, and of crucial importance for urban design, the argument that consumers get what they want through the market signals does not apply to public space, because public space is extremely hard to purchase as a commodity for sale. The point here is that cities exist for processes of communication and exchange between people — that is the only reason for having them in the first place — and public space is a key medium through which these processes take place. In capitalist contexts, it is easy enough to commodify communications media in general; as with the mail, the telephone, the fax and so forth. Still, face to face contact is crucial in many situations; and to achieve this, people have to traverse public space, which can therefore never be eliminated from the urban *raison d'être*. Strenuous efforts are made to commodify public space itself, and to charge admission to it, either directly or indirectly: this is one reason why recent urban form is so full of culs-de-sac, malls, atria and the like. A further approach to the privatisation of the public realm is seen in the ever-increasing use of automobility — mobile bits of the *private* realm — as private cocoons in which to traverse it. Still, there is an irreducible (and large) proportion of space which has to be left as *public* if the city is to function effectively as a setting for communication and exchange; and this space has to be freely available, literally, to its users. And in regard to that public space — the space which is conventionally taken as constituting the very ground of urban design practice — there can therefore be no capitalist market through which users can signal what they love and what they hate. The consequence of course, is well known: the concentration of design effort on the (saleable) building — 'the piece' in recent architectural parlance — and the reduction of the public realm to (literally) 'worthless' SLOBB: mere Space Left Over Between Buildings.

Many urban designers would see urban design itself as a response to this situation, attempting to compensate through professional efforts for the lack of users' influence on the design of public space.

The Responsive Environments approach, for example, talks of urban design as following 'the same idea as that which has inspired most socially-conscious designers of the last hundred years: the idea that the built environment should provide its users with an essentially *democratic* setting, enriching their opportunities by maximising the degree of *choice* available to them'. This is a position where practical consequences, as John Punter shows in a comparative review of urban design writings, seem broadly acceptable throughout the current urban design literature.

Though these approaches represent positive attempts to think about how to design as though people matter, mainstream urban design culture is still largely an introverted area of 'expert knowledge'; quite opaque to ordinary users, and with few mechanisms for testing users' reactions to the practical, built results of its people-centred theorising. This means that, in principle, there is an ever-present danger of urban designers repeating the modernists' classic error of mistaking their own particular values for universal truths. Indeed, there is an air of rabid and unquestioning certainty about many recent urban design pronouncements, which is strongly reminiscent of the architectural avant-garde of the 1930s; and we all know where that led.

The worst dangers of this dogmatism are mitigated, in many cases, by a design practice which relies heavily on public space types and morphologies which have a proven track record of public approval. These well-established types, however, have always to be re-interpreted for modern situations; and in the process it is, in principle, all-to-possible to lose the very characteristics which give them their public value. Unless we are forever to reproduce exact historical prototypes — not a practicable option in many situations, even for those who think it desirable — we therefore have to find some way of getting the consumers of public space to inform the design debate about what is important to *them*.

For a number of reasons it is urban design work in existing areas of local authority housing which offers the easiest opening into ways of developing user-involvement as a normal part of urban design practice. First, the people to be involved are relatively easy to identify and to contact in these areas, as compared with, say, edge city or new settlements. Second, there is increasing pressure both from local and from national government, in the UK at least, to require user-involvement to take place. Sometimes this pressure is economically motivated, for it has become all too apparent that public housing which is hated by those who live in it is also a spectacularly bad investment. Sometimes it is politically motivated, as when tenant involvement is seen as a way of building up grass-roots social organisations, to contribute to developing the richer and more animated 'civil society' which might eventually lead to more fundamental social change. Third, because of this broad-based political support, it is in the context of local authority housing regeneration that funds for user-involvement are most easily available: access to Estate Action funding, for example, is contingent on the involvement of tenants in the design process. Urban design work in estate regeneration is therefore a crucial arena for developing a culture of user-involvement which might eventually bring a breath of fresh air into the stuffy introversion which currently passes for urban design debate.

The potential here is greatest in those estates which are large enough to have real political clout, and where there are already active local groups

73

working to improve tenants' conditions. One such is the Angell Town estate in Brixton, South London, where the Oxford Brookes Urban Regeneration Consultancy (URC) has been working for a tenants' organisation called Angell Town Community Project Ltd (ATCP) over the last five years.

Angell Town, designed by Lambeth Borough architects' department, was developed during the 1970s. In its morphology, it represents an intermediate stage in the shift from 1960s modernist blocks towards the more traditional street-orientated layouts of the 1980s; for it has something of the plan geometry of the traditional perimeter block, but modified to form a rigid pedestrian/vehicular segregation because high levels of car ownership were predicted. To this end, the ground level was largely given over to car use, whilst pedestrian access was concentrated on pedestrian decks or 'pedways' at first or second floor levels. These pedways were linked from block to block by bridges; and originally these were intended to link across the busy Brixton Road to the neighbouring Stockwell Park estate, which houses all the social facilities such as shops and a doctor's surgery. Sadly, the bridge was never built, so Angell Town for years had no communal facilities at all for its 4,000 people.

Despite this disadvantage, Angell Town's first residents were happy to go there. The estate is conveniently situated in relation to Brixton as a whole, and expectations were high. In the words of one early tenant, who moved to Angell Town from bedsit accommodation, 'we saw it as a luxury pad'. Though the morphology was unfamiliar, the first residents were not suspicious of it: 'we knew it had been designed by experts, and we trusted them to know what they were doing'.

Soon, however, the lived experience of the estate began to overwhelm these favourable first impressions. First, residents began to notice that there were few chances to meet people in casual ways; because there were no windows opening onto the pedways (*Figure 23*). 'In ordinary houses, you can see people in the street through the kitchen window, so there's a chance to see what's going on, and maybe say "hi" if you want to – but we soon found out you can't do that here'.

The blindness towards the public realm also made it difficult to control children, who wanted to play there with their peers. The ground-floor garages were

hidden from view, so the residents never used them from the start: they soon became vandalised, and this quickly contributed to a depressing image for the estate as a whole. (*Figure 24*) Soon people gave up requesting to live in Angell Town, and the only new arrivals were those whose problems meant they had no other choice: Angell Town with its problems exacerbated by the management problems of a well-meaning but bureaucratic local authority, had become a sink estate; widely seen as a disaster even before its construction was complete. 'Angell Town becomes Hell Town' said the South London Press.

To make matters worse, the complex network of upper level pedways and bridges quickly turned out to provide a wonderful series of escape routes for criminals from outside the estate itself, who could easily run in and evade the police. The first attempt to improve the estate consisted of removing the bridges between the blocks, to seal off these escape routes. This change was carried out by the local authority, with police advice and with a minimal level of tenant involvement, consisting of no more than an agreement from the tenants' association: at that stage, little more than a social club for elderly white residents. Though well-intentioned, the change had unexpectedly negative results.

First, the bridges had been used as play areas by children, for these were the public spaces which enabled them to meet their peers from other blocks, a little out of earshot of the dwellings themselves. With the bridges gone, children wanting to stay near their home had only the pedways themselves to play on. Now the noise they generated was right outside people's flats, and in some locations over the tops of bedrooms, and this led to all sorts of social conflicts.

Second, not all the blocks had refuse chutes, and with the bridge gone, people found that they had to make sizeable detours if they were properly to dispose of their rubbish, say on the way to work in the morning. Inevitably, some people didn't bother, refuse began to accumulate, others began to see little point in taking the trouble to be tidy themselves, and local authority management problems compounded the situation. Not only did this lead to an ever-worsening image of neglect and decline, but also cockroaches and rats became an endemic part of the Angell Town milieu.

Third, the loss of the bridges meant that people from some of the blocks had to walk through dark

Figure 23. A pedway with no signs of life.

Figure 25. A consultation drawing for recreating streets. (Urban designers: Urban Regeneration Consultancy)

Figure 24. A row of abandoned garages.

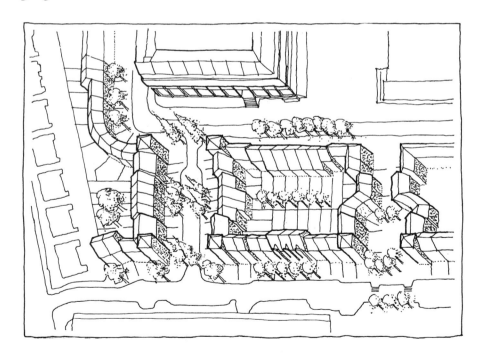

Figure 26. Making streets and perimeter blocks. (Architects: Suakin (left), Burrell Foley Fisher (right).

and unsurveilled garage areas to get out of the estate, unless they were willing to make lengthy detours. This raised the level of apprehension and fear on the part of many residents.

All in all, then, the results of the bridge demolition were perceived by the tenants as overwhelmingly negative. 'If they'd asked us, we could have told them what would happen. It was aggravating, man'.

Partly as a reaction to experiencing the negative result of being excluded from decisions about their own living environment, a group of concerned residents began to push for a greater degree of tenant participation in the much-needed process of improving the estate. Beginning with voluntary youth work, then taking over the tenants' association and eventually forming the Angell Town Community Project (ATCP) residents began to take ever greater initiatives; first on their own, but eventually recognising the practical need to work with consultants of various sorts. As part of these initiatives, Oxford Brookes Urban Regeneration Consultancy was asked by ATCP to set up and manage a tenant consultation process, to help them articulate first what was wrong with the estate in design terms, and second what could be done to improve it.

In taking this initiative ATCP saw the need for urban design expertise, but was also aware of the potential danger of the professionals taking over. The process was therefore set up on the model of 'two sets of experts', where the tenant took the role of experts about life on the estate and its problems and opportunities, whilst URC provided expertise about what was possible in terms of design, rather than pushing a particular line about what *ought* to be done.

This philosophy of keeping ATCP firmly in the driving seat was attractive to URC as well as to ATCP, both on grounds of political conviction and also because it clarified whose side we were on in a situation fraught with potential conflicts. It was reinforced in the practical arrangement of the consultation process at four levels. First, our consultancy contract was directly with ATCP. Though our funding came ultimately from Lambeth Council, it was paid first to ATCP; and it was the ATCP management committee who decided whether to pay us or not. Second, a group of residents was to be trained to take an important role in running the process themselves. Third, the consultation process was to be designed as far as possible to involve *all* the people on the estate;

as far as possible the process would have to be taken to *them*, rather than just involving those who could be persuaded to come to *us* by taking part in public meetings. And fourth, the process was to begin with a clean sheet of paper, rather than with URC making proposals to be discussed.

The clean sheets of paper — long rolls of lining paper — were put up on the walls of a community room which ATCP had already managed to carve out of redundant garage space, and an initial series of agenda-setting public meetings began. ATCP made strenuous efforts to get as many people to each meeting as they could, by energetic door-knocking and leafletting, and to ensure that people from different age groups, genders and ethnic backgrounds were always present. This represented a considerable organisational effort, including the provision of an impromptu crèche (where the children were encouraged to draw their ideal homes) and escorts to see the old people safely home. Usually, these efforts resulted in a turn-out of about 30–50 people at each meeting — a tiny proportion of the 4,000 Angell Town residents, but a start, and understandable given that people were being asked to put time and effort into something which had no guarantee of success.

The 'clean sheet of paper' policy meant that there was no structured agenda of design issues to discuss — rather residents were asked to talk first about their experience of problems on the estate. Not surprisingly these were not issues whose links with urban design were immediately obvious, so our role was to help uncover whether such links existed, and if so what they were. An example may help to make this clear. At the first meeting, we were disconcerted to discover that dog shit was the topic which people were most anxious to discuss. The links between this prevalent nuisance and urban design were initially unclear but were uncovered as the meeting progressed, through a process of give and take between the two sets of experts. 'Why is there so much dog shit, anyway?' we asked. 'Because there are so many dogs' came the reply, delivered in a tone of voice which made it clear that the speaker found this a pathetically stupid question. 'But why are there so many dogs then?' At this point, the answers began to uncover a dog-culture which was utterly new to the middle class urban design consultants, to whom 'dog' had hitherto been equivalent to 'family pet'. It became clear that to many dog-owners at Angell Town, the dog was at least partly a cost-effective, high tooth-powered security device; and someone recited what was later to become a familiar *bon mot* about neighbouring Stockwell Park: 'The estate where even the Rottweilers patrol in pairs'

— 'But why do people feel so threatened anyway?'
— 'Because the place is always deserted'
— 'Most of the time nobody can see what's going on when you're outdoors . . .'

By now, we were clearly into urban design issues, which the consultants felt able to grasp. And the point is that these were issues about community safety, the perception of threat in public space and so forth, which our previous urban thinking had only engaged in the most peripheral way. These are issues, after all, which are almost entirely ignored by the *Responsive Environments* frame of reference; and yet they were massively top of the residents' own agenda. The frame of reference itself was thereby subjected to a powerful critique and was subsequently enriched, much to the benefit of URC's design approach as a whole. It is hard to see how that could have happened without engaging with this previously un-familiar culture in a process of action-research. And it is hard to see how that could have happened without the residents driving the design process, according to *their* agenda, from the outset.

This is not to say, of course, that we did not involve *our* own agenda into the process: merely that we tried hard not to introduce our own pet concerns until a basic framework of issues had been articulated by the residents, and we did our best to avoid man-ipulating the situation to make it come out how we wanted. In the nature of things, we probably failed in this to some extent — it is difficult to become a 'neutral instrument' after all — but the fact that we are still around, still with a positive relationship with ATCP, five years later, suggests that the residents feel they are getting enough of what they want.

This initial series of agenda-setting meetings con-tinued, with a shifting group of participants, until a point was reached where new issues seemed to be emerging so infrequently that the general consensus from the participants was that we should get on to thinking about how the issues already identified should be addressed in design terms. At this stage, we used simple wooden block models, which the

participants could easily manipulate, to explore what could be done at a strategic level, with 1:50 scale models to explore options for complex areas in more detail.

Again this process continued, trying to develop a wide range of options which each had several resi-dents prepared to argue for it, until the majority of participants felt that the process was becoming a waste of time because few new ideas were emerging. At this point, attention shifted towards bringing these options, and views about their respective pros and cons, to the attention of the wider community.

This process began by mounting an exhibition of work done so far, set up in the community room which had a large expanse of window in a prominent position on the estate. The exhibition was staffed by paid workers who had taken part in the public meet-ings which had generated the options, who were trained in workshops to be able to explain and answer questions about the exhibits. These workers took their job so seriously that they tended to hang about outside the hall, dragging people in off the street, and making sure that they filled in simple question-naires to record the visitors' impressions of each option. (*Figure 25*)

Armed with the information from the meetings and the exhibition, the next step was to prepare a questionnaire to be administered to all the house-holds on the estate. This was produced through dis-cussions with a paid group of 12 of the residents who had taken active roles in the process so far, drawn from different interest groups, with URC producing drafts on the basis of these discussions. These drafts went through a lengthy and sometimes hilarious process of revision, largely devoted to changing them from what the residents called 'Oxford Polyspeak' into language which they felt would be understood by the prospective respondents. Together we had to arrive at a trade-off between precision and com-prehensibility; and this was no easy task.

To the professionals of Lambeth Council, who were monitoring the consultation process as a whole, the final form of the questionnaire represented some-thing of a threat, because it was designed to elicit residents' reactions to specific design proposals as well as to general design principles. The Council's own architects and landscape architects felt that this would remove the potential for them to use their creative ability to do the best job for the residents, and wanted to be told about problems rather than guided towards solutions. The residents, on the other hand, were worried that this would allow the Council's professionals to import their own agenda into the design process: the very problem which the consultancy process had been designed to avoid. As the residents saw it, the purpose of the questionnaire was to generate a design brief which would (inevitably) call for a great deal of detailed design interpretations, but would be as prescriptive as possible about key issues of site layout, relationships between buildings and public space, access to dwellings, locations of uses and so forth. This conflict ran deep, and was never amicably resolved: in the end the residents, with our help, just did it their way; but at the cost of worsened relationships between ATCP and the Council officers concerned.

Once agreed by ATCP, the questionnaire was administered by the members of the working party who had been involved in its design, who were in the best position to help respondents fill it in. Despite shrinking Council funding, which meant we could not approach all households, the level of interest in the project as a whole can be gauged from the fact that return rates of these complex questionnaires, which took about an hour to complete, were as high as 70% in one block.

When analysed, the results showed a very clear pattern of preference for street-orientated housing laid out in perimeter-blocks, and clearly linked into the surrounding areas of Brixton to reduce the 'ghetto' effect of the current layout. This preference seems to be inspired by two main concerns. The first, to say it again, is security: what urban designers might call 'perimeter blocks', the residents call 'stockades'. The second concerns the relative cultural associations of street-orientated developments as compared with modernist layouts: 'Everyone knows homes on proper streets are better than estates. Estates are where they put people like us' as one resident put it at an early public meeting. Interestingly, though the forms which these values generate are similar to those of the Responsive Environments approach, the rationale for them is only loosely connected with the 'choice' ethos which underlies that approach itself.

The results of the consultation process have so far borne physical fruit at two levels. The first concerns design work carried out by the architects Burrell Foley Fischer Associates in a series of projects now largely completed on the estate, including shops, workshops, café, bar, training centre, recording studios and housing. This work was carried out in parallel with the consultation process itself, and links between the two were maintained through the involvement of URC as 'export clients', working on ATCP's behalf, in design meetings held on the estate.

The second level of linkage between the consultation process and physical design involved using the questionnaire results to construct a design brief with a very closely-argued rationale, with statistical backup for each step in the argument. Far from this proving a strait-jacket for architects working with it, experience so far suggests the reverse. As a first step towards implementing the brief, ATCP commissioned Suakin Architects to carry out a detailed design study for the demolition of one of the estate's worst blocks, and its replacement by new buildings. Funded by the RIBA Community fund, and with URC monitoring the design process as urban design consultants, Suakin say they found that the brief's clear guidance enabled them to home-in quickly on the most difficult design issues, and tackle them in depth, without wasting time 'reinventing the wheel' so far as other issues were concerned. Perhaps more to the point, ATCP also profess themselves delighted with the results. (*Figure 26*)

In conclusion, then, what are the lessons of the Angell Town experience, so far as the practice of urban design is concerned? First, it opens urban design up to criticism from outside the closed circle of the established development agencies and other professions, and keeps it in empirical, practical contact with the public concerns which are supposed to be urban design's whole *raison d'être*. Second, the Angell Town experience has thrown a new light, for us, on the qualities which should be sought in urban design. It interests us that the values of the Angell Town residents support both qualities with which we had not previously been concerned, and a new perspective on making trade-offs between the established quality of the *Responsive Environments* approach. The residents' prime concern is for security, but they see this as being achieved through the presence of other people in public space: 'most people aren't psychos, they're perfectly decent, so ordinary people put the muggers off' as ATCP's project director puts it. This means that the residents see safe

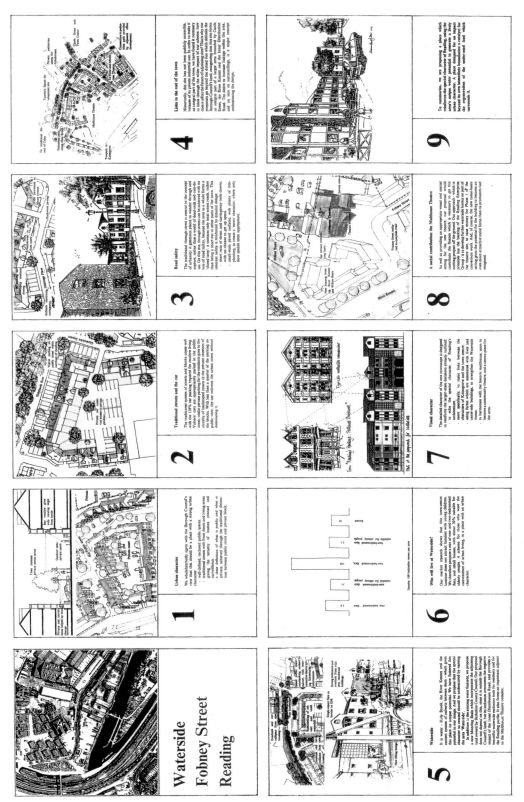

Plate 1. An initial rationale for Fobney Street, Reading, Urban designers: Bentley Hayward Murrain Samuels (see p. 19).

Plate 2. A variety of public spaces, from top left, clockwise: Birmingham's Centenary Square brings heritage alive, whilst at the Park of the Americas, Sao Paulo, Brazil the scale of multi-purpose space is scarcely softened by the sculpture; quality investment not matched by imaginative design at Harwich and a traditional street in Totnes that manages to provide a robust setting for urban life (see p. 57).

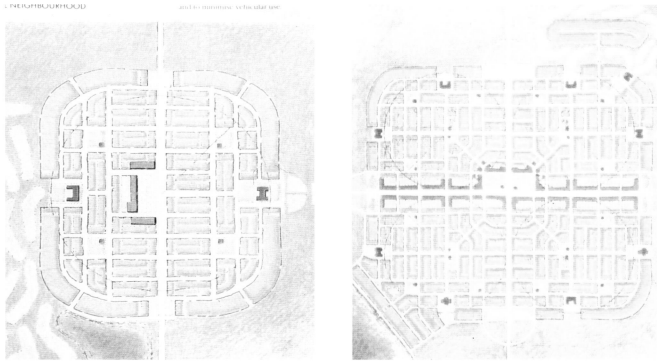

Plate 3. Individual and combined neighbourhoods (see p. 91).

Plate 4. Expansion of West Sacramento, California: regulating plan (see p. 91).

Plate 5. Expansion of West Sacramento, California: public transit plan (see p. 91).

All diagrams, Duany and Plater-Zyberk

Plate 6. Asnières sur Oise seen across the flood plain of the Oise with the forested escarpment of the Ile de France in the background (see p. 113).

Plate 8. Model of a project for housing for sale and rent designed according to the new POS regulations (see p. 120).

Plate 7. Asnières sur Oise: a typical street showing how the buildings are set at the back of pavement line and a secluded private garden at the back of one of the houses (see p. 114).

Plate 9. Sandpit adjacent to marked parking bay, Maastricht, Netherlands (see p. 123).

Plate 10. Pedestrian route marked out along desire line across the road, Julich, near Aachen, Germany (see p. 128).

Plate 11. Design of median strip prevents overtaking whilst enabling manoeuvring, Aachen, Germany (see p. 128).

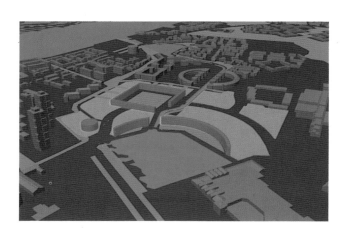

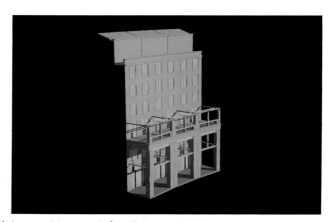

Plate 12. Development of Surrey Quays from conceptual model to architectural detail (see p. 135).

Plate 13. The apotheosis of the 'six-pack'? A view from the street in Brisbane, Australia (see p. 141).

Plate 14. Bayside, Port Melbourne Community Planning Forum, led by Paul Murrain, Wendy Morris and Jon Shields (see p. 141).

public space in terms of permeable layouts and active interfaces with adjoining buildings: roughly the opposite of the 'defensible space' ideas of much urban design theory, or the 'target hardened cul-de-sac' of the police's 'Secure by Design' initiative. The concept of 'vitality' with which we have tried to encapsulate this insight, seems to us an important addition to the Responsive Environments frame of reference. Third, the work at Angell Town utterly disproves architects' fears that public involvement in the design process must lead to uninteresting design products. Architects of the artistic tendency, who have seen the work so far completed, say they approve of it on artistic grounds — a view which the residents seem to share.

Finally, the Angell Town experience has led us from a conviction that urban design ought to be concerned with community-led design, towards a current position of *wanting* to work in this area because we've had more fun with it, by a whole order of magnitude, than with any previous design experience. For us, it even beats lager; it refreshes the parts — intellectual as well as emotional parts — which other approaches cannot reach.

SECTION THREE
THE URBAN FRINGE AND BEYOND

Within the Joint Centre probably no issue has generated such fierce exchanges as the benefits and disbenefits of what we have here termed the 'urban fringe'. Murrain believes that 'there' should not be designed any differently from 'here' and follows through with cogent arguments for sustainable development that at least recognise the virtues of traditional form. Simmonds, on the other hand, goes for broke, with an impassioned plea for progress and the new personal transport based city.

Samuels concludes this section with a review of one phenomenon of the city of dispersal: the employment park. He includes examples that start arguably to become new urban quarters, with a range of support uses including even housing.

Paul Murrain

URBAN EXPANSION: LOOK BACK AND LEARN

The urban fringe, edge city, new settlements are the places where most urban designers dare not or refuse to go. The legitimacy of the professional title is accompanied by a rejection of any expansion; new development has to be in the existing city. This chapter acknowledges that urban expansion is inevitable and new settlements not automatically bad. Every existing place we defend with 'inner urban passion' was new once. Equally, this chapter does not deny the vital role urban design can and has to play in keeping our existing towns and cities diverse and interactive.

Our primary concern should be arresting the retreat from interactive urbanism in both the existing inner city and the 'suburb'. If we acknowledge that they are both symptomatic of the same isolationist tendencies in society, we will address that issue rather than engage in arbitrary locational arguments. Urbanism then, is not about size (other than sustainable thresholds; an issue not to be overlooked but beyond the scope of this chapter). Instead urbanism is about an attitude supportive of interaction and exchange, be it inner city, suburb or small town. The essential spatial qualities of the 'traditional city' do this so much better than contemporary suburban and 'edge city' models and those qualities are vital to the sustainable success of new development. (*Figure 27*) It is the retreat from public interaction, and all the economic and political structures that attend it, that makes the task of producing new expansion similar to the traditional city so complex and extraordinarily difficult. The more we retreat, the worse the traditional urbanism we leave behind becomes. We use that as evidence and retreat further, in a monumental self-fulfilling prophecy.

Our towns and cities are not just growing in population, they are spreading out and changing their structure into a looser, more widespread urban pattern, and to what extent is this dispersal consumer led? As Feagin and Parker (1990) argue, the conventional view is that suburbs, be they housing, business parks or retail malls, are somehow the spontaneous result of consumer demands expressed through a rational market system. It assumes that the consumers were free to choose among several alternatives, particularly in residential areas and that their choices reflected real preferences. They point out that, 'Absent from this rosy portrait is any mention of several other factors that have profoundly shaped (US) suburbanisation, including investment decisions of industrialists, developers, financiers, land speculators, and government housing officials in connection with suburban migration and job creation' (p. 208)

The more we put distance between each other and the uses and activities we take part in, the better our environment is argued to be. As long ago as 1958 Hannah Arendt in *The Human Condition* warned us of this trend: 'The public realm, as the common world, gathers us together and yet prevents us falling apart. What makes mass society so difficult to bear is not the number of people involved but rather that the world between them has lost its power to gather them together, to relate and separate them at one and the same time.' (Arendt in Glazer and Lilla 1987, p. 7) Sadly, we are still suffering from the mistaken judgement of a century ago that the *form* of the city was responsible for the undoubted ills, inequalities and environmental degradation present at the time. What is more alarming is that we continue to blame it today.

Technology, Transport and Town Form

Thirty years ago Melvin Webbers renowned paper *The urban place and the nonplace urban realm* (1964) was attempting to convince us that the traditional role of urban places as the setting for interaction and exchange were no longer necessary. Advances in communication technology from video phones to rapid transport systems would render 'urban place' if not exactly urban centre, irrelevant. Of all the predictions Webber made, the massive increase in the private vehicle has been the only significant 'advance', confirming that the need for interaction does not disappear. Instead, we believe it acceptable to spend a sizeable proportion of our personal income to say nothing of the enormous expenditure through the state to allow us to take part in exchange of a sort via personal private transport. In the last few years explosions of information technology have caught up with Webber's forcast with the prediction of millions of people eventually working from home.

Those who believe in the low density strongly zoned suburb use this phenomenon as an additional supportive point. Their position is that once the commuting imperative is taken away, the arguments against 'sprawl' diminish. In contrast to this and much more convincing, is the argument that if people work at home then there is even greater need for a range of facilities and diverse settings in close proximity to minimise the increased isolationism resulting from the loss of the urban experience. This view is strongly held by Andy Harris, formerly of Apple Computers now the founder of Telemorphix, who has done a great deal of research into the organisation and potential of telecommuting. So much so that whilst I was working with Duany & Plater-Zyberk proposing traditional urbanism for the expansion of West Sacramento, he came to add support to their ideas and circulated a paper (Harris, 1991) in which he declares:

The more high-tech we become, the greater our need to come together. Teleworkers don't want to be isolated in their homes . . . (their) biggest complaint is 'cabin fever'; physical isolation, lack of community and continued dependence on the car. What's lacking in these workers' lives is unintentional face to face interaction, the ability to just walk out of the front door and encounter other people as a normal part of living, rather than having to plan and drive to every single social activity.

Meeting friends and co-workers on the way to lunch or the day care centre is what teleworkers most keenly feel they are missing by not being part of a big busy office.

Sadly, even pathologically, many daily commuters cling to their distant offices and ersatz neighbourhoods, their last remaining refuge for spontaneous friendship and conversation amidst the decimated human ecosystem and loneliness of suburban sprawl. Ironically, it's the older downtowns that have the most to gain . . . It is the very low-tech, pedestrian nature of these older parts of their cities that now makes them attractive to information workers.

Significant as this quote is from someone not directly involved in the design of towns, it must not be overlooked that this is special pleading for those who no longer travel to a 'centre' to work. It does bring into focus just who is and who is not empowered by contemporary town form which separates functions, isolates and reduces accessibility. As Alison Ravetz reminds us with her categorisation of the 'transport poor'; 'Car ownership is heavily biased against the young, elderly unskilled and the female as well as the handicapped and disabled . . . It is biased in favour of skilled or professional workers, of people aged between thirty and fifty-nine, and of men' (1980 p. 136).

Even assuming commuting to work can be reduced, figures as high as 15 car journeys a day in suburban USA just to carry out family tasks, belies any significant transport saving. Without the car, survival itself would be a serious issue! Tied into all of this too is the need for multiple car ownership for separate members of the family to fulfil the daily routine. The capital and revenue costs of owning that second or third car can be equivalent to an additional mortgage component that the institutions would not lend in the first place, increasing the need to purchase a cheaper house out on the fringe; clear evidence of the wider conspiracy that perpetuates the problem.

The relative costs of producing denser, integrated mixed-use town as opposed to suburban sprawl are hotly debated and to delve into the criteria and assumptions behind one method of calculation as opposed to another is complex indeed. But, few seem to argue that the way we are expanding our cities has much to commend it on economic grounds beyond the usual short-term expediency.

Twenty years ago no less, a study for the US Government by the Real Estate Corporation declared: 'Sprawl is the most expensive form of residential development in terms of economic costs, environmental costs, natural resource consumption and many types of personal costs.' (Roseland 1992) Attempting to estimate an overall direct and social cost for the automobile and put it into a Deutschmark equivalent West German studies in the mid-1980s found annual costs to range between 50 and 110 billion DM. (The Canadian Urban Institute in Roseland 1992) San Francisco found that doubling residential density or population density reduces the annual car mileage per capita or per household by 20–30% The study claims consistency with studies in Canada, United Kingdom and other urbanised areas of the USA. When comparing San Francisco's Nob Hill with the suburban sprawl of Danville-San Roman, using the Hertz Corporation estimates of car ownership and operating costs per mile, the average Nob Hill family spends approximately $14,000 less on cars, with 66% less petrol and emits 14kg less hydrocarbons, 12kg less nitrogen oxides and 98kg less carbon monoxide than the average suburban family equivalent. (Holtzclaw in Roseland 1992)

Examples of this kind are at their most dramatic in countries such as the USA and Australia where the anti-urban Anglo Saxon attitudes found plentiful space and rapidly expanded in the heyday of the car. None the less the same mentality is evident in the UK and has been for some time. We are more confined by space relative to population size but we are essentially committing the same mistakes. Furthermore if anyone counters the above 'sensational' arguments with claims of roughly equitable costs for both forms of development they have then to argue against the increased choice and empowerment that more concentrated integrated mixed-use areas bring to everyone, regardless of whatever form of mechanical transport. The car itself is not the villain of the piece but if we continue to produce town form that makes the car *essential* as opposed to optional, we have failed.

Fine Grain Mixed-use Town: Towards a Definition.

Sustainability is most certainly concerned about extravagant use of finite resources and the efficient management of the ecosystem; greenhouse gases, storm water pollution, efficient food production and so on; as well as fundamental concerns for social equity and social justice. It also addresses the need to ensure that what we do now does not negatively affect what future generations may wish to do. No less important, but perhaps at a smaller scale and more pertinent to the role the urban designer can play, sustainability is about structuring town form such that the individual has choice but never at the expense of the collective, thus empowering as many of the citizens as possible to successfully determine the outcome of their daily lives in so far as the layout of the town and the location of uses can assist. A good many urban designers have been arguing for a return to a more democratic urban form long before the sustainability debate gave a welcome boost to these and related matters of social justice and ecological balance. The Joint Centre for Urban Design can legitimately claim to belong to this camp (Bentley *et al.* 1985). It is general but fair to represent what they all advocate as being 'fine grain mixed-use town;' not just in relation to the inner city but equally for the urban edge and new settlements. This chapter will focus on what this might mean for urban expansion, drawing on contemporary authors and practitioners who seem to have considerable overlap in their definitions and proposed solutions.

It is not possible to define 'fine grain mixed-use' in precise terms. In many ways it is undesirable because it will vary in different situations and cultural conditions. Pioneering works such as Jane Jacobs' *Death and Life of Great American Cities*, thirty years old and even more valuable and relevant today than when first published, found it hard to give a precise and thorough definition of what *good* mixed-use is, though much can be gleaned from her requirements of a town. The 'why' of mixed-use will lead to an easier definition of 'good' mixed-use. Precision and measurement will still be difficult. So why does it matter?

As David Engwicht reminds us, 'Cities were invented to facilitate exchange of information, friendship, material goods, culture, knowledge, insight, skills and also exchange of emotional, psychological and spiritual support' (1992 p 17). He logically asserts that for a truly sustainable environment, we need to maximise this exchange whilst minimising the travel necessary to do it. All this implies as much variety of activity as possible easily available within a reasonable walking distance of where people live and work. Clearly, exchange is limited without the variety of uses and activities, but there is a fundamental quality that gives the basis for the empowerment. It is the key quality missing from almost all urban expansion and it is in abundance in the traditional city; the quality of permeability, the extent to which the street system is connected, integrated and intelligible. (*Figure 28*) Within this permeable network, frequent public transport should be available within the same walking distance to carry people beyond comfortable walking distances. In turn the public transport needs a nearby concentration of people, living and working, to help it function as an efficient and economically viable system.

All this implies densities far greater than that currently advocated in contemporary edge city and new settlement proposals; not only a greater density but a fine grain of mixing within that increased density. That would better ensure a 24-hour presence of people for different purposes within more or less the same place. A great deal of design prescription would be needed because the greater the proximity of a variety of uses, the more difficult the compatibility can be. There is little point denying that but equally there is little basis for assuming it is automatically a problem. The 24-hour presence would ensure greater vitality and subsequent safety.

If the all-encompassing nature of sustainability is to be truly addressed, then the biotic side of the debate must be incorporated into the human interactive side and a balance achieved. Sadly, it cannot be denied that the ecological and landscape movement has had a good deal of anti-urban bias in its arguments and propositions throughout the twentieth century. But now there is growing support for the resource effectiveness of integrated and denser mixed-use town. The biggest challenge is the quantity, nature and location of green spaces within those environments such that they contribute in terms of human activity, climate amelioration and ecological diversity *without* separating and isolating the concentrated pedestrian proximity necessary for human interaction. Combining urbanism and nature is an enormous challenge but fundamental to true sustainability. So, fine grained mixed-use is sought in urban expansion in order for those environments to be lively, safe, sensorily rich, choice laden, eco-

nomically and spatially efficient and ecologically diverse; sustainable in as far as the built environment *per se*, can believably be. When these objectives are applied to what we have been producing in contemporary expansion and new settlement proposals we are nowhere near achieving them. Good mixed-use can therefore be defined as a finely grained mix of primary land uses, namely a variety of housing and workplaces with housing predominant, closely integrated with all other support services, within convenient walking distance of the majority of homes.

The Fundamentals of Good Mixed-use

A challenge indeed, but to achieve this in physical terms there are two fundamental qualities necessary: permeability and variety. As sub-heads under variety we need concentration and proximity. From the combination of these qualities we already will have a great deal of legibility, namely an understanding of what is available, but minor adjustments may give added benefit. Finally we need robust built form that can easily adapt to a reasonably predictable range of alternative futures. This chapter will elaborate on the two fundamentals with examples from designers pledged to change contemporary trends for urban expansion and new settlements.

Permeability

This is a quality very familiar to students at the Joint Centre for Urban Design. Permeable cities must be the basis for any democratic sustainable urban layout simply because if you can't reach a place you cannot use it. Contrary to popular belief, this does not deny privacy nor does it deny restricted access to things that may legitimately benefit from relative security. That is possible through the management of the grid; for it is the grid town that affords the potential for choice and change. It may be orthogonal or deformed, the difference is worthy of note but not fundamental to its value. The connecting of the grid should be consistent through a variety of scales down to the finest grain to allow perimeter blocks of development to exist with clear distinguishable public and private sides. (*Figure 29*)

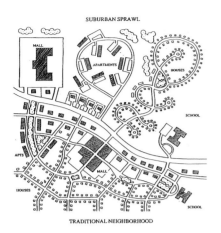

Figure 27. The contrasting models. (Duany and Plater-Zyberk)

Figure 28. Medieval and baroque Prague: spatial integration transcending different periods.

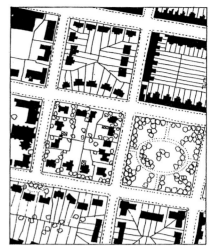

Figure 29. The perimeter block (Bentley *et al*, 1985).

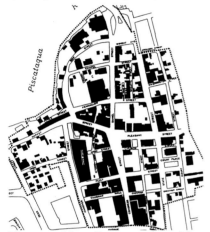

Figure 30. Portsmouth, New Hampshire, USA (White Mountain Survey Company Inc, 1991).

Figure 31. Contemporary proposals. New Parks, England above (Gazeley Properties Ltd/David Lock Associates) and right, Lyndhurst, Victoria, Australia. (Jennings Group Ltd).

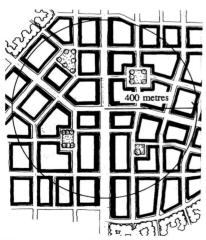

Figure 32. The neighbourhood unit: a module of mixed-use.

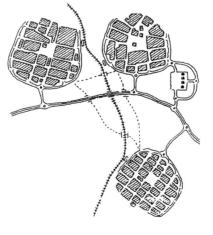

Figure 33. Urban villages: the enclave tendency (Richard Reid in Aldous, 1992).

As Hillier reminds us:

In a grid people start and finish everywhere. Origins and destinations are everywhere, with different levels of intensity. This by-product of movement is to generate as many happenings and interactions as possible . . . Enclaves are almost, by definition destinations which are not available for 'natural movement'. They are discontinuities in the urban grid and disruptive of the movement economy. Any tendency in an urban structure towards 'precinctisation' must also be a tendency to a lessening of the useful by-product of movement. (1992a p. 1.10)

It is the connectivity and integration that turns an accumulation of things into something called urbanism. Hillier (1992b) sums up the true nature of sustainability in that it is about parts and wholes. Either a new part to an existing whole or a new whole made of parts. Traditional connected cities tend to succeed on both counts, and this is nothing to do with beauty. The grid is so often accused of being boring. Bearing in mind the grid is the basis of just about every 'beautiful' historic city in so many cultures, how on earth can the grid be held responsible for someone being bored!

Of course, the traffic engineering fraternity holds its hands up in horror at the chaos and carnage that will result from a return to such layout principles. Here is a crucial issue; that of the crossroads. In her studies of traditional grid layouts as opposed to suburban sprawl settlements in California Susan Handy (1993) emphasised the number of four-way intersections and the consequent connectivity that allowed clear and direct access to local facilities. Despite no clear evidence that regional trips were curtailed she was strongly of the view that the local facilities were surviving because of that direct, walkable access. But not all highway engineers are fazed by this. Chester Chellman, one of the most forward thinking highway engineers in the USA has collaborated with Duany & Plater-Zyberk on numerous occasions in their attempts to bring traditional urbanism to the urban expansion of North American cities. In a recent letter as part of an ongoing dialogue with me, resulting from working together in California, he openly acknowledges that there is an insufficient amount of Duany & Plater-Zyberk's work built at present to satisfactorily model the effects on traffic generation. However, he wholeheartedly agrees that a different set of goals are needed, encouraging

pedestrian traffic, bicycle movement and forms of transport other than private automobiles. Logically we *must* then, have different design criteria. Chellman goes on to say (*figure 30*):

'I was able to analyse an (existing) neighbourhood in Portsmouth New Hampshire, which very closely emulates a Duany & Plater-Zyberk new town in density, building mass and interconnected streets . . . we found that the daily trip generation rate for vehicles was one half of what would be expected and projected using ITE projection methods which are usually quite accurate when used for otherwise conventional development (suburban sprawl). Very important from a traffic management perspective, we also found morning and evening peak hour reductions in traffic of 60 to 70%. *Such peak hour reductions are phenomenal and engineers I have discussed this with know of no other way to effect such a reduction.*'

With Friends of the Earth (Elkin *et al.*, 1991) reminding us, the British Government's own forecasts for car traffic in the UK predict an increase of between 83 and 142% by the year 2025, the implications are obviously horrific and Chellman's observations highly significant.

The grid is also seen as essential by those promoting public transit. Peter Calthorpe, based in sprawling California has produced a series of Transit Orientated Design Guidelines. He strongly advocates multiple and parallel routes to the transit stop at the core of the neighbourhood. 'Cul-de-sac and dead end streets should be avoided . . . A street pattern which is circuitous and complex will discourage pedestrians . . . Clean, formalised and inter-connected street systems make destinations visible, provide the shortest and most direct path to destinations and result in security through community, rather than by isolation' (1990 p. 48).

As to the nature of the grid, an abstract model of an orthogonal grid devoid of a specific location would have equal integration throughout. In reality, the site and its features would influence the grid as would the distinction between the streets that connected into the more global system, and those that had local connection. This in turn, supports the social logic of where global and local facilities would wish to locate and the relative densities and concentrations of each.

This 'social logic of space' (Hillier 1984) is distorted when the isolated single use relying solely on private transport becomes the alternative, empowering only those who have the time and means to get there, relying on further car journeys between uses. Public transport cannot conceivably operate efficiently with such spatial rules. Designing a fine grained grid town has to be learned again, valued again and insisted upon as a prerequisite for sustainable town form. (*Figure 31*)

Variety, concentration and proximity

The grid then, gives a social logic to the location of uses resulting from the spectrum of global and local connections. But, if pedestrian proximity is a true measure of empowerment, then it would seem appropriate to try and achieve as great a variety of uses and activities within reasonable walking distance of where most people live. Therefore, it could be argued that a further layer of ordering is placed over the grid to direct policy and control towards that end. This concern has brought with it a rediscovery of the much maligned 'neighbourhood', but with a legitimate and *fundamental* difference that must not be compromised.

The 'neighbourhood' as a planning device has been roundly condemned for its interpretation as a specific entity with precise thresholds, often visually and spatially separate from one another, with minimised entry and exit points. This had little or nothing to do with true networks of social interaction. Recently in both the USA and Britain this base 'unit of variety' has been proposed as a structuring element of urban expansion. Both the positive and negative sides of the abstract model have been in evidence.

At its simplest, a basic neighbourhood unit has an approximate 400 metre radius which equates to an area of approximately 125 acres (50 hectares). (*Figure 32*) This radius represents a comfortable walking distance for able-bodied people; a general measure used in retail design and as a good capture distance for pedestrian access to public transport. The 'centre' will vary from local facilities and a public transit stop to a local high street or a new town centre depending on location, the nature of the road network, overall densities and absolute size. The logic of this structure also implies an increased density gradient towards this centre allowing more people to be within a close distance of uses and public transit.

This is in fact a description of many traditional city districts or neighbourhoods. That is not surprising however when the social logic of space at that time had a great deal to do with pedestrian proximity and contemporary arguments call for a return to the same social logic. Andres Duany makes the aim explicit and acknowledges that it would take time for these areas to develop the sophistication of complementary mixed-use.

The neighbourhoods are mixed-use communities balanced to a degree which permits the overall town plan to become self-sufficient to the extent of extremely high trip capture rates . . . Over the period of a generation, this will provide to all its residents the theoretical possibilities of housing, jobs, shopping, entertainment, education and civic institutions within extremely short driving distances

(Duany & Plater-Zyberk, 1990 p. 1)

There is a trap to be avoided. As soon as dimensions, areas and centres are prescribed, introversion and enclave raise their heads. Combined with this are claims of self-sufficiency that imply no need to look or go beyond the cosy little neighbourhood that has been created. The principle in no way demands or proposes such a solution as the above quote from Duany makes clear. This dangerous response tumbles us back to all that was misguided in neighbourhood concepts of 30 years ago and more. Sadly a worrying diagram creeps into the publication *Urban Villages* (Aldous, 1992) and despite many good, sustainable intentions, gives warning of these dangerous interpretations. (*Figure 33*) Rather, these pedestrian scale neighbourhoods overlay the integrated grid, they do not chop it off every 400 metres.

This unit of variety provides a logic for a district scale of land use promotion and control. But interactive urbanism needs more and therefore how such 400 metre radii relate to each other in groups and absolute numbers becomes of vital importance. What must be non-negotiable is the frequent, street oriented connections between however many of these neighbourhoods there are.

Again this will vary and at times the frequent connection in the form of streets may be limited by the locations of sizeable public parks towards their periphery. Once more this is the effect parks and linear green systems tend to have in the traditional city and are themselves treasured enough to sacrifice some of the connectivity. During daylight hours they

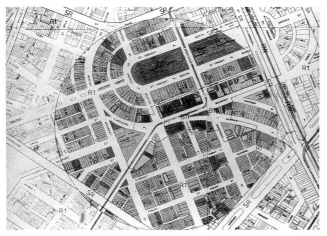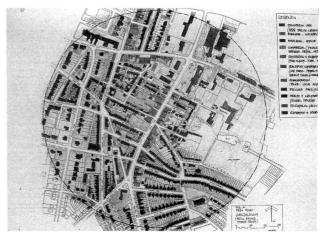

Figure 34. Existing mixed-use areas – a valuable source of research. Left, Albert Park, Melbourne, Australia (Urban Design Unit, Department of Planning and Development, Government of Victoria, Australia) and right, Cheltenham (Neda Stevenson).

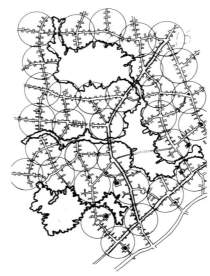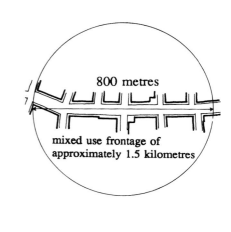

Figure 35. Pedestrian proximity: an integral part of city structure: Oxford.

Figure 36. The structure of larger open spaces.

Figure 37. The major streets and mixing of uses.

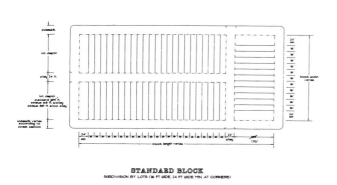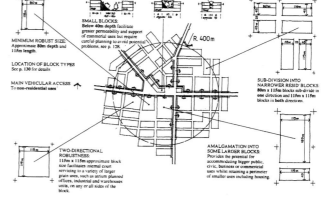

Figure 38. The size of blocks: Duany and Plater-Zyberk's (1989) 'standard blocks', left, and a range of mixed-use blocks, right, (Baulch, 1993).

need not limit connectivity unduly but need to be well peopled to be safe. If this cannot be guaranteed then street alternatives have themselves to be within reasonable walking distance of the unsurveilled parkland paths.

To produce abstract models of mixed-use for pedestrian proximity is inevitable and necessary to aid the debate; certainly until sufficient place-based design examples can serve to illustrate the model. It is also problematic because the models tend towards a placeless rationality that may imply an enforced spatial order that will never be absolutely necessary or even possible. The two diagrams used by Duany & Plater-Zyberk have this problem; not helped by implying the neighbourhood is *totally* surrounded by open space of one form or another. (*Plate 3*)

In reality, this need not and rarely, happens. A recent project I was involved in with Duany & Plater-Zyberk for an expansion of Sacramento, California demonstrates the value and flexibility of the model showing the relationship between global connections and the foci of the pedestrian radii. The combination of these two components gives an operational logic to the public transport network. The open space network does bring some discontinuities to the street connection as it does in any city, but that network is extensive and varied, respectful of existing and proposed water courses and vegetation. In addition, the streets, squares, neighbourhood parks and private spaces all contribute to the greening. (*Plates 4, 5*)

It is a fruitful exercise to attempt overlays of pedestrian proximity on existing mixed-use areas of towns and cities, gleaning principles for new places. (*Figures 34, 35*) This is not to say that every aspect will be favourable or appropriate as these areas were usually developed at least a century ago. But the common connection is that their social logic of space produced and relied far more on pedestrian proximity and we need to re-discover those principles and then address contemporary conflicts.

To further emphasise the energy efficiencies, the work of Sue Owens (1985) concludes that the single most important factor is the low physical separation of activities. This has to take account of the degree of mixing and the density of development, both extremely complex and highly political issues, where the urban designer has a central role to play in demonstrating the possibilities but needing far more

detailed research and design application than hitherto. What is an appropriate density is beyond the scope of this chapter, but it must be acknowledged that it is central to the ultimate performance of an area of town as far as the distance necessary to travel between activities and other people is concerned. As Newman and Kenworthy (1991) point out, low density cities are suffering from congestion because of car dependence and there is no real way of avoiding the problem. High density cities undoubtedly have congestion problems but for them, *alternatives exist*. Friends of the Earth go towards densities that would shock many in the UK let alone the USA or Australia; when they propose that, 'overall housing densities in town and cities ought to be at a level equivalent to the typical three and four storey urban street; a level at which it is still possible to provide each dwelling with its own front door onto a public street and to provide gardens for all family dwellings . . . these can lead to high quality housing at densities 50% greater than those typical of new urban housing'. (Elkin *et al* 1991). Depending on mix, dwelling size and contemporary parking standards (hopefully reducing in time) a net density of twenty dwellings per acre is well within reach with these criteria set by FOE.

Valerie Rosencrantz (1992) of the Sacramento Transit Authority emphasises the combination of density and proximity in making public transport viable. She would prefer to see 20 to 30 dwellings per acre within 200 metres of fixed track transit, yet accepts 10 to the acre as a minimum density to support a bus service. As with all such figures she fully acknowledges the trade-off between density and operating subsidy. Similar trade-off criteria apply throughout all aspects of the sustainability debate emphasising the complexity and potential danger being too specific in any one.

Peter Calthorpe (1989) emphasises concentration and mixed-use and supports the 5 minute/400 metre rule of thumb. Within this approximately 125 acre/ 50 hectare area is housing, offices, retail, day care, recreation and parks. Calthorpe is of the view that some 2,000 units of housing and one million square feet of office space can be located within three blocks of the transit station without high-rise apartments or offices any higher than four storeys.

For a true mixed-use town to give a 24-hour presence and the enhanced safety this should provide, residential is the only use that can offer that presence. Within the approximate 400 metre radius, residential should be the primary use and distributed throughout the grid, albeit with varying net densities and varying balance with other uses as the social logic of the spatial integration directs. Jane Jacobs' fourth condition for the generation of diversity alludes to this. 'There must be a sufficiently dense concentration of people for whatever purposes they may be there. This includes dense concentration in the case of people who are there because of residence' (Jacobs 1961).

Clearly the only exception to this requirement of residential predominance would be arguments for a specific special quarter or district if centrality and related land values continue to operate as they have done traditionally. The downtown may well have a greater predominance of commercial, cultural and retail such that housing did not predominate. Nevertheless as existing downtowns testify the more housing they contain, the better they are. The recent fiscal crisis has demonstrated that when commercial land values slide to match residential, there is a strong market for residential and a development sector only too keen to supply. Robert Adams, manager of Architecture and Urban Design for the City of Melbourne, has achieved considerable success attracting residents into the CBD in a remarkably short amount of time — this in a culture which apparently regards the traditional city as somewhat profane.

The product is traditional, the change radical. Richardson gives us the good news and then the bad news.

The good news about these and other steps towards urban sustainability is that they fit very well together. More efficient structuring of urban growth, higher densities, better use of urban sites, and a shift from cars to transit, all work together to protect land resources, conserve energy and improve air quality. The bad news, of course, is that all this is very difficult to do . . . But they are not technical problems. In a technical sense we know pretty well what needs to be done, and how to do it. The problems of achieving urban sustainability arise out of the nature of our society and the way it is organised (Richardson (1991) in Roseland, 1992 p. 127)

This chapter has demonstrated some ideas as to what the product of urban design should be. But as usual, the lists of laudable and soundly researched intentions all too often fall short of demonstration and

certainly demonstration with precision. By way of a conclusion it is necessary to be as prescriptive about the product and the process as well as being precise about what still needs to be further researched and determined and to offer the following to further the debate.

The Location of New Development

Recent research for the Department of Environment (Breheny et al., 1992) concluded that there are three broad locations that can support sustainability; all with varying implications, of course.

- Intensification of existing cities
- Expansion that is grafted on to existing towns and cities
- New settlements with a minimum population of 30,000 people and far enough away from an existing town or city to prevent it having a dormitory function

The least sustainable solution of grafting small numbers of housing on to existing villages or producing new settlements of a relatively modest size (900 or 1800 dwellings) are sadly the ones that are being promoted and endorsed in the UK. It is hard to imagine where in the UK a new settlement of a *minimum* population of 30,000 people would be politically acceptable and far enough away to minimise commuting. It is equally hard to imagine the private sector being willing or able to finance towns of this size with the necessary public structure, management and advanced infrastructure.

This raises the spectre of something akin to the defunct New Town Development Corporation scale of public initiative, albeit with a markedly different agenda, emphasising the need for major political intervention and considerable public finance.

The Grain of the Grid

- The global connecting system; the main streets will obviously be dictated by the location of the area being developed. But they will be the most integrated streets. They need to be thought of as high streets wherever possible with an active building frontage. If slip roads are necessary to achieve this then it has to be.

— The global connectors will be where the majority of retail and office development locates providing they are conceived and promoted as streets and not as traffic conduits with no frontage development. Some residential will be there too.

— Public transport will focus on these routes.

— Densities will increase towards them.

— Local connectors will feed into them at intervals as directly and frequently as possible.

Pedestrian Proximity

— Some centrality along the global connectors will be a necessary focus for the initial public and commercial buildings, associated with all forms of public transit.

— As much variety as possible will then be targeted within an approximate 400 metre radius of the initial focal place.

— These areas of approximately 125 acres will be duplicated to form larger towns and key into and incorporate existing adjacent areas.

— The existing landscape will influence where focal places and the consequent districts will settle and connect as well as influencing the location of major public spaces.

The Structure of Open Spaces

— In addition to the fine grain grid of public streets a range of open spaces will be needed,

— In principle the pedestrian-oriented 400 m radii should have major open spaces to their periphery for at least one quadrant of the circle but never more than two, to minimise the tendency towards isolation from other development. This appears a crude rule of thumb but allows major public space to be no more than 1.2 km away from the majority of people and allows for linear continuity of open space where necessary. More localised neighbourhood squares and small parks can be located within the grid, as has been the tradition in most grid towns, but never more than 200 metres from the majority of people. They too should be at the junction of the better-integrated local connectors. (*Figure 36*)

The Mixing of Uses

— A pre-requisite is that the global connectors are frontage streets with a strong emphasis on the public interface, wide pavements and street trees. If so, a 400 metre radius (125 acre area) with only one main street running through it will have a potential commercial frontage of something approaching 1.5 km. Some of this can and must be residential but it will take some time for that one commercial street to establish. Add to this the tradition of such streets to turn corners and develop commercial uses some 30–50 metres down all the streets that connect, then the run of edge increases further. (*Figure 37*)

— None of this precludes further intermixing on the streets deeper into the system; at junctions and/or associated with home working and small enterprises, but it demonstrates that mixed-use, with a social logic to its location along the main connecting streets is quantifiable, considerable and never more than a reasonable walking distance from its hinterland.

Robust Building Form

This is not a specific topic for this chapter, but it cannot pass without brief mention. A robust building typology of four storeys maximum, 9 to 15 metre depth with frequent entrances along its frontage will best ensure a mix of uses at any one time and over time as well as being resource efficient in reducing the need for mechanised air handling and illumination.

In essence, this is the recipe for mixed-use town; sustainable town, and consensus is growing. There is still much to be done on a range of supportive issues posing major questions for urban design to research.

Plot and Block Size

How does the spacing of the street structure divide developable parcels of land such that a variety of uses can pragmatically function in close proximity? Approximately 90 metres was proposed by Bentley *et al.*, (1985). Duany & Plater-Zyberk propose approximately 165 × 83 metres in the USA based on a subdivision system of 4.8 metre frontage, capable of combining in various ways to accommodate a substantial range of standard building footprints with rear alley access.

More recently work at the Joint Centre for Urban

Design has itself offered different dimensions based on slightly different assumptions. An approximate 60 × 140 metres was proposed by Thorne (1993) assuming a plot width of 9 metres and no rear alley access. Whether or not plot frontage width matters at all is an interesting area of study in itself, particularly in the UK where a subdivision system does not exist currently. An MA study by John Baulch (1993) proposes 80 metre depth and 115 metre length as optimum for fine grain mixed-use based on close examination of a range of mixed-use studies in existing towns and cities. Clearly the *depth* of the block and the consequent back to back dimensions are crucial. If the grid is deformed and not orthogonal then critical minimum dimensions become very specific issues. (*Figure 38*)

Overall Mix and Carrying Capacity

The amount of residential as opposed to other uses in order to be mutually supportive within the approximate 125 acre district demands more focused research. Equally, what is the right amount of development to be placed in a particular landscape to strike a truly sustainable balance?

The Will to Deliver

What does all this mean at the wide political level; the persuasion or enforcement to deliver; the emphasis on more centralised structures; intensive land-use, pedestrian proximity, restraints on high speed traffic and the provision of far better public transport? It would certainly require the greatest change from the status quo in government policy and management programmes and would require a great amount of government regulation. Governments will have to remove the conflicting incentives and act globally. If not, regions adopting more forward thinking policies will suffer dramatically from those who perpetuate the status quo for short term political and economic expediency.

Urban design cannot allude just to geographical locations like 'the inner city' because what I have outlined is as vital to new expansion. It cannot allude to the 'public realm' without qualifying the nature of *being public*. Perhaps it is naive to suggest that what is proposed in this chapter is achievable within our broad political economy as it exists. Up until the last 50 years it was the norm. In rejecting traditional urbanism we have achieved exactly what Hannah Arendt warned against, namely that the world between people has lost its power to gather them together, to relate and separate them *at one and the same time*. There is no conflict between this human interaction and ecological concerns of sustainability in new 'traditional urbanism'. There is no possibility of *uniting* them in the dispersed city of the late twentieth century.

Roger Simmonds

THE BUILT FORM OF THE NEW REGIONAL CITY: A 'RADICAL' VIEW

'Conservative' Versus 'Radical' Reformers

A New Kind of City

A new kind of city has been emerging in the growth regions of the USA. It is regional in scope, involving the transformation of existing urban areas into new patterns of land use, as well as the emergence of new kinds and forms of development on the urban fringe and beyond. In retrospect, we can see that this evolution has been taking place since the war with many of its roots going much further back in time. Similar patterns of built form are emerging in Europe, though belatedly and in more muted form. Following Lewis Mumford's classification of the evolutionary stages of the city (Mumford 1961), it is clear now that this new kind of city will be as different from the nineteenth century European city as it was from the Baroque and as it, in turn, was from the Medieval.

Responses

A few years ago it was common for European professionals to deny that the emerging patterns of development in the USA had any relevance for them. Such things were not expected to happen in Europe for a variety of reasons; car ownership would not reach US levels; Europeans would never abandon the conventional city in the way Americans have; high agricultural land values in Europe would enforce building at higher densities; local governments in Europe were able to provide greater protection for local employers, thus keeping them in less cost effective locations in the inner city, and so on.

As most of these claims proved unfounded and the new kind of city began to emerge, European professionals turned from denial to confrontation. Two quite different styles of confrontation, belonging to two distinct schools of thought and practice, can be found among urban design theorists and practitioners today. I will call them:

- The 'Conservative Reformers'
- The 'Radical Reformers'

The 'Conservative Reformers'

Conservative reformers confront the emerging form of the new city by seeking to suppress it; channelling pressure for new kinds of growth into traditional built forms. Their deep pessimism about the potential of the built form of the new city seems to be partly aesthetic; as they contrast its chaotic built results with the built forms of earlier historical periods. It seems partly social; as they worry about further social polarisation and compare its fragmented and disrupted public realms with those of the traditional city.

Their response is often political; it being often claimed by the conservative reformers that they are unable to trust the emerging city because it is so much a product of a destructive late twentieth century capitalism. It is not clear how seriously we should take this last claim, however, as it is rare for the conservative reformers to address the effects of past political economies on the historical forms from which they draw their inspiration. It is often observed by critics that some of the environments which conservative reformers use as models were produced under regimes of almost venal political economies.

Other conservative reformers argue that, because the city is still emerging in a capitalist political economy as in the past, it is false to make claims about the emergence of a new kind of city. What appears to be a new city is simply the product of incompetent management by local and regional governments, who have failed to control new development pressures along the traditional lines they have used in the past. Recent writing by critics like David Harvey (1989), who might have been expected to support this point of view, seem to dispute it. He makes a significant distinction between the capitalism of the early and late twentieth century, claiming that new kinds of social and economic practices have been emerging with new kinds of built form.

There appear to be two distinct kinds of conservative reformer. The first are those who have a deep commitment to the traditional nineteenth and early twentieth century city. Most urban designers earn their living from nurturing and repairing these traditional cities, and it is not surprising that conservative reformers derive their urban design principles and their inspiration from studying them. Jane Jacobs' *Death and Life of Great American Cities* (1961) seems to be the model approach for this group while *Responsive Environments* (Bentley et al., 1985) is, perhaps, the most impressive attempt to formulate a general theory of urban design practice, based on studies of the traditional city.

In their desire to channel pressure for new kinds of growth into traditional built patterns, this group of conservative reformers seem to hold two approaches. The first seems to be predominantly deterministic, believing that by forcing new social and economic activities into traditional patterns of built form it is possible to reform them in the process. The second approach seems to focus on aesthetic qualities, believing that traditional patterns are robust enough to accommodate the changed social and economic practices of the new age, while the built form and its links with the past remain essentially intact.

The second group of conservative reformers are typified by the work of Leon Krier in the UK and the 'neo-traditionalists', who have become so popular in the USA through the work of Andres Duany and Elizabeth Plater Zyberk. Working more often with green field sites on the fringe the main basis of their rejection of the built form of the emergent city is its 'unsustainability'. They build at higher densities and integrate traditional style commercial centres into their developments. Unimpressed by claims of the

radical reformers about the way the automobile and new information technologies are transforming the built form of the city, the neo-traditionalists base their designs on the 'robust' built pattern of small towns in the late nineteenth and early twentieth century. It is a pattern which emerged before the automobile, the telephone, or the radio were even invented.

The 'Radical Reformers'

A new perspective is beginning to emerge in opposition to the conservative reformers. As yet it has little coherence, but it is possible to detect an emerging theme of ideas and practices with a small but growing body of followers. I have called them the 'radical reformers'. Radicals confront the built form of the emergent new city not by seeking to transform it but by embracing it; believing that, through intelligent and caring interpretation by designers, it can become the basis for a new and better kind of city in the future.

There is a thin thread of this willingness to embrace the new city running through the history of urban design theory and practice. An early example can be found in *Learning From Las Vegas* (Robert Venturi, *et al.*, 1972). Here the authors urged readers to study the ordinary everyday built forms of the contemporary city. Only through such studies, they argued, could the designer expect to understand the city sufficiently to design it.

Today, the work of Rem Koolhaas is becoming a focus for those who seek to embrace rather than turn away from the contemporary city and its products. Koolhaas also urges designers to study the ordinary pieces of the contemporary city because it is here that a collective experience can be discovered and learned from. This experience, he seems to argue, is of the utmost importance because it emerges from the interaction of a range of actors, including unsung professionals of various kinds, each embedded in one way or another in the social and economic life of the city and involved in producing its built form. In his studies of New York city, he claimed to find a kind of collective genius which had led to the emergence of its block structure and building type (Koolhaas, 1978). Later, studies of the urban fringe and its ordinary and chaotic landscapes produced the insight and inspiration in his competition entry for the Parc de la Villette (Lucan, 1991).

Typical of the emerging concepts of the radical

reformers, the work of Koolhaas displays a greater concern with the relationship between urban form and function than one encounters in the ideas of the conservative reformers. There is something distinctly Modernist about the radicals; expecting that changes in social and economic practices will almost inevitably produce and be produced by new cultural landscapes and patterns of built form.

In the above sense Koolhaas argues that the uncertainty, which is such a feature of social and economic practices in contemporary society, is accompanied by a degree of 'chaos' in the processes and built form of the new city. It is, he argues, necessary to have an attitude and a response to it, if you want to design today's city. Here we find the sharpest of all possible contrasts with the approach of the neo-traditionalists.

In spite of their preoccupation with matters of function, most radical reformers find themselves accused by conservative reformers of being uncritical of the political economy lying behind the production of the environments they study. While being soft on capitalism is certainly not a required condition for being a radical, one rarely meets one who is not more optimistic than the conservatives are about the potential of the late twentieth century version of it. Similarly, it is rare to encounter a radical reformer who is not optimistic about the potential of the new information technologies for contributing to the achievement of a better society. Sometimes this optimism can sound like the most naive form of technical determinism and wishful thinking. Sometimes it is informed by a deeper attempt to see how such technology is translating into the emergence of new systems of deprivation and control. At such moments radicals make claims along the lines of Castells (1989), about the relative merits of this system over the system it has replaced. The radical reformers can often sound like an electronic version of the Italian Futurists, who placed such store in the potential of the machine.

The Character of the New Regional City

Introduction

Conservative reformers dominate urban design thinking in Europe and the USA and their deep pessimism about the built form of the new city prevents most designers from even seeking to understand it and its potential. Radical reformers, in their willingness to embrace the new city, can provide insights which the conservatives would never be able to discover for themselves. Then again, conservatives are fond of accusing radicals of not being willing to put their proposals on the table. Until they do, conservatives say, there can be no debate.

This section aims to begin that debate. It is an attempt to pull together insights and proposals of radical reformers about the emerging new city. At this stage, they are generalised and analytical and they are weak on images and vision about what this new kind of city can become. Where such images exist, however, I have tried to draw them in.

Communications Investment and Associated Growth Poles

Cross town movement has always been difficult in cities with radial road structures. Most larger radial cities and towns thus end up building by-passes or ring roads to prevent the centres clogging up with through traffic. As soon as this happens, certain kinds of retail and manufacturing investor seek to locate on them. The junctions between them and the existing radials become the focus of investment, as indeed cross roads have been throughout history. This tendency is reinforced here by the ring roads being limited access roads and, thus, only accessible at their junctions. (*Figure 39*)

As these developments have grown, they have begun to generate a quite different kind of regional movement system: no longer dominated by the familiar periphery to centre movement of the past but movement from one part of the periphery to another. It is a pattern which is very difficult to serve by conventional mass transit systems but, as densities increase, systems with the required flexibility will emerge.

Towns and cities which prevent locations at such junctions simply lose employers and services to those that allow it and, in an increasingly international and competitive marketplace, this can mean losing investment not just to the next town but to the next country. No government, central or local, dare risk such losses!

These development nodes become critical new

pieces of town. Sometimes they take the form of introverted malls, with their origins in the farmers markets of an earlier period (Rowe, 1991). Sometimes they are business nodes, the modern equivalent of development around the railway stations and goods yards of the last century. In both cases they raise many questions, presently unanswered by urban designers, about how such fragmented pieces of town should be integrated with the public realms of the fast and slow roads which serve them.

Grid structured cities usually have much better cross-town movement and it is less common to find ring roads. They do, however, need to be connected in to new motorway systems, usually with junctions at the major grid roads. These then become important growth poles, for the same reasons.

Airports are the second major transport investment which have become generators of growth at the junctions between their entry points and the existing road system. Again they are outside the old cities and have given rise to developments of a kind that is unique to their function. The airport is about to increase its share in the freight market by some three- or four-fold, with obvious consequences for its immediate locality, and is fast becoming the functional and symbolic link between the region and the global marketplace within which it must survive. As such, the airport is becoming a commercial node in its own right, not just a transport terminal.

Growth Poles Based On Quality of Place

The environmental quality of a potential investment location has, for almost all kinds of company through history, been secondary to the quality of its connectedness to markets, materials, and labour pool. Today, more companies are trading in information products which, where the infrastructure exists, can be received as raw material and transmitted as finished product along the fibre optic cables of air waves. Spatial connectedness, except to the pool of labour is, thus, increasingly irrelevant for certain kinds of company or certain departmental functions within them. This means that companies (or departments) can choose locations because they are cheap or beautiful or offer the kind of recreational resources which company employees and their families prefer. This gives rise to at least two kinds of growth pole;

those centred on special cultural or historic locations, and those centred on other recreational or scenic locations.

The first are often old urban centres which, depending on their resources, are in the process of being transformed by city governments into lucrative 'theme parks' (Sorkin, 1992)), borrowing their management techniques from Disneyland. Such areas often become formalised as 'cultural' or 'historic' planning districts aimed to attract regional and sometimes international tourists. Certain kinds of service company need and can afford to locate at these nodes. Centres which lack the resources to become 'themed', find their land values plummeting and once again become the locations for employers, especially those who employ unskilled workers who cannot afford a car or high mass transit costs.

The second kind of growth pole can be found in some wilderness or rural areas, where companies have been buying land as a setting for their operations and then pouring money into nurturing and sustaining it. These individual buildings and 'science parks' are beginning to break down one of the land use segregations which were a particular feature of the traditional city; namely the distinction between 'urban' and 'rural' or 'wilderness' activities.

The New Roads of the City

Looking at aerial photographs, taken every five years, of development along the link road between Dulles Airport and the Washington Beltway a certain pattern becomes clear. It is a pattern, once recognised, which is emerging everywhere on the fringe and in the inner city. To begin with the motorway or limited access road corridor is not considered to be part of the city and buildings are designed with their backs to it and their fronts to their access road. In recent times, however, buildings have begun, tentatively at first, to relate to travellers on the motorways by presenting some kind of formal 'face' to them. (*Figure 40*) Often this includes a symbolic entrance linked by an atrium to the real entrance off the access road on the other side of the building. Sometimes it involves bringing the access road alongside the motorway so that buildings can address themselves to both roads at the same time. Sometimes existing buildings are dressed up with supergraphics for the attention of the motorway user. Sometimes buildings surround themselves with manicured landscapes (often integrated with parking) to be seen by travellers on the motorway with three dimensional Modernist style buildings standing in their midst.

As buildings begin to address the motorways in this way, these roads become social spaces of the city. The nature of this space and its function is mediated by the fact that it contains no pedestrian travellers. It is a world made up of people in vehicles receiving information about the city in sight or out of sight and only accessible from the next junction. The best examples are the French autoroutes, with their huge scale but simplified facsimiles of important buildings close to but not visible from the road. To travel through France on these roads is to travel through a cultural exhibition (based exclusively on virtual images) at 120 km/hr. (*Figure 41*)

The radial roads (or main grid roads) function according to different rules. These have evolved to become the commercial 'strip', which achieves its full flowering in the USA and has much more muted expression in most of Europe. The strip itself is partly an information system about what is immediately available on the road and is geared to a different traveller speed, though here also the signs are more important then the buildings. Today these roads carry a higher percentage of office and manufacturing investment and now not just facing the road but leading back from it in 'parks' or 'estates'. The 'strip', so much derided by the conservative reformers, has emerged as the 'high' or 'main' street of the emerging regional city, providing almost the only continuity between the old urban centres, the periphery, and beyond.

Most cities in the developed world are struggling to keep these radial and major grid roads functioning as they clog up due to the increase in car numbers and the problem of vehicles turning across oncoming traffic. Of the many solutions which have been tried, two seem the most sensible:

- The provision of a central reservation with 'frontage' (or 'access') roads parallel to and on either side of the main road to create a kind of boulevard style landscape. This must be linked, via the main road, to traffic roundabouts facilitating vehicles turning back in order to gain access to facilities on the other side of the road.
- To function effectively, these frontage roads must

be designed as complex parking facilities and bus stops with parking vertical to the road on both sides and overspill parking to the side or rear.

This kind of built pattern, as one approaches motorway junctions, can provide a rival to the mall in benign climates and this built form is becoming the basic organising principle for busy continuous commercial high/main streets of the fringe as all local centre activity is directed onto them. (*Figure 42*)

Public transport systems on these 'strip' high streets will intersect with transit systems on the ring roads to form the basis of a new public transport network with its interchanges at the motorway junctions.

The New Open Spaces of the City

Throughout history, major growth spurts have often led to new development well beyond the outskirts of the city. Subsequent phases of more modest growth have led to filling in of the land between these outposts and the urban edge. In the short term there was, thus, a large amount of 'rural' land within the emerging urban' area. The only rural spaces which survived in the long run, however, were those owned by municipalities; these were often the original market spaces outside the city gates in successive phases of wall building. By the nineteenth century a few cities were assembling land for municipal parks.

Today, the growth poles adjacent to airports, at the junctions of motorways and ring roads with the existing road system and in rural settings, as discussed, have stretched the urban area in new and even more dramatic ways. Often, huge swathes of open land remain between these new poles and the old urban edge. As these areas begin to fill up with urban activities, the new residents, attracted to these locations because of their rural character, become fierce conservationists, seeking to protect open land and the character of local roads. In political situations where there is a small and relatively autonomous local government, such groups can be successful, with large swathes of farmland and wilderness areas surviving within the urban area. In contrast to the past, most of these are privately owned but, because they have been preserved as open land in perpetuity by local public initiative, through development rights transfer, Areas of Outstanding Natural Beauty,

99

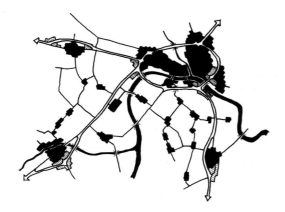

Figure 39. Existing and planned development (hatched in) at the ring road and by-pass junctions of a UK 'regional city.'

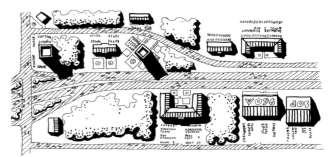

Figure 40. The motorway, ring road or by-pass as a 'social space' with buildings addressing it in different ways.

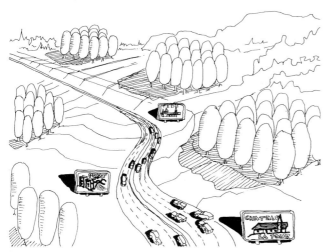

Figure 41. The French autoroute as cultural museum seen at 120km/hr and based on virtual images.

Figure 42. Retro-fitting the American strip with central reservation, frontage roads and integrated high density housing.

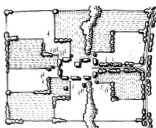

Figure 43. Design for hobby farms and small holdings in redundant farmland areas on the fringes of New England regional cities, using local suburban zoning of 1 unit per 2 acres. (Source: Schuster et al, 1990)

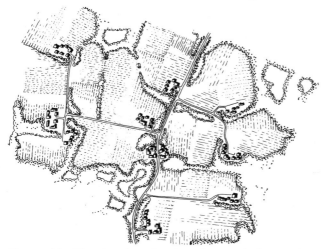

Figure 44. Housing in redundant farmland; designed to conserve the rural landscape and promote productive use of the land. (Source: Schuster et al, 1990)

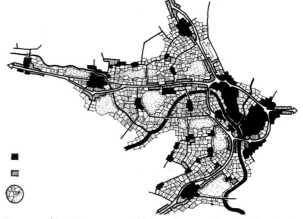

Figure 45. Diagram of the future 'regional city' of Oxford, UK, showing fields with new employment and retail directed to major ring road and by-pass junctions and 'A' road 'high streets' between Oxford and Witney, Woodstock and Abingdon.

community forests, and programmes like them, they often have access for residents.

Dramatic though the impact of such initiatives is in producing open land within the city region, it does not compare with central, regional, and local government initiatives to protect air and water quality, and to eliminate pollution through run-off and waste disposal. In combination these programmes can result in over 50% of all open land in the regional city being preserved in something like its agricultural or wilderness state. As with land which is protected on account of its beauty or special ecological quality, this land then becomes a quite new kind of resource for the resident of the city region. Much of it becomes 'public realm', but of a very different kind than the realm of the municipal park.

Radicals discover much potential in these kinds of realm, finding fruitful relationships between mixes of so-called urban and rural land uses. One of the most obvious, of course, is the amount of resources companies or people with urban lifestyles can find to pour into land preservation. Many farm their land as a genuine supplement to the urban incomes. (*Figure 43*) In the devastated old urban centres which did not have the necessary resources to be themed, poorer residents, particularly those from a rural background, are taking over under-utilised public and private land on which to grow vegetables and keep chickens. As agriculture becomes increasingly industrialised, a lover of the countryside in the future will be more likely to find it in the old city and its fringe than in the land beyond. (*Figure 44*)

In short, we are seeing the emergence of what Neutelings (1991) calls a 'patchwork metropolis'; a landscape with a completely different relationship between urban and, what used to be thought of as, rural activities. This relationship is chaotic and happenstance in formal terms but it provides endless opportunities for individuals and corporations to experiment. Fishman (1990), in his attempt to interpret these landscapes, finds them evocative in certain ways of Frank Lloyd Wright's 'Broadacre City'.

The Residential Areas of The New City

Tree-structured road hierarchies that are beloved of traffic engineers and found in most UK design guides are a freak of central government imposition and they rarely appear in the ideas of the conservative or radical reformers. Radicals, however, are less dogmatic in their approach and tend to support a very limited version of the pure traffic engineer model, in that they tend to accept the need for limited access roads at one end of a potential 'tree' and are open to the use of residential courtyards at the other. In the middle, where it really matters, both groups favour the grid.

What really separates the groups is their approach to the public realm of residential areas and its density. Conservatives advocate building at sufficient densities so that most of the ground floor spaces of buildings can sustain some kind of public use, nourishing the public realm of the street in the process. Once net densities fall below a particular high threshold, however, the commercial facilities have to be directed to one or two areas, the local centres. Conservatives argue that these should be roughly in the geographic centre of a housing area, in order to minimise the travel distance for pedestrians and cyclists and to maximise the interdependence between residential and commercial activity.

Radicals tend to want to direct the commercial activity into the nearest existing commercial corridor, adding to the emergence of a kind of strip leading out of town on major radials and grid roads. This strip, then becomes the location for public transport systems and higher density housing linked in to the commercial areas. The virtue of this approach for the radicals is that it works with the market forces already under way in all developed countries, where retail trade can only survive in large centres or on roads with a heavy passing trade. (*Figure 45*)

This concentration of the local centre function into commercial strips does not mean that the public realm of housing areas in the emergent city are condemned to build on the single land use of dwelling. In place of the failing dynamic between dwelling and retail, a much more promising but very different land-use dynamic is emerging; namely, the mix between dwelling and work that is based in the home or immediate neighbourhood. This represents yet another kind of new land use mix which radicals see to be the basis of new kinds of public realm in the emergent city. In one sense it evokes images of the public realm of the medieval city, the last period in history when work, other than domestic work, took place in the home.

Conclusion

The above represents an attempt to assemble some of the insights and partial visions of the group I called the 'radical reformers'. These perspectives are only emergent but it is fair to assume that those who are beginning to think this way are going to mount an attack on the way conservative reformers dominate urban design thinking and practice. If they are to be effective, however, the radicals will have to develop or borrow some new and sharper analytical tools for dealing with this kind of city. For example, conventional categories like 'work' and 'leisure' are deeply confusing in the context of the new city, as are 'town' and 'country', 'public realm' and many others.

Conservatives have rightly argued, that until radicals start to put things on paper and begin to talk about real decisions about built form on the ground, it will be impossible for a dialogue between the two groups to begin. I have seen my task here to be to begin this process. I have tried to put down some markers so that an informed debate can begin. Without the rethinking of concepts, however, it will be a debate held on the opposition's turf; a debate which the radicals will find it hard to win.

Ivor Samuels

WORKING IN THE PARK: CHANGES IN THE FORM OF EMPLOYMENT LOCATIONS

Changing Context

The past decade has been marked by a change in the nature of the workplace. The intention of this chapter is to outline recent experience, particularly British, in the provision of new types of workplace and to consider its application in other contexts. Historically when work moved out of the dwelling it became located in two distinct environments – the office and the factory and the planning profession since its emergence at the beginning of this century has been concerned to separate these activities from residential uses. Today this distinction has become blurred. For example a plant for the assembly of electronic instruments requires the same clean environment, high light levels and controlled ambience as an office for the processing of data associated with the financial services sector. (Worthington, 1989)

Another factor influencing change in the workplace is a shift from long assembly lines to small batch production where jobs may change with greater frequency. This is linked to the commercial applications of new technologies and a realisation that industry needs access to high level research if it is to remain competitive.

The workforce in modern industries is also changing. More technical, professional and managerial staff are employed. They often have work commitments which require buildings to be open 24 hours a day seven days a week. They are also concerned about both the quality of their immediate work environment and the wider setting in which their family life takes place.

A further drive towards a concern for high levels of design and maintenance is a realisation that customers as well as staff need to be wooed by quality environments both inside and outside buildings. Against this background attitudes towards property for industrial use have changed in Britain during the 1980s. Greater attention is being given to the image of the development and its marketing. Hence the use of the term 'park' to suggest surroundings of a level of delight not normally associated with the workplace (Carter, 1989). While the individual building occupier can control the quality of his own property, any attempt to control the quality of the public spaces implies a need for some form of collective management.

A Taxonomy of Parks

To meet these needs employment areas have been developed by private and public agencies which enjoy a bewildering variety of names.

Following definitions adopted by the US National Association of Industrial Parks (Spink, 1975) and allowing for differences in that country's practices, it is suggested that the elements essential to this type of development are:

- a comprehensive plan,
- compatibility among industrial operations in the park,
- compatibility between industrial park and existing activities and character of community,
- design controls on streets, plots, buildings and landscape provision,
- openness and park-like character,
- harmonious integration into neighbourhood,
- zoning to protect surrounding area,

- continuing responsibility of park management to preserve compatibility between park and community and to protect investment of developer and tenants.

In Britain the blurring of the division between the traditional use classes of industrial, commercial and office has been acknowledged by the introduction of the Business Use Class or B1 which came into force in June 1987. For the first time this allows activities ranging from office, research and development to light industrial to be treated as one land use category. It allows developers to provide a building within which a user can change the proportion of floor space devoted to particular uses without reference to the local planning authority for permission for change of use.

This practice makes the labelling and definition of these workplaces often ambiguous. As a general guide to buildings the following categories have been suggested (King, 1989):

- Office   more than 75% office
- Hi-tech   25–75% office
- Mid-tech   10–25% office
- Low-tech   less than 10% office

Henneberry (1987) points out that in all these categories two-thirds of the firms are in the service as opposed to the manufacturing sector.

In practice the definition of parks is less easy and the description chosen is usually dependent on the marketing strategy adopted by the developer. The following nomenclature is based on a number of authorities (Monck, 1988, Worthington, 1989).

The first four categories of 'park' may be distinguished by reference to a number of variables:

1 The extent to which they devote space to research activities.
2 The split between administrative (used in its widest sense to include training and marketing) and production activities.
3 The degree of concern for the quality of the environment and the image projected by the development.
4 The extent of links with academic institutions.

Business Parks

As the broadest category of new workplace, the Business Park, a term introduced in the 1970s, is the most familiar of these developments. It can accommodate a wide variety of activities such as manufacturing, showrooms, distribution and training. There is unlikely to be a link with a higher education institution.

The most prestigious of these enjoy good road and air communications and lie within a metropolitan catchment area. Stockley Park adjacent to Heathrow Airport is a good example of this category. (*Figure 46*)

Innovation Centres

These are generally small developments which provide accommodation and support facilities to enable new enterprises to start up and develop ideas. They do not aim to provide accommodation for these enterprises once they have grown, nor are they intended for existing medium sized or larger businesses or production plants. They are sometimes located close to academic institutions with the intention of encouraging academic research groups to engage in commercial enterprise.

The EEC as part of its regional development activity is actively promoting the 'small and medium sized sector' through a programme of Business Innovation Centres (BIC) which has been running since 1983.

Science Parks

These aim to provide accommodation for both start up and medium sized enterprises including small scale manufacturing. Generally on 'green field' sites the often quoted US prototypical examples are either spontaneous (Boston) or managed and emphasise the amenities of the area (Stamford). In the US a minimum of 8 to 12% of the workforce are technical or scientific professionals.

The United Kingdom Science Parks Association seeks to distinguish the true science park from other locations for high technology firms by emphasising three aspects: the operational links with a Centre of Higher Education; the presence of a management function concerned with the transfer of technology and business skills to the enterprises on the site; a concern to encourage the formation and growth of knowledge-based businesses.

There are a number of variations of the term science park which are commonly quoted:

Research Park   This is used to distinguish a science park which may have covenants on the leases which prohibit manufacturing activities.

Technology Park   This term is often used synonymously with science parks, but in a more precise definition can mean a commercial development as opposed to a science park which is, at least partly, a venture by an academic institution.

Office Park   In the spectrum of employment locations this usually defines a commercial development with some restriction on the activities permitted so as to exclude manufacturing or storage categories. There are normally no links with academic institutions.

Upgraded Industrial Estate   Many of the so-called high technology developments fall into this category. They represent an attempt, for marketing reasons, to upgrade the image of the standard industrial estate. In this process the industrial sheds have a 'high tech' facade applied and tree planting and other landscape works are carried out around the perimeter of the sites.

Retail Park   Although this category is not covered by the US definition quoted earlier with respect to uses, its physical and management characteristics are in essence identical to those of industrial parks and they have therefore been included.

It was estimated by estate agents Hillier Parker in 1989 that 50% of all new shopping space completed in 1989 in Britain was in retail or retail warehouse parks. The same authorities define this type of development as offering at least 4,500 square metres of gross retail space and containing at least three single storey retail sheds of not less than 1,000 square metres. In 1988 alone 45 opened bringing more than half a million square metres of retail space onto the market. There were 90 retail parks in Britain in 1989.

Business Parks in Britain

The development of the new workplaces in Britain was stimulated by the improvement of motorway networks – notably the completion of the M25 around London, and the massive shift from manufacturing to serve employment between 1971 and 1982. In the south-east of England alone half a million manufacturing jobs were lost while half a million new service jobs were created.

There were 575 schemes calling themselves business parks in Britain at the beginning of 1989 and it was estimated that 16,000 hectares of land were either under development or planned which could eventually provide more than 18 million square metres of floor space (Jones, 1989). Thirty-nine % of these schemes are in the south-east of England. Between 1980 and 1989 2.7 million square metres of building has been completed in these developments and over this period it is suggested that there has been a tendency for schemes to become larger in order to generate sufficient support for ancillary facilities. At the same time density of development is falling.

Of the space constructed in Britain, while 74% is used for high tech and pure office uses, there is an increasing tendency to include retail warehouses, hotels and sports buildings on the Parks. Three sectors dominate the high tech and office category – computer manufacturers with 250,000 square metres taken up in 1987–8, electronics (with an equal split between administration and sales and manufacturing and assembly) with about 100,000 square metres (1987–8) and telecommunications also with a take up of around 100,000 square metres in 1987–8. (King, 1988).

A further feature of development is the shift of headquarters buildings of large corporations from their traditional city centre locations. In 1987–8 130,000 square metres were programmed to be occupied by 1991 (King, 1988). This group includes service industry giants like Barclays Bank and Pearl Assurance.

Science Parks in the US

The science park concept originated in the 1950s with such well known developments as the Stanford Industrial Park (California), the Research Triangle Park (N. Carolina) and the concentration of enterprises along Route 128 (Boston).

The Office of Technology Assessment (Monck, *et al.*, 1988) has identified five contexts where development has taken place.

1 High Technology Centres such as Silicon Valley and Massachusetts where there is a strong base of high technology firms, research universities and venture capital.

2 Diluted High Technology Centres in major cities where firms have grouped together in highly visible centres to achieve a critical mass within larger, less specialised economies like New York or Chicago.

3 Spillover Communities where the attractive environment of small towns on the edge of centres has succeeded in attracting firms to low cost premises and a less competitive labour market (Wang headquarters locating at Lowell).

4 Technology Installation Centres where subcontractors are attracted to a single large production and research installation. Boeing at Seattle and the Kennedy Space Centre, Florida are examples.

5 'Bootstrap' Communities which cannot offer all the conditions attractive to high technology firms but can provide low costs and a high quality of life (Colorado Springs, Phoenix and San Antonio).

Science Parks in Britain

Perhaps the best documented of all Business Parks, Science Parks now occupy over 300 hectares and accommodate 907 tenants (CBI News, May 1990) in Britain and there are 38 members of the United Kingdom Science Park Association.

Started in 1973 the Cambridge Science Park was the first and is the largest of its type in Britain. Covering 130 acres (52 hectares) it employs around 1,900 workers occupying nearly 50,000 square metres of space. Built on green belt land its development was carefully circumscribed by the Local Authority which insisted on a number of conditions:

It should be limited to scientific research associated with industrial production, light industrial production would only be allowed if the research, development and design staff are also located in the Cambridge area or scientific staff from local institutions are involved in the enterprise.

The second British example, Heriot Watt University Science Park near Edinburgh is much more restrictive in its criteria for location so that tenants not only have to be engaged in research and development, but their activity must be linked to the work of University departments.

The small scale of British Science Parks should be noted. Monck, *et al.* (1988) point out that the whole of the Cambridge Science Park could fit into the car park of the Hewlett Packard factory at Palo Alto, California. A 1986 survey of 232 occupiers in the three sectors (Science Parks, high technology developments and contentional industrial estates) in Britain (Henneberry, 1987) confirms the small size of enterprises accommodated in Science Parks. These took on average less than 600 square metres of space as against an average of nearly 18,000 square metres in high technology business parks and over 2,100 square metres in modern industrial estates. The typical science park unit is 185–500 square metres while in the other categories the norm is 900–4,600 square metres.

French Technopoles

The Technopole is much less an instrument of real estate investment and more one of regional development than the Business Park in Britain or the US. They have been established in peripheral regions (Rennes-Atalante in Britanny) or in regions where the economy is dominated by one sector (Sophia Antipolis established in a tourist area). (*Figure 47*)

Management associations with mixed public and private ownerships have been set up to develop the technopoles and Central Government was instrumental in the early stages by directing such institutions as Air France to Sophia Antipolis and Telecoms to Rennes. State support is also given through the inclusion of teaching establishments such as *lycées* or special schools within the developments.

Particularly characteristic of the French scene are the networks of business parks established around the country by large consortia. Europarc, the largest chain, is developing 20 while Parc Club has established fifteen. These are sometimes established within the confines of a Technopole. (*Figure 48*)

Figure 46 and 47. At Stockley Park (left), the doyen of UK business parks, and Sophia Antipolis (right), the main design issue is coping with the large car parking areas.

Figure 48. The French business parks are dominated by a small number of developers offering an identifiable product across the country Parc Club development, Montpelier, France.

Figure 50. The road network at Sophia Antipolis which is required for the high car usage.

Figure 49. Water features are a common characteristic. Above, Warwick Science Park, England and below, Labège Technopole, Toulouse, France.

Development

In Britain, Business Park developments have been regarded as long term investments and were initially often promoted by institutions with a continuing interest in the land – Trinity College at Cambridge Business Park, a pension fund at Stockley Park or the Luton Hoo Estate at Capability Green.

These were followed by property developers with shorter term interests who fuelled the boom in Business Park development of 1987–8. This coincided with a surge in business investment in the UK (but which is now running at a much lower level with future prospects gloomy [*Financial Times*, 1990]) and the change in planning regulations already noted.

Although difficulty is being experienced by some Parks the success of this type of development is demonstrated by the fact that in some areas like Bristol and Reading, Business Park office rents are higher than equivalents in the city centre.

Science Parks have not attracted the financial institutions normally associated with property development because they do not meet their usual requirements for investment. These institutions look for strong evidence of rental growth, long leases (21 years), low voids and few planning restrictions. They are also anxious to attract well established companies with a sound financial base. Almost none of these criteria apply to the short lease, emergent company, high risk profile of the typical Science Park tenant.

The great majority of Science Parks have therefore depended on the partnership of a local authority or regional development agency. It has proved easier to establish these enterprises in northern areas of Britain where there is greater accessibility to public funds and a higher involvement of public bodies in development activity. Yields may be low but this is justified by the public agency concern to create jobs. The only notable exception is the Surrey Research Park created in the London green belt where land values were £1 million per acre in 1988 and very high rents could be demanded. These circumstances attracted private capital into the venture.

Science Parks in the US did not have a particularly good record in the first two decades of their establishment. Between 1960 and 1980 it has been estimated that three out of four were unsuccessful. (Monck, *et al.*, 1988). A successful Park is considered to be one where land is occupied at a rate of two to three tenants per year. Like their British counterparts they have depended on State and City participation for their survival.

The arrival of a single firm has often been instrumental to the progress of a development. An example of this was the North Carolina Research Triangle Park, now quoted as a market leader but which experienced slow growth in its first decade and only took off with the IBM decision to move in its 9,000 jobs Research and Development facility in 1965.

Management

The traditional industrial estate has roads and footpaths (often the only public spaces) maintained by the local authority, with individual tenants responsible for caring for the separate plots. This often leads to widely diverse painting and landscaping schemes (if they exist at all) and a mix of different levels of maintenance.

In contrast the management and maintenance of the public domain are crucial to the successful projection of the quality image to which business parks aspire. The developers of some of the earliest parks, Warrington New Town at Birchwood or Trinity College at the Cambridge Science Park, already had experience of land management. Private developers have had to develop their own skills often by setting up a specialist company to carry out this function. It is argued that the cost of maintenance is more than offset by the increase in values accruing to the property and reflected in higher rents at reviews and relets.

Site management often assumes responsibility for marketing and letting in addition to site security, signs and advertising, road and footpath cleaning, refuse collection, street lighting, landscape maintenance and, where they exist, recreation facilities.

In letting plots and buildings emphasis is usually placed on controlling the activities of tenants through covenants on the leases by which they hold their land. This restricts their activity and allows a greater degree of flexibility to the Park management than a blanket exclusion or zoning would permit.

Master Planning

The plan aims to provide a framework within which different architects, and on occasion, different developers, can work while still maintaining the coherent image which tenants expect. It also has to allow buildings to be occupied at an early stage without disturbance from the construction activities which may extend over several years.

The framework generally lays down a road and infrastructure network which is reinforced by a landscape structure. Given the long time scales involved, different architects and varied clients, the coherence and image of the Park often depend on the skill with which the landscape elements have been disposed. The co-ordination of street furniture, signs and surface finishes also clearly plays an important role in maintaining a quality image.

In sizing roads and infrastructure care has to be taken to maintain development options while minimizing initial capital investment and allowing a range of plot sizes to be offered. In the US plot sizes average about 1.5 hectares with around one-third of Parks specifying a maximum size of 8 to 10 hectares.

Building densities in the US are generally low with buildings covering 25 to 30% of the site area. In Britain 35 to 40% of the site area is occupied by buildings. Given the high level of car parking provision (close to one space per employee or one space per 27 square metres of office area at Aztec West) this allows little space for the landscape framework.

Plans are usually based on a ring road of a more (Aztec West) or less (Cambridge Science Park) formal layout which gives access to plots of similar depth. Larger sites may have two access points but developments up to the size of Stockley Park or Cambridge may be entered from one controlled access.

Roads are often lined by planted mounds in order to screen buildings, construction sites or car parks. In this way it is hoped to impose some sort of order on the appearance of the site while acknowledging that it may be difficult to control the appearance of individual buildings. The mounding will be more difficult to achieve in higher density sites where it is difficult to avoid the appearance of buildings, however carefully designed, floating in a sea of car parking.

Normally those sites at the front of a development command higher rents than plots at the back. By devising a landscape framework which can add value to these sites, higher rents can be obtained. Features used in this way include water gardens, pedestrian malls, promenades or sports grounds. (*Figure 49*)

In the US the minimum land area available for landscaping is usually around 50% rising to 60% in Princeton Forrestal Center and 68% at the North Carolina Research Triangle. British equivalent areas range from 30% (Capability Green) up to 40% (Solent Business Park). (Holden, 1987). In Sophia Antipolis 60% of the area will remain open space.

Holden suggests that the relatively high density and relatively small size of British business parks leads to great difficulties in emulating the campus like feeling of their US or French counterparts. This problem is exacerbated by an inability to afford multi-level car parking where a demand needs to be met of providing one car space for every 20 square metres of gross floor space (around one space per employee). In the US with more space per employee, car parking standards vary between one space per 25 square metres and one space per 30 square metres. (*Figure 50*)

Conclusion

The British Context

King (1988) suggests than an over-supply of space could lead to a buyers' market in Britain by the turn of the century and that this will lead to polarization at each end of the employment park spectrum. At one end some Science Parks and a limited number of the better endowed Business Parks (those with a quality image and good location) are likely to succeed while Industrial Parks will fulfil a need at a lower end of the scale. Parks with a range of building types and therefore no clear image and those badly located could remain empty for long periods.

To avoid this situation in regions currently less well endowed with employment parks, a careful market survey should be carried out in advance of development and then the construction and promotion should take place of products which have a clear identity related to the survey findings. It also suggests that attempts to cater for the whole spectrum in one development will not be successful. The prestige corporation headquarters building is unlikely to be attracted to the same development as the basic service industry warehouse.

There are indications that it is becoming difficult to attract labour to some out of town locations. This is most apparent in areas of low labour availability where female part-time workers need to be enrolled in the workforce. Good public transport links may therefore assume a greater importance in the future although, surprisingly, this tendency can already be noted in the US. Public transport can most effectively serve higher densities nearer concentrations of population which contradicts the current tendency to reduce densities.

Another influence which could propel employment parks towards stronger links with public transport networks, is the growing concern for the effects of motor car use on the global ecology. If governments force car users to pay more of the social costs of using their vehicles an effective public transport service will become an important asset of a business park.

Finally, linked with the need to reduce movement is the phenomenon (already noted at Sophia Antipolis) of employees actually living within the Business Park. The new clean industries, especially if traffic movement is reduced, do not need the exclusive zoning which currently operates. If this tendency continues we may witness attempts to build communities which seek to achieve a balance between residence, work and leisure activities — nothing less than the re-invention of the New Town!

The Business Park as a Model?

With its emphasis on car access, image, ease of development, simplicity of funding and prestige clientele the Business Park and its derivatives are very much a product of the United States. While it is understandable that Britain in many respects follows North American paradigms it could be argued that in all matters, apart from language, European models might be more appropriate, not least because the US economy is certainly not as flourishing as that of many European regions. Those regions that have demonstrated particularly high rates of growth (Southern Germany, Tuscany, Emilia and the Veneto in Italy) are distinguished by networks of closely integrated small businesses, often run on a family basis. There are undoubtedly a number of reasons for this success. Among those suggested are government support through special banks offering favourable loans to small enterprises and a peasant culture that, unlike the industrial workforce of older industrialised areas, is unused to production line manufacturing and is much more entrepreneurial.

It may be also that the spatial organisation of these areas is particularly supportive of these enterprises. The hypothesis is offered that the urban fabric, by integrating rather than separating uses helps integrate the firms and the families that run them. Obviously work needs to be done on this issue but it could be argued that, given the particular characteristics of Europe, a closer integration of activities would be worth considering as an alternative to the North American business park model.

SECTION FOUR

DOING IT

The entire book is peppered with examples of direct involvement in urban design but in this section we concentrate on four examples of exploration by intervention.

Samuels starts us off by a demonstration of the application of years of theoretical and practical work in morphology to a clear instrument of legal guidance and control. The work is all the more fascinating for its shift to another culture.

So much of our concern is with the public realm, and Graham Smith's extensive work on the policy and practicalities of humane streets is indicated here in a chapter that truly shows how positive and crucial is the management of traffic and the furnishing of the public realm it inhabits.

The importance of computer aided design to urban design has long been recognised in the Joint Centre with little progress in the educational programme. At last we are making some small progress, so at the same time it is a pleasure to present Hammond's account of her work, aided by, amongst others, another colleague, Roger Evans.

Hayward concludes this section, and the book, with some observations about the effects of context on the urban designer and the opportunity unfamiliarity gives for simple reflections.

Ivor Samuels

THE PLAN D'OCCUPATION DES SOLS FOR ASNIÈRES SUR OISE: A MORPHOLOGICAL DESIGN GUIDE

This project brings together, three different approaches to the problems of devising codes for controlling urban form in a way that we believe is completely new. In other words designing the city without designing the buildings – an enterprise which the authors consider to be at the core of urban design. The three approaches used are the British tradition of urban design guides, the practice of urban morphological analysis and the procedures of the French Local Land Use Plan – the *Plan d'Occupation des Sols (POS)*. The opportunity resulted from an invitation by Paul Lassus, the mayor of Asnières sur Oise, to the author, to put together a team to prepare a new POS for his commune. This followed an *Action Pilote* undertaken in July 1991 by a group of staff and students from the Joint Centre for Urban Design at Oxford Polytechnic under the patronage of the *Patrimoine Historique et Artistique de la France* (PHAF).

Over the last ten years Madame Abravanel, the President of the PHAF, has worked with staff and students from Oxford Polytechnic on *Actions Pilotes*. These are urban design projects which have involved up to a dozen staff and students spending an average of three weeks preparing proposals for a locality. This might be the entirety of a small village (Donzenac, 1986), part of a town (Provins, 1981, Honfleur, 1989) or a complex of buildings (Hôpital Saint Louis, 1985). The results of these projects have included programmes for environmental improvements and town trails in addition to specific building proposals which in some cases have been implemented.

At Asnières the proposals of the *Action Pilote*

were presented in July 1991 at a seminar held at the conference centre of the Abbey of Royaumont. The work presented included recommendations for the enhancement of the settlement edges, embellishments to the public spaces, outline proposals for an abandoned industrial area and a suggested framework for a design guide which would help to maintain the character of the settlement. It was this last proposal which was to be developed into the POS, although there is no doubt that at this stage it would have carried little conviction in the absence of the other work.

Asnières sur Oise

This 1400 hectare commune of 2,400 people is located 35 km north of Paris on the northern boundary of the region of the Ile de France. In addition to the main settlement it includes the hamlet of Baillon and the former Cistercian Abbey of Royaumont, all set within a matrix of forests and fields. It has an attractive location on the forested northern escarpment of the Plaine de France which overlooks the flood meadows and arable fields bordering the River Oise. (*Plate 6*)

The village of Asnières grew around the gates of the medieval Chateau de la Reine Blanche de Castille (the mother of St. Louis) and extends along east–west routes following the contours of the escarpment with the connecting north–south streets following the lines of watercourses. The patrician characteristics of the settlement have endured (a neo-Palladian

113

villa was built by the Pereira brothers whose bank financed Hausmann's rebuilding of Paris) and it continues to be remarkable for the number of large houses with their surrounding parks which seem to bring the forest into the centre of the pre First World War built up area.

The form of the historic core, like most villages in the Ile de France, is based on the traditional street lined continuously with buildings which have access directly from the back of the pavement. (*Plate* 7) There are some variations to this pattern where farm yards open onto streets, but in general the building forms the barrier between the public and the private realms. Nineteenth century and early twentieth century factory buildings, in two industrial areas totalling approximately six hectares, depart from this pattern, and more significantly, so do the latest areas of detached single family housing — the *pavillions*. (*Figure 51*)

As a desirable place to live, half an hour by car from Charles de Gaulle Airport and with good public transport connections to Paris, Asnières has received some attention from the *pavillion* builders. Not enough to destroy the quality of the village but sufficient to motivate the Mayor to take action to prevent the creeping suburbanisation of the northern fringe of Paris from swamping the commune. In many ways this is a situation analogous to that of pre Design Guide Essex.

At a time when everywhere is becoming like everywhere else, the problem of the maintenance of local identity has occupied much staff and student attention at the JCUD. It is not only a question of designing an environment which replicates the details associated with a locality without descending into a Disneyworld pastiche. Over centuries traditional building forms and tissues (buildings with their associated access arrangements and adjoining spaces) have proved capable of accommodating social and economic changes and they embody an accumulated wisdom that can be lost when they are replaced by other forms. For example, the single detached houses in the centre of small plots, offer far less privacy in their garden space than the traditional row house lining the street. While the detached house gives the illusion of being separate and independent it in fact destroys the distinction between the public and private realms and creates a homogeneous semi-private world surrounding the buildings. It was their aware-

ness of these issues that commended the JCUD team to the Mayor of Asnières who shared the same preoccupations.

The Development Control System

In France a single permission which incorporates planning and building controls is needed for development (for an account of the French Development Control system see DOE, (1989). This is called the *permis de construire* and has to comply with the legally binding local plan — the POS. Unlike the British system, where the development plan is only one of the factors to be taken into account in determining an application, if a proposal accords with the regulations of the POS then it must be approved. There is no discretion, at least in theory, to deal with a project on its own merits.

In 1989, having defeated an incumbent who had run the commune for several years, the newly elected Mayor, Paul Lassus had inherited a POS which had been prepared by the *Direction Departmentale de L'Equipment* (DDE) and adopted in 1987. The DDE is a local office of the *Ministère de l'Equipement* (responsible for planning matters as well as housing and public works) and provides a planning service for the communes in the department. In addition to plan preparation it also can carry out the processing of the *permis de construire* for these communes which are, in general, too small to employ their own technical staff.

Because a POS has legal significance it is clearly the key to achieving that improvement in the quality of the environment to which the Mayor was personally committed and which he had used as a major plank in his election campaign. But at Asnières the 1987 POS was proving a frustration to these intentions.

Like many plans prepared by the DDE this plan conforms to a model which, through its standardisation, neglects the special characteristics of each locality. This is partly due to the pressure on staff — it is easier to put together a collection of standard clauses rather than worry about interpreting the particularities of each town. It might also derive from the professional background of a staff more concerned with the administrative efficiency than with *genius loci*. Although there are some architects in the plan making teams, DDE officials are usually engineers and administrators – as befits an agency which is the direct descendant of the *Corps d'Ingénieurs des Ponts et Chaussées* founded by Louis XV.

A further source of concern was the way the heavy work load of the DDE and the distance of the office from Asnières (25 km away in the new town of Cergy Pontoise) often obliged decisions to be reached by officials with respect to authorisations without the benefit of even a single site visit.

French mayors represent a mixture of the British Chief Executive and Leader of the Council and have considerable freedom to initiate policies. It was a growing dissatisfaction with the service that was being provided by the DDE that had led the Mayor to take advantage of the 1983 decentralization law which allows planning controls to be transferred to the communes in those cases where a POS has been approved. There are only two other Communes in the Department of the Val d'Oise which have assumed the execution of these powers and they are both large enough to employ their own technical staff. Asnières is too small to do this so that the detailed development control negotiations are handled by the Mayor and the Commune secretary during Saturday morning surgeries. As in the UK most of the proposals for extensions and alterations do not involve the use of an architect. Even where architects had been commissioned they did not demonstrate much regard for the context in which they were designing and seemed more concerned with personal interpretations of the latest deconstructivist mode.

The Mayor, a commercial lawyer who is extremely well informed about architecture, therefore found himself having to demonstrate, without any supporting documentation, the principles according to which Asnières had evolved and how these could be followed in new buildings and alterations. He was obliged to negotiate from a position of weakness since his arguments were not backed up by the POS and therefore had no legal force. He had therefore resolved to prepare a new POS even before the *Action Pilote* took place. One advantage of initiating a new plan was that the Mayor was able to postpone making decisions on a proposal for up to a period of two years if he considered that an application was likely to jeopardise the successful implementation of the new plan. This has proved to be a formidable weapon in the negotiating process.

There are two agencies of Central Government which could have given some technical support to Asnières. They both proved unsympathetic to the Mayor's intentions. The first is the *Conseil d'Architecture d'Urbanisme et d'Environnement* (CAUE). In 1977 these were established in each department to promote the quality of the built environment and to give advice to the communes. In some departements the CAUE have published design guides to traditional architecture. In this case architects of the CAUE of the Val d'Oise expressed a hostility towards the embryonic proposals on the grounds that architectural creativity would be restricted. They also labelled the degree of control that the Mayor was seeking as undemocratic. Both are familiar arguments to proponents of design guidance.

The second possible source of support was the *Architect des Bâtiments de France* (ABF). Since there are two listed buildings in Asnières, the church, which is *classe*, and the Château of Touteville, which is *inscrit*, all developments proposed within a 500 metre radius of these two are subject to special controls. The protected perimeter includes most of the built-up area of the main settlement and this means that the ABF, the official at departmental level responsible for historic buildings, has to be consulted about all applications for a *permis de construire*. The Mayor felt that in any debate the ABF would tend to side with his professional colleagues and, at the Royaumont seminar, the ABF proved hostile to the Mayor's intentions and supported the arguments of the CAUE.

The 1987 POS

Following a formula established in 1973 with the intention of limiting land for urban expansion the 1987 POS is an essentially negative document and followed the standard four part formula laid down by the *Code d'Urbanisme* consisting of:

1 A Report setting out the physical, demographic and economic context leading to the general development policies – the *Rapport de Présentation*.
2 Plans – in this case a 1:10,000 scale zoning plan for the whole Commune with 1:2,000 scale inserts for the built up areas of Asnières and Baillon.

3 Regulations for each of the zones identified in the Plans — the *Règlement*

4 Appendices tabling, in map and written form, *Servitudes* which cover such matters as lines for road improvements or sites reserved for future public infrastructure investments.

The first three of these sections were to be radically modified in the 1992 POS.

The 1987 *Rapport de Présentation* tackled the physical form of the settlement in a very general way and was mainly concerned with assembling the quantitative data pertaining to the commune. It then projected the land needs necessary for the rate of growth assumed and made no reference to the new administration's central preoccupation — maintaining the character of the settlement.

The commune was subdivided into 'urban' and 'natural' zones. There were four urban zones defined according to a mixture of morphological and land use criteria. Thus all the older areas of the village were defined as one zone (UA) of continuous building for housing, services, trade and industry. All the newer areas were defined as individual houses (UG) while the bigger individual houses, whether old or new, were zoned separately (UH), where a narrower range of uses was permitted in a zone which was described as being of residential character. The two industrial areas formed the fourth urban zone.

The possibility inherent in the POS system of adopting a scheme of zoning according to building form rather than land use proved to be of great importance for the 1992 POS. It was the key to the use of morphological concepts in a way which would have been impossible in a British Local Plan.

In the Regulations each zone, as defined in the Plans, was covered by fifteen articles in three sections dealing with land uses permitted and excluded, physical conditions to be met and permitted plot ratios.

The second section included articles regulating access, siting with regard to roads and adjoining buildings, site coverage, building heights, parking and external appearance. This last article covered aspects of form and permitted materials. This appears to be a comprehensive list of all the aspects of urban form that an urban designer could possibly need to control but in fact it proved deficient for a number of reasons.

First the Report did not present a detailed argument setting out the reasons for adopting certain provisions while rejecting others which did not contribute to the goal of maintaining the essential character of Asnières. This made the mayor's assertions in development control negotiations appear subjective and whimsical. In fact they sometimes were less than convincing and it was only the process of preparing the new POS that tested his views and convinced him to reject a number of them as untenable.

Second, the lumping together of all the older area of the village reduced the subtle but very real differences in form and materials between the different districts. By adopting similar regulations for all parts of the village the 1987 POS would have had the effect of reducing the diversity of the Commune.

A similar objection can be raised to the rigid nature of some of the prescriptions. For example, a maximum height to eaves rule will probably, over a longer term, eventually result in all the buildings being of the same height. This is in contrast to the present street scene which is notable for a variation of heights within a range of maximum and minimum limits.

Some prescriptions which appeared to be very precise did not in fact lead to acceptable forms. The plot ratio, *Coefficient d'Occupation des Sols* (COS), is the most striking example. It is critical for realising the development potential of any site and an architect will in general be urged by his or her client to build up to the maximum prescribed. Unfortunately the results can be buildings of a proportion which are unacceptable against the goal of maintaining the existing character.

Finally, the effort needed to make specific regulations often resulted in the article dealing with building appearance to be couched in such vague terms as 'should be coherent' or proposals should be 'in harmony' with the traditional building forms.

THE 1992 POS

The new POS (Mairie d'Asnières sur Oise *et al.*, 1992) had to be an instrument that the mayor could use to show to lay people, professional builders and architects the characteristics of the village and the bounds within which solutions to their specific development problems could be found. Thus far very much the specification for an Essex-type Design Guide. But in addition, since it would be a legally binding document, it had to demonstrate the legitimacy of the prescriptions it was putting forward. Unlike an advisory design guide it would have to put up arguments that could be tested in a Court of Administrative Law.

The didactic quality of the British design guide was very attractive to the Mayor. In particular he was much taken by the possibilities of illustrating both unacceptable and acceptable solutions to building design problems.

While recognising the usefulness of design guides as models the team were concerned by their common lack of rigour. They often take the form of random collections of subjective responses to place and sometimes put forward proposals based on implicit design attitudes which would be considered doubtful or untenable if made explicit.

Within the expressed intention of the client to produce a POS which was concerned with maintaining the character of the commune, it was the task of the team to first define that character in terms of built form and then formulate prescriptions which would ensure its continuity into the future. To do this we had to work within the constraints of the *Code d'Urbanisme* and more generally of Civil Law, particularly where it deals with property rights. We also had to work within the bounds of political feasibility given the Mayor's desire to be re-elected. It was only possible to achieve these two objectives by including the Mayor, with his legal skills, as an integral part of the team. Although this might seem an irregular practice, it is not unusual in France where there is much less distinction between political and technical roles.

The other key step was the adoption of a methodology that enabled a systematic argument to be built up. For this we turned to the concepts of urban morphology and its application to questions of urban design which had been pursued for a number of years at the JCUD (Samuels, 1985, 1990). A member of the team, Karl Kropf had become interested in the application of morphological concepts to urban design while on the MA programme at the JCUD (Kropf, 1986) and the Asnières POS was an opportunity to develop a structuring concept based on levels of resolution that he had derived from the work

for example of Conzen (1969) and Cannigia (1981) as part of his PhD work at Birmingham University (Kropf, 1993).

Using a simplification of this method the urban form was subdivided into six levels of resolution each of which forms the basis for analysis and prescription: the whole commune, districts, streets and blocks, plots, building form and elements of construction. The process of analysis was undertaken by a mixture of direct observation, discussion with local experts and desk research into the local vernacular architecture. The first four levels of resolution also used the eighteenth and nineteenth century cadastral plans available in the Mairie.

The Rapport de Présentation

The first part of the POS (Mairie d'Asnières sur Oise, *et al.*, 1992) describes the characteristics of the settlement according to the categories described above. It puts forward an argument for identifying seven districts in Asnières and one in Baillon and then proceeds to discuss the characteristics of the streets, blocks and plots in each district. Under the headings of Building Forms and Elements of Construction characteristic and unacceptable forms are illustrated. (*Figure 52*) The latter section is divided into two parts reflecting the way the work was managed. Each team member had assumed responsibility for one of the major subdivisions but the complexity of the Elements of Construction led to their division into roofs (including chimneys and dormers) and walls (including openings and door and window details).

Joinery and ironmongery details were covered as were garden walls, hedges and colours. This was considered necessary since the alteration of window openings and frames which had already taken place demonstrated the way the character of street, and ultimately the whole village, could be altered by an accumulation of small and, seen in isolation, apparently minor modifications to the fabric.

The Report concluded with a brief summary of the main objectives of the commune:

- to protect and realise the potential of the historic, architectural and natural heritage of the commune.

Figure 51. Typical recent *pavillion* development at Asnières sur Oise.

Figure 52. A corner plot in the district of Les Fermes.

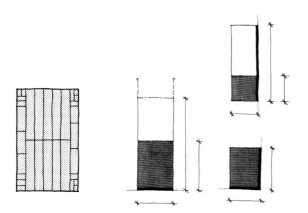

Figure 53. The range of acceptable plot dimensions and the extent of buildable area vary according to the location of the plot in the urban block.

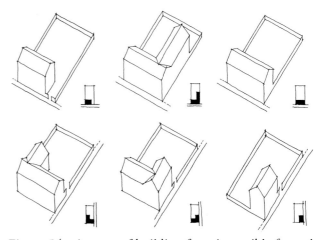

Figure 54. A range of building form is possible for each plot type; some of the combinations possible in Les Fermes.

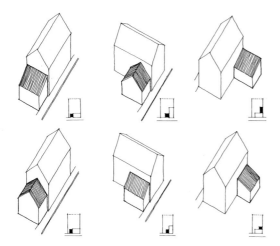

Figure 55. Some of the possible extensions in Le Village.

Figure 56. Acceptable forms of dormer windows in Le Village.

Figure 57. Acceptable and unacceptable forms of shutters in Le Village.

- to regenerate the older districts and to reinforce the traditional shopping.
- to revitalise the abandoned industrial areas with a mix of trade, services, industrial and residential uses.
- to integrate the new residential estates with the rest of the settlement.

The settlement would be kept within its existing built perimeter with new building needs being met in the underused industrial areas. The Commune intends to promote small housing units for the young and the old in these areas together with the new productive activities which contribute to the Professional Tax levied on all businesses, which is an important source of revenue for communes.

The Règlement

Under the seven zones (plotted on a plan at 1:2000 scale) corresponding to the districts identified in the *Rapport de Présentation*, prescriptions are laid down for the range of uses acceptable. These correspond closely to those of the 1987 POS with the exception of the former industrial areas where the area of residential uses is required at all times to be at least one-third of all the floorspace constructed — an attempt to design a mix of uses.

A principle is then established that the only sites where construction is permitted are those alongside the roads indicated on the zoning plan. This was a measure introduced by the Mayor as a method of preventing the subdivision of very large properties. The Civil Code, which is superior to the provisions of the Town Planning Code, allows the subdivision of plots every ten years, and thus this device was necessary to prevent these subdivisions being developed.

For each zone a range of acceptable plot types is then established together with minimum dimensions, plot proportion, buildable area and plot coverage. The permitted type varies according to the plot position in the block — front, side or corner. (*Figure 53*) These plots are defined on a plan of the older areas of the village drawn to 1:1000 scale. Each plot type has a range of permissible construction types — typically there are between three and five possible variations for each plot type. (*Figures 54, 55*)

There are common regulations for the constructions in each zone. These cover the range of permissible dimensions for length of facade, type and degree of roof pitch and length of gable wall. There are no limitations on height but a range of permitted storeys is defined as are the range of proportion between building height and building depth.

While each zone is separately defined as far as the form of buildings on plots is concerned there is one chapter which sets out a common range of details for all the districts. Thus only red plain tiles are permitted with the exception of buildings of public significance which can be roofed with slate. Gutters, chimneys, dormers, facade opening arrangements, types of door and window frame and shutter are covered in addition to wall materials and a range of permitted hedging shrubs. (*Figures 56, 57*) These regulations only pertain to the public fronts of buildings. On post-1914 buildings there is freedom to use different opening arrangements and materials on the rear or the sides of buildings which cannot be seen from the public realm.

There is, in effect, a far more restricted range of choice at the lower levels of resolution than at the higher levels, that is a greater choice of plot size and building arrangement than of window detail. If this seems unduly restrictive then it is only replicating the diversity of a traditional settlement which is derived from variations in building size and form rather than building materials. In a modern speculative housing development any attempt at diversity usually results in a reversal of this situation — a variety of details but a limited range of building forms and plot types.

A position was taken towards the *pavillion* areas which sought to use the carrot of rebuilding at a higher intensity of site use to tempt builders to adopt plot types derived from the older parts of the village. The restriction on details was relaxed with the exception of those which could have an impact on long views of the settlement. Thus roof tiles, wall colours and planting are required to be the same as in the older zones.

Conclusions

As the POS moves through the stages of the adoption process and, by a procedure of anticipated adoption, is currently being used in *permis de construire* negotiations, some observations on its efficacity can already be made. As a didactic instrument it has proved to be a powerful aid in persuading non-professional applicants of the range of possible choices open to them.

It should be noted that the regulations never propose a model building but rather a series of choices at each level of resolution – a set of possible parts with instructions for their assembly. The intention was to promote a diversity of response in an attempt to ensure that the diversity of the form of Asnières is maintained. It is too early to judge the extent of any success in this respect and the crucial test will only come with a proposal by a single developer for a group of buildings.

In an exercise mounted towards the local school children of around ten years of age they were also able to understand and to design within the framework of the regulations. Professional applicants have had more difficulty in coping with an unfamiliar guidance document. In detail they have been particularly upset by the absence of a plot ratio or a height restriction and in general they have been unable, or unwilling to accept the simple principle of public fronts and private backs. In a limited competition for fifty small flats to be built on an existing school site by a social housing agency, only one of the four invited architects was able to grasp the potential of the code to produce a group of buildings with a scale and variety appropriate to that part of the village. (*Plate* 8) But the winning project has demonstrated both the functional and financial feasibility of the code. It also suggests that the greatest problem which concerned us, that of coding for variety in a situation where development occurs in large units, is also capable of resolution.

The familiar criticism that innovation will be excluded and creativity denied has been raised by both architects and journalists commenting on the unusual format of the POS. There are different degrees of innovation possible in different parts of the Commune but these are always set within limits and working within a set of rules could be considered as a challenge rather than a hindrance to creativity. There is the suspicion that this criticism is, at least partly, owing to a reluctance on the part of designers to expose their values and assumptions to discussion, but given that architecture is a public activity designers need to subject their arguments,

which may include pretentions to innovation, to public scrutiny.

Furthermore it has to be emphasised that the preparation of the plan has been a democratic process with work in progress being presented regularly to a commission of both elected members and co-opted members of the public nominated by the different parts of the commune. The decision to maintain the character of Asnières is therefore a democratic choice and the complaints of the would be innovators and the possible loss of their projects has to be weighed against this choice.

Elsewhere we have noted the time consuming nature of urban morphology studies (Samuels, 1985) and the preparation of the POS took a great deal of time. This was partly because we were inventing a new method but also because the preparation of drawings is time consuming and therefore expensive. There was also a tendency to do more work than was strictly necessary at each stage. It often proved difficult to keep within the discipline of the levels of resolution – it seemed too simple to keep within the scope of the category being discussed whether plot, wall or opening. Another problem was a tendency to define elements by use for example houses rather than two storey blocks with a roof ridge parallel to the street.

In order to devise the prescriptions or codes it was necessary to have a set of design intentions or a future image of the settlement. Only in this way was it possible to make the value based choices between alternative models for future development at each level of resolution. These choices were arrived at by discussion around a hypothesis for each element which covered such issues as to whether the proposal was necessary for the continuation of the character of Asnières and whether such a decision was capable of being implemented in 1993 for reasons of functional or financial feasibility.

In these debates it was sometimes difficult to abandon cultural preconceptions. For example, the long blank walls enclosing the gardens to the large mansions do not encourage street vitality and regulations were considered to reduce their length – until it was pointed out that it was a characteristic of the village and indeed of many villages in the Ile de France, which was acceptable to the population and should be maintained.

At a more general level two observations can be

made which question some of the conventional wisdom about the French planning system as seen from this side of the Channel. First, that the POS is inflexible (cf. the Royal Town Planning Institute tape *Planning in France*, RTPI, (1991). This is clearly a view of authorities who have not had the opportunity to work within the system and test its limits and is not supported by local comment (Rey, 1993). The draft plan has successfully negotiated a special commission at the Departmental Prefecture to test its legality and initial publicity about the new Asnières POS and has raised a great deal of interest from other Communes and Central Government agencies, which suggest that it is widely applicable. From a technical point of view we believe that the method is applicable to more complex settlements than Asnières and that the key to its application would lie in increasing the range of acceptable types to match the wider diversity of a larger settlement.

Second, in response to the claim that the French system does not allow for participation (RTPI, 1991) it has to be pointed out that no British village the size of Asnières would have the possibility of preparing its own plan. Quite apart from the commission which reviewed the POS as described above, it is difficult to imagine greater participation than in a small Commune which has taken advantage of the possibilities of decentralisation — Asnières even has its own works department of five which looks after the roads, lighting, trees and parks. Communal matters are an everyday topic of conversation — we heard a great deal of comment on the POS in the *boulangerie* particularly as to why it had been necessary to employ English architects!

Graham Paul Smith

TRAFFIC CALMING: THE SECOND WAVE?

Mixed-use areas of the city and mixed-use buildings require a mixed-use public space to enable choice of use to the widest public. It is perceived that public space is generally dominated by the demands of motorised transport. Better public places are ones where the broadest range of users have a degree of equity. This paper focuses on concepts and installations which are designed to change driver behaviour. These changes are effected using both more subtle and dynamic, sometimes, more fixed and brutal means than the now familiar first phase of traffic-calming using a recipe of narrowings and humps. Urban designers need to understand the benefits of these concepts and installations to aid them in achieving better places.

The measures described are presented for their effectiveness at empowering vulnerable users of public space. They are established and successful.

Dynamic Traffic Calming

Dynamic traffic calming uses uncertainty as a principle to demand care from dominating road users. This is an important component of urban design which contributes to the concept of a mixed-use city. Just as the mixed-use concept confronts many of the development orthodoxies of recent decades, the idea of 'mixed-use' in the highway, a major part of all public space, is treated with profound distrust by many highway design professionals.

American examples are often quoted as foretelling practice in Britain. Car based development here has followed New World models with, *inter alia*, motorway based retail malls, theme parks and edge cities. Whilst these may be regarded as mixed blessings there are features of the American driving environment which induce calmness on the road and which could be (re)introduced with British levels of motorisation. One now waits for acceptance, as common practice, of successful dynamic traffic calming ideas such as crossroads and the abolition of the 'keep to the left' rule for motorways.

Crossroads, with 'stop all way' signing, give no priority for any traffic stream and have the effect of forcing drivers to roll along at steady speeds. Drivers take turns to cross and consequently streams of traffic are broken which increases pedestrian crossing opportunities and slows traffic speeds.

The absence of a 'keep to the left' rule on American motorways has the effect of smoothing and controlling the speed of traffic. This is because drivers tend to hold their position in traffic lanes and approaching, faster moving drivers know that they have no right to demand that preceding drivers give way by changing lanes. Thus, faster moving drivers are obliged to match the speed in adjacent traffic lanes to overtake. Dramatic car chases in American films show cars careering wildly across streams of steadily moving traffic but the daily experience of the rule in operation is that, especially in denser traffic, the majority of drivers tend to travel in a gentler more resigned, manner.

A number of examples of designs, whose philosophies could be taken up as a distinct second phase of traffic calming in Britain, can be seen in continental 'dynamic calming' which have the following features:
- children's play spaces located in areas where cars park
- pedestrians invited to accept priority on the road
- cyclists invited to accept priority on the road
- providing for servicing and parking in the centre of streets

Traffic Calming: Controlling Behaviour

The second part of this chapter considers installations which, by their physical nature, demand conformity with a required model of behaviour. Indeed the engineer, given the responsibility of advising on road safety, sees danger in any confusion over activity and rights of way in the highway. Thus pedestrians (especially children), all vulnerable road users (especially cyclists), trees, lampposts, signposts, telephone booths and indeed anything which can be hit by a motor vehicle, are to be removed from the road because they could cause injuries.

The apparently logical alternative of reducing the dangers of impact by reducing the speed of motor vehicles has, hitherto, had too little legitimacy. New work has explored the counterintuitive area of increasing what we have learned to perceive as apparently 'dangerous' measures as a means to achieve improved 'safety' because of consequent behavioural change. Recent research in England has focused on the visibility standards at T-junctions and their impact on cyclists' safety. The finding is that greater visibility is associated with a greater number of accidents. Much work needs to be carried out to convince engineers, let alone the general public, that reducing visibility is a good thing (Henson and Whelan, 1992)

The descriptions which follow concentrate on main road installations that:

— prevent overtaking when public transport picks up passengers at bus stops
— prevent overtaking on the open road

Children's Play Spaces Located in Areas where Cars Park

One of the greatest concerns in road safety must be the fear of harming children who, whilst distracted by play, are involved in an accident with a vehicle. One of the features of the 'battle' to reclaim road space from moving vehicles has been the counterintuitive location of play space in the highway. The

'woonerf' established the idea of insisting that road space was public space and play is one of the legitimate activities promoted by the designation (Traffic Department, ANWB and Road Safety Directorate, 1980).

For many visitors to the Netherlands the woonerf reconstructions are fascinating installations which, in an almost sinful way, mix uses in old areas. Surely new installations do not need to so outrageously combine play and cars? In Maastricht the De Heeg estate (constructed c. 1980), to the south of the city, has just such an installation. The sand-pit in the photograph is located directly adjacent to parking spaces. The safety record of this city has twice won a national prize for road safety improvements, measured by year on year records. The sand-pit is so dangerously located that the behaviour of all users is extra careful. (*Plate 9*)

Children's rights in the highway have been eroded in a kind of inverse proportion to the rate of increase in car ownership and use. To make better places for children, or even for recreation space for all ages, the vehicle dominance of public space calls for a reconsideration of the limited range of uses regarded as lawful and legitimate in public space.

Pedestrians Invited to Accept Priority on the Road

The woonerf legislation of 1976 sought to control vehicular speed to give a 'low maximum speed limit, compatible with pedestrians and cyclists . . . The whole of the highway within a 'woonerf' is a pedestrian's domain . . .' (Smith, 1987). The intention and general practice has given rights to pedestrians which had been forfeited by common practice and the design of street surfaces which had motor vehicles in mind. The 1984 reassessment of the regulations and their re-issue as 'erf' (a shortening which expands the purely residential connotation of woonerf, and applies to mixed-use areas including residential and business uses, school areas and villages), confirmed the rights of pedestrians in the road space. With growing concern over the costs, of reconstructing areas as erven, regulations were issued covering 30 km h zones which aimed to achieve 90% of the improved accident rate benefits for only 10% of the costs. In a 30 km h zone pedestrian's rights do not extend ubiquitously over the highway but are ensured by the reduction of traffic speeds to a level which allows more freedom to cross the carriageway. At-grade junctions, built-out footpath pinch points and frequently spaced humps give pedestrians a more secure and a shorter possibility of crossing the road.

The benefits of the *woonerf* have been extended, by the 30 km h zones, to cover around 80% of residential streets in some cities. One logical extension of giving parity to pedestrians has been to affirm their rights on collector-type roads by marking crossing routes which respond to desire lines and not to a traffic engineering notion of 'safe' crossing points. (*Plate 10*) Too often we find examples in the UK where a crossing is located near to, but not at, a pedestrian desire line. The thinking in these situations is that pedestrians may recklessly tumble into the carriageway, if footways are marked out in continuation of a desire line, without noticing moving traffic. These are the same pedestrians who, presumably, manage to walk along without colliding with each other! The consequence is that many pedestrians cross roadways away from the zebra, pelican, etc. which has been provided.

The two examples shown both connect residential and shopping areas with a direct paved route designed for pedestrian convenience, which takes precedence over the asphalt carriageway surface. The driver, presented with an unusual paved surface crossing at an oblique angle, is obliged to expect people walking over the road. When pedestrians are absent the difference in paving, and colour, acts as a reminder of the permanent invitation being made to pedestrians. These installations are located after a corner, in places where drivers have already been slowed.

With their explicit safety benefits these examples invite one to speculate on the question: for whom are our British regulations made? If pedestrians are inconvenienced by the dislocation of desire lines, which the crossing regulations demand then perhaps the benefit accrues to motor vehicle drivers? Because pedestrians are obliged to move to 'safe' crossing points, which tend to group desire lines or be located where drivers have to slow anyway, the consequence for drivers are longer unhindered lengths of roadspace. This is intuitively reasonable if one thinks of drivers (or even the national economy) benefiting

from the speed capabilities of motor vehicles but results in a worse place from a walking point of view. (These ideas are further rehearsed in Davis, 1993)

Cyclists Invited to Accept Priority on the Road

Cyclists' journeys are relatively pollution-free, quiet, undamaging to others and healthy for the rider, yet cyclists are among the most vulnerable of road users. Their journeys are also efficient for the kinds of trip which predominate in existing cities and in the kind of denser mixed-use city which is espoused by urban design. The main danger to cyclists are fast moving motor vehicles, especially buses, in the act of overtaking (Joshi and Smith, 1992). If cycling is to be taken up by a greater proportion of a city population then the routes which are most threatening to cyclists, especially the busiest central streets, need to be redesigned to offer more safety to cyclists. There are many options which, given available space, can define threat free routes.

In terms of dynamic traffic calming, designs which invite the cyclist to take space rather than merely to occupy a designated space, add a counter-intuitive twist to highway design.

For more than a decade main road planning in towns and cities in Germany and the Netherlands has been notable for the space, marked out on the road surface, for cycling. Major junctions with traffic lights are shown, in the new version of the main road design manual (EAHV, 92), with lanes marked for cyclists in every possible movement direction. There is a clear allocation of road space for the vulnerable two-wheeler. The lack of such explicit direction in Britain is interpretable as either an expectation that cyclists and vehicles will find a way to cohabit or a veiled invitation to keep away from major roads and road junctions. Road Safety officers are to be heard explicitly saying that the only safe way for cyclists to use 'dangerous' junctions is to dismount and use the footpath. What seems out of order, in the main road context, is the expectation that one form of transport should be allowed to dominate another.

At junctions where traffic lights are not appropriate and flows, whilst heavy, do not require separation of cycle and motor vehicle there is still a need to control the behaviour of general traffic to ensure safety for cycling. In Hennef, Germany the main road through the centre has been redesigned so that overtaking is made almost impossible because of the narrowness of the newly reconstructed dimensions. A maximum of 3.25 metres is available in separated carriageways with a 1.3 metre dividing strip of rough stone blockwork designed for occasional use. Around the bollards and their surrounding kerb the stone blockwork narrows the available 3.25 metres by visual and tactile means. Here the cyclist acts as a dynamic traffic calming device. (*Figure 58*) Cyclists occupy around 1.0 metres so, with some 2.0 metres remaining, there is simply too little room for motor vehicles to pass a cyclist along most of the length of the Frankfurter Strasse. This seemingly dangerous reconstruction gains its calming and safety effects from the design which, with obvious clarity, defines the available roadspace and invited drivers to recognise that they are expected to proceed in single file. Observation reveals that this is indeed the case. For the cyclist who is not prepared to take this role it has been made permissible to join pedestrians on the footpath but in this case the presence of the cyclist is signed as subordinate to that of the pedestrian.

The Dutch BREV experimental scheme in the village of Benschop supports cycling on a busy, but narrow, highway by marking cycle lanes continuously at 1.5 metres on both sides. The consequence for general traffic is that only some 3.5/2.9/2.8 metres of asphalt remains for two way traffic. At varying intervals from 200, to 40, to 10 metres, the cycle lane priority is reinforced by islands between the cycle and general vehicle lanes. The concern which UK traffic engineering eyes would see is that the cycle lane could be brought into 'disrepute' by the necessity for vehicles to encroach on the cycle lane. The answer to this concern is that the islands are located sufficiently regularly to force vehicles out of the cycle lane. Inevitably as the road becomes busier the potential for congestion, induced by the narrowed installation, becomes real.

In many British cases the solution to cyclists' problems needs only a small change to benefit from the experience to be observed in Hennef and Benschop. The British cyclist does act as a mobile traffic calming 'device' but has little or no protection from physical engineering measures. To legitimate the calm effect that would ensue if motor vehicles were not making threats and causing accidents by pressing to overtake the cyclist (DoT, 1992; Automobile Association 1993), much clearer indications of legitimate behaviour are required.

Providing for Servicing and Parking in the Centre of Streets

Solutions to design problems in the street environment require consideration of types of transport, movement volumes, uses and junctions. For pedestrians to feel better supported, whilst travelling around, the 'gulfs' of carriageway which separate the pedestrian realms could be filled and the carriageway raised to make the footpath continue across junctions at grade.

There are now various examples of such treatments, sometimes grudgingly engineered, which reinforce pedestrian rights of way. Arguing for an uninterrupted footpath is acceptable in the British context but arguing for the same thing for cyclists is much more contentious. Cycle lanes are often painted onto the margin of the carriageway, usually just outside double yellow lines. Since loading is allowed in these restricted places, where is the cyclist expected to go? Some 70% of accidents, involving cyclists, occur as they travel forwards and with motor vehicles 50% of which are also travelling forwards. The danger points are often precisely those occasions when a rider moves out from the nearside to overtake a stationary vehicle. For faster moving vehicles approaching from behind, the overtaking manoeuvre coupled with the relative slowness of the rider can appear to be a sudden lunge into a stream of traffic. Clearly an answer to this problem lies in continuity of provision for cyclists, taking account of the likelihood of parked vehicles. Cycle lanes which share road space with double yellow lines are not satisfactory. This is especially the case in High Streets.

The example illustrated, (*Figure 59*) from the French town of La Trinité, Brittany, shows a sea front street with a delivery space, marked '*livraison*', astride a central divider strip. Stone bollards further prevent vehicles crossing up to the point of the

Figure 58. Town centre road space reconstructed to prevent passing manoeuvres – the cyclist as dynamic traffic calming, Hennef, Germany.

Figure 59. Delivery space – *livraison* – marked astride central divider strip, La Trinité, France.

Figure 60. Parking spaces grouped on the public side of development to ensure frontages adjacent to routes.

Graham Paul Smith

markings. Only large wheeled vehicles can easily mount the strip which is aggressively dimensioned. When a vehicle pulls on to this location traffic in both directions is inconvenienced by the narrowing of the carriageway. The driver of the vehicle becomes a vulnerable road user when climbing down from the cab and when crossing the carriageway to a destination. Since the driver's presence on the road is legitimated by the goods vehicle, the 'pecking order' of normal relationships is confused. As a pedestrian the driver offers no threat to other motorists but being a goods vehicle driver conveys a status of a powerful kind (AA, 1993). The position of the stationary vehicle and the activities associated with it are a form of dynamic traffic calming. Meanwhile the footpath is left clear and the side of the carriageway is also free of obstruction for cyclists.

There are numerous locations where just such a confounding design proposal could be beneficial. Many relatively narrow High Streets are obstructed by vehicles parking on both sides when it is legal to deliver. For cyclists such locations are a source of danger when other traffic is weaving around and drivers' attention is overloaded. Often these streets have central pedestrian refuges which could be regularly located along a central loading zone. It would be unnecessarily dangerous if traffic were allowed to proceed at the normal urban limit so formal traffic calming measures would be appropriate in these places.

The idea of central parking or even servicing is not new, many market towns have central parking in the old market area of the 'Market' or 'Broad Street'. An idea which could be newer is to make provision for parking, for private commercial or residential users, in public space. This runs counter to local authority thinking in that, generally, parking space for private users is not 'adopted'. Were such changes to be adopted the efficiency of shared use could liberate perhaps 30% of the land required in many local plans for car parking requirements. This would ease the path to making better places by allowing denser development of sites.

Providing for statutory parking standards tends to result in large parking lots within development blocks. Consequently the activity of arriving at a building is removed to a semi-private rear realm. As Hillier and Hanson (1984) have shown, one of the determinants of security in public space is the num-

ber of entrances into buildings. The more entrances the greater are the number of 'strangers' who will use a given length of street. The strangers 'patrol' the street and ensure the security which peopled streets are recognised to provide. But streets which are edged with large parking lots are isolated from building fronts and thus are not overlooked and are inactive. To allow building fronts to be adjacent to pedestrian routes requires that, in areas of high parking demand, one side of some streets needs to be facing car parks which could occupy a whole block. Then the activity of one side of such a street could be assured and the street itself would be crossed by drivers and passengers approaching entrances. This fact would necessitate traffic calming to ensure that the street was safe to cross. (*Figure 60*)

Prevention of Overtaking when Public Transport Picks Up Passengers

If public transport matters, if its passengers are important enough for their safety to be important, is there a benefit in allowing vehicles to pass the bus when it stops? Passengers hurrying to reach the bus stop and those dismounting and moving away are in danger if general traffic is rushing past. In the UK it is current practice to give priority to moving traffic and thus it is generally preferred to move bus halts off the carriageway. In the USA the school bus has an individual and highly recognisable design and its yellow colour makes it stand out. When the bus is transporting children and halts at a stop the federal regulations demand that all traffic stops. On some buses a swing-out arm reinforces the message. In Germany there are now schemes where a 'cape' rather than a lay-by is built out into the highway to give a degree of priority to buses over other traffic. The 'cape' is also raised to ease the step into the bus. Overtaking a stationary bus is further denied by a median strip extending before and after the stop.

This installation achieves a dynamic effect in terms of reordering priorities in moving traffic. The focus is the pedestrian and not the driver. The physical clarity of the design also controls the behaviour of other bus drivers who can also contribute to the experience, for pedestrians, of the road being for drivers.

Prevention of Overtaking on the Open Road

The drug of speed, released by the mechanical and engineering discoveries of the modern age, has intoxicated and holds enthralled much of the developed and developing world (Marsh and Collett, 1986). Not only does speed affect the lives of all road users but, with some 12% to 14% of the workforce involved with vehicle production and use, the livelihood of our industrial societies seems to depend on continued abuse of this dangerously exciting addiction. In Britain the speed limits which would indicate a national desire to control behaviour are a custom more honoured in the breach than the observance. On the road the expression of speed is seen as an individual freedom, overtaking is widely seen to be normal but the public road is too aggressive for vulnerable and unprotected users with so much freedom being expressed. The divisive and threatening nature of vehicle speeds and volumes is well documented (e.g. Appleyard, 1981) and measures to curb the worst excesses can now be seen installed in many continental locations.

Measures to limit speeds on main roads in small towns can be found in Dutch experiments in towns such as Weiteveen and Almere (DVV Road Safety Directorate (the BREV projects, 1985). In France some of the notorious three-lane *Routes Nationale* are being reduced to two-lane working and measures to prevent overtaking both in towns as well as without can now be observed in many countries.

The scheme illustrated, *plate 11*, extends for many kilometres on the Bundersstrasse 258 south of Aachen. Rough white stone is used to establish a broad dividing band between the carriageways. This division is enforced by regularly placed planted areas with bollards defining four corners. Overtaking stationary vehicles and obstructions is possible, but only with great care, by crossing the rough blockwork into the oncoming carriageway. There was an accident record along this road which regularly carries large amounts of tourist traffic into beauty spots in the Eiffel Mountains. Control of speeding and

reckless overtaking has been effected by road narrowing rather than road widening.

Conclusion

In a human world one of the ways in which change occurs is to reveal, to people who have power, new and legitimate ways of increasing that power. This has been the case with traffic calming. In recent years the imagination of highway engineers and planners, in particular, has been fired by an apparently new way of doing things. The evidence described above, of new achievements on the continent, should ensure that the pace of change which contributes towards making a better place in the road environment will continue.

Government has been less quick to respond to the idea of traffic calming but, as the accident reduction benefits have become more obvious and as the clamour from residents for dangers on their roads to be reduced has grown louder, new money has been forthcoming. This has to be seen in perspective and the £50 million, announced in January 1993, dims to relative insignificance alongside the annual billions spent on new road building. Such expenditures, whilst welcome in themselves, tend to conceal the corrosive effects of supporting car growth. This paper has dealt only with installations to calm traffic but it is implicitly understood that we already have too much traffic and too ready an assumption about its use. There is also a concern that traffic calming may be seen as a 'green smokescreen' by using traffic calming measures to legitimate on street car parking arrangements in such a way that more spaces are available, thus allowing more traffic (Whitelegg, 1990). Urban design can only be aware of this problem, but efforts to calm traffic will be wasted if traffic increases are the only consequence. Changing driver behaviour so effectively that new, denser, patterns of development are accepted is the goal.

Traffic calming can now be experienced by most citizens but better places with calmer traffic, or even an environment in which less travelling is necessary, is still a distant prospect for many. Mounting concerns about both the sustainability and the dissociative effects of our modern developments are rising through the urban design agenda. In the USA the implementation of the Environmental Protection Act (1990) and the Intermodal Surface Transport Efficiency Act (1991) will, it is hoped, stem the profligacy of current development patterns. At Seaside, Florida, notwithstanding the comments on architectural style or elitist development, might we be witnessing an American rediscovery of a denser urban form? The question of whether 'traditional neighbourhood development' will work, with modern traffic as well as its potential for denser developments, is being asked with increasing frequency.

British guidance for new layouts for residential roads (DoT, DoE, 1992) has changed significantly to enable networks rather than the hierarchical layouts of the first (1977) edition. This is because it is now accepted that traffic calming can change behaviour. The task for urban designers is to show how each small, winnable battle with car promoting orthodoxies can result in environments which are safe, responsive and sustainable.

The range of traffic calming implementations discussed here represent bold steps forward in urban design terms.

Barbara Hammond

COMPUTER AIDED DESIGN AS AN URBAN DESIGN BRIEFING TOOL

The urban design process in the public sector is concerned with the promotion and control of change in the built environment rather than with the direct implementation of change. It may be said that the Urban Designer's role is to protect the public interest in ensuring that the new development contributes to the communal life of the city; that places are made which are responsive.

The product of the urban design process is most often in this case a briefing document of some kind. This briefing document will probably be aimed at the private market, whether the land is publicly owned or not, so that not only must it describe an urban design vision of the site or sites which is responsive, but it must also be acceptable to the market in showing a level of development which is economically viable.

The general problem faced by urban designers attempting to brief for a site, an area or a neighbourhood in this situation is that it is very difficult to communicate design ideas effectively in outline, although it is acknowledged by urban designers themselves that it is not their business to design buildings and spaces in detail. This difficulty is felt most strongly at the negotiation stage, where it often becomes apparent that there is a gap in communication; the urban design brief which confines itself to outline, diagrammatic expression is not seen as the basis for negotiation but as only one, arbitrary option for development which the developer feels quite comfortable in more or less ignoring. The temptation, in order to gain a negotiating position of strength, is to work up one particular proposal in some detail and to present it to the market as the only available option. This type of site specific, prescriptive briefing may be successful in situations

where the public body has a great deal of control over the land, where the economy is buoyant and where the site has a relatively simple context. The problems with this type of briefing are that:

— it is labour intensive and so means that some areas are covered in much detail whilst others are not covered at all
— it is seen as being restrictive by developers and their designers, especially in a difficult market, and so may create a climate of conflict rather than of certainty
— it is not responsive to change
— it tends to cover a specific site thoroughly but does not deal very well with large, complex areas
— on large sites, it tends towards a homogeneous environment whereas the nature of towns and cities is pluralistic and heterogeneous
— it is restrictive of the activity of urban design in confining the urban designer to site specific work, like a sort of architect on the large scale, rather than allowing her or him to concentrate on the whole urban system, the inter-site issues, the co-ordination of which is probably the urban designer's major role.

It appeared to urban designers in the London Docklands Development Corporation that CAD might present some answers to these problems in facilitating an iterative, interactive briefing process

— which could respond quickly to change
— whereby many varying options for development could be investigated fully but quickly and resource-efficiently
— which could be used to communicate design ideas effectively to non-professionals; developers

and public alike could thereby be involved more closely in the design process

- which could help to make the negotiation between briefing and final planning application more effective and less confrontational
- which could deal with large, complex sites effectively

The idea was that a piece of city could be modelled on the computer; an urban design study could then be carried out on it which would test varying options for development, resulting in an outline, but three-dimensional, model for a site, or sites, which could then be used in a three-fold manner: as a briefing tool, as part of a marketing exercise and as an effective tool for co-operative negotiation at the planning stage. The model would, we thought, be particularly effective at the planning control stage because it would be possible to 'insert' new proposals into it, so that everybody could see the proposals in context and so that new proposals could be quickly investigated to test both their responsiveness and their viability. It might even be possible to try 'hands-on' revision at meetings!

These ideas seemed to match very well work being done by Roger Evans Urban Design; the practice has been developing techniques for using CAD in the design process since the mid-1980s which have been used for 3D impact studies on Docklands sites at St. George-in-the-East, Limehouse Basin and the Royal Docks. In order to demonstrate the effectiveness of CAD as an urban design briefing tool, Roger Evans was asked to carry out a study on a set of sites at East India Docks with input from urban designers within the LDDC. The complex relationship between the sites and new infrastructure had not been fully investigated. This infrastructure consists of the Docklands Light Railway Extension and the East India Dock Link Road both running on flyovers to the south of the sites in question. The relationship between the sites and the new infrastructure was of particular interest, in terms especially of access, aspect and prospect views and the relationship of the built form and space to the new forms of the road and railway.

The study divided into three stages:

- Contextual Studies
- Site Development Studies
- Visualisation and Briefing

The first stage covered the sort of urban structure studies — figure/ground, aspect/prospect, tissues, etc. — often covered at the initial survey and analysis phases of a project. They are obviously of great importance in helping the urban designer to understand how the city is working. They are, however, essentially 2D paper studies following visits to sites to which CAD does not add much in either speed or depth, although it might be convenient to draw up these studies on CAD if a good set of Ordnance Survey bases is held on the system. What CAD does offer in terms of 2D mapping is the possibility of setting up a Geographic Information System. This type of 'topological data structure' allows graphic data (on maps) and alpha-numeric data to be integrated in a way which enables 'what if' maps to be generated automatically, e.g. census and transportation data sets could be queried to produce maps showing the accessibility of public transport to groups with low car ownership, (from *Introduction to the LDDC and Information System*, Roger Evans Urban Design). Investigation into the social structure of the city can be quickly undertaken using this system and can inform the urban design process.

The second stage really began to exploit the strengths of CAD: the quick testing and revision of many options for development within an overall built form/public space proposal. The layout shown in the existing brief was revised by Roger Evans and then modelled in 3D to a notional height within a context model showing the surrounding area. This model was revised to .test different ways of treating the mass of the buildings and these options were tested:

- visually, by walking through the model, driving along the road, arriving at the station, etc.
- financially via a spreadsheet working from given values and reacting to different plan areas calculated from the model
- in terms of sun and shadow via ray-tracing software

These activities are all of immense value to the urban designer in working up a briefing document which will have some robustness and some reality. They allow the urban designer to cover a range of options within the preferred framework, so that the implications of different types of proposal can be quickly known. The urban designer can then enter the negotiation phase of the development process with some confidence because it will be known with some precision what level and type of development the framework will stand before its quality as a piece of city is compromised.

The third, visualisation and briefing, stage exploited the work already done on CAD in the second stage to produce a briefing model and marketing materials which 'design the city without designing the buildings'.

In this case, the briefing model showed three main types of control, (taken from the *East India Docks Briefing Study*, Roger Evans Urban Design):

1 Envelope Controls showing
   – build-to planes where the edges of the built form should be
   – build within lines
   – height controls
2 Architectural Devices showing
   – key elevations
   – landmarks
   – gateways
   – corner responses
   – arcades
3 Public Realm showing
   – pedestrian areas and routes
   – vehicular access
   – sites for artifacts/sculpture
   – structural planting

This briefing model is the main tool for negotiation and can be used as the base for testing new proposals since, given compatible software and disc formatting, a new building design can slot into position within the briefing model and be considered and tested within its context.

The briefing model can also be used as the basis for more sophisticated visualisation and can therefore become a marketing tool. The wireframe briefing model can be rendered to a greater or lesser degree of 'photo-realism' and can even be animated to show particularly important routes through the site. This requires a fine balance to be struck at this stage between producing images exciting enough to 'stimulate' the market and images seemingly so real that the market feels that it is being given no room for manoeuvre. (*Figure 61*)

The aim is to achieve a 'climate of certainty' over a large or complex set of sites, so that varying developers and designers can operate individually within them whilst still contributing to some sort of urban coherence.

The potential of CAD as a briefing tool was clearly shown in the East India Docks study. A presentation to senior management gained support to apply the approach to another set of complex sites, the Surrey Quays Centre sites, for which no brief had yet been written. The exercise was thus intended to be a full-blown urban design study whose output would be:

– a form/space strategy which would fix the public realm whilst defining parcels of development which would be attractive to the market
– a briefing model to be used through the negotiation stage
– a marketing video produced using the CAD briefing model as a base

Koetter Kim and Associates International Ltd. as urban designers, with Arup Associates as Computer Animation/Video interface, were commissioned to carry out this study following a tender process.

The Surrey Quays Centre sites cover 20 acres in the heart of the Surrey Quays peninsula. They are the last major development sites in this part of the Surrey Docks area of London Docklands and were intended to be the 'town centre' serving the substantial areas of new and existing housing in the peninsula and feeding from the existing, but new, Surrey Quays Shopping Centre. The town centre would also feed off the proposed Jubilee Line station at Canada Water with its links to the West End in one direction, Canary Wharf and Stratford in the other. It seemed inevitable that the sites would serve a much larger catchment area than the Surrey Quays peninsula because of these new public transport links, especially given that the Canada Water station will be an interchange between the Jubilee Line, the East London Line and the bus network.

Careful studies had already been carried out as to the development potential of the sites in terms of density and use, given a difficult road transport situation, a difficult development market and a complex set of constraints including large surface allied to the new Canada Water underground station. The further study was intended to work from this base and explore the problems and potentials of the site in terms of its three-dimensional urban fabric given the intended density of development of between 1 and

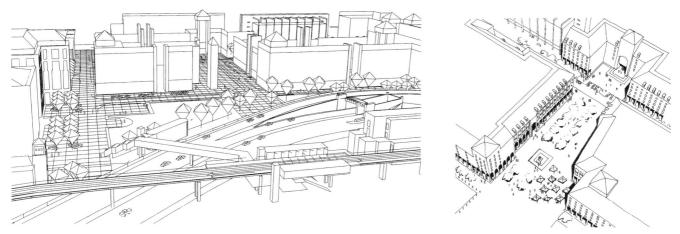

Figure 61. General view of the basic wire frame briefing model (left) and a hand rendered detail showing architectural treatment for presentation purposes.

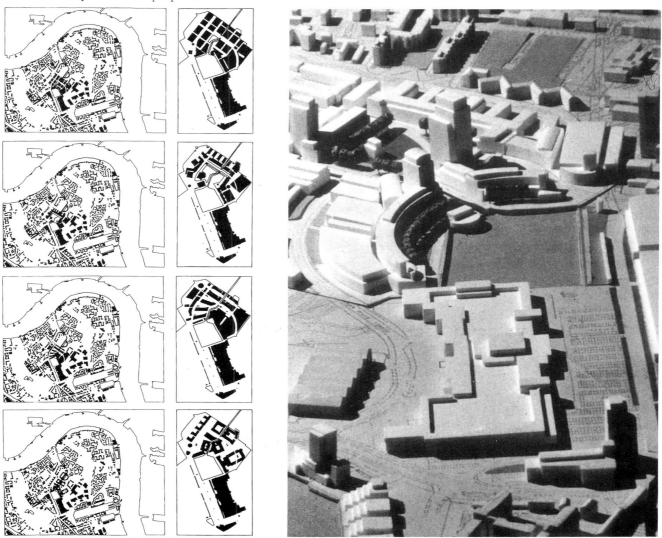

Figure 62. Surrey Quays: figure ground plans in context and enlargement of the four development options (left) and model showing preferred scheme 5 (right).

1.5 million square feet and the range of acceptable uses, from housing and offices through speciality shopping to leisure and community uses. The object was to keep as flexible as possible within these parameters, whilst achieving a certain urban quality.

In the first part of the study Koetter Kim did not involve CAD other than for base information but used a rapid foam-modelling technique to explore many different form/space strategies for the sites. CAD does not lend itself well to this sketch stage because it requires a precision rather alien to the idea of a sketch and a relatively long time is needed to set up each different option.

A range of five basic form/space strategies, all with multiple sub-options, arose from this process and are shown in *figure 62*.

These strategies are all responses to a particular set of problems imposed by the infrastructure framework; namely Canada Water and the Surrey Quays Road. Normally, Koetter Kim's initial analysis stage would test the 'correctness' of this infrastructure and would propose options for form/space strategies arising from different changes made to the infrastructure. In this case those changes were not on offer, so all the options explore ways of making:

— a gesture to the water
— a gesture to the road
— a gesture to the existing housing
— a linking, via public space, between the existing Surrey Quays Shopping Centre and the new bus and tube stations
— a location for 'streetwall' and taller, landmark buildings.

The eventual preferred approach was the double figure shown in Scheme 5 with its curve to the water, an internal square and links to surrounding housing. This particular armature/street wall configuration was chosen by LDDC designers as offering the clarity and elegance appropriate to the sites' position as town centre and heart of the Surrey Quays peninsula.

Koetter Kim see this sketch, option-testing phase as the fundamental activity of the urban designer; it leads to an understanding of the forces that shape urban conditions, and it forms the basis of strategic briefing (guideline) documentation. In order for this stage to be rapid and effective, the designer needs to have a wide, deeply understood set of form/space

typologies to draw on combined with a 'feel' for current market forces and how they shape buildings, so that the options produced have some conviction, some reality and are not just three-dimensional patterns. This 'options' stage sets the 'edges' within which the urban designer works and at which the individual building designer will subsequently work.

CAD was introduced at this point to help test two or three options for density and use behind the edges set by the double figure of Scheme 5. Again, as found in the pilot study, this is where CAD comes into its own. The parcelling and plan configuration stages have been done; this stage is all about making quick revisions to a basic wire frame massing model which can then be quickly analysed in terms of plan areas, parking strategies and feasibility. The overall robustness of the general plan configuration can thus be tested in terms of its development viability.

Within the edges of the armature/street wall detailed studies were also carried out on the spaces to establish how different options for development might affect them. Again, this activity is well suited to CAD in being a continuation of the revision/testing activity described above. This set of studies included:

— aspect/prospect studies
— sun/shadow studies
— landscape structure
— landmarks and focus points

The interface between public realm and building mass was then analysed in terms of testing various 'street wall' typologies:

— solid/void ratios
— continuous lengths
— repetition of pattern

Out of these detailed studies, it is possible to start creating a 'pattern-book' of typologies, or design guidelines, which can govern the development of a piece of town, giving it some coherence without being totally prescriptive. Again, this activity requires an extensive vocabulary of typologies from which to draw. An attempt was made to use the technique at Canary Wharf but, in the end, the resulting guidelines were only applied in a limited way. Although not developed to any great extent for the Surrey Quays Centre study, this is an interesting briefing tool whose potential should be explored, one of the major questions being whether it can achieve coherence whilst still allowing the chaotic richness which can be one of the best features of city life.

The options tested on CAD were used in the final visualisation stage. The output from this was a video which intended to make the case for the basic form/space strategy whilst stimulating interest in the market by showing various ways of developing it. Stills from the video show the general line of argument and the development of the wire frame models into rendered, animated images. (*Plate 12*)

In the original brief this stage was seen as having a much simpler output; the transfer of two or three minutes of animated walk-through sequences from CAD to video which could be shown to interested developers to stimulate further their interest in the sites. As the study progressed, however, this stage grew in complexity and importance because of the potential it was perceived to have in terms of the explanation and promotion of the urban design as well as of the sites themselves. The video was to be the bridge between the urban design and the strategic marketing of sites, to the benefit of both.

This sort of marketing product has not been attempted in the UK before and it produced some interesting results at the LDDC. A gap in understanding between the designers on the one hand and the property and finance professionals on the other became obvious. The former appreciated the video for its explanation of the urban context, the urban design response to that context and the illustration of varied options for development within the urban design framework. The latter perceived the video as only showing one option for development, and therefore as being over-restrictive in a difficult market. The result is that the video is not being used as a free-standing marketing tool but will be issued as part of a comprehensive package including briefing documentation based on the CAD study. The video thus becomes part of a process rather than a finite product, as does the CAD study. It is arguable that this result is a positive one because it keeps the products of the urban design briefing process flexible and so makes more possible the iterative, interactive process which was a major ambition at the beginning.

This difference in perception between design and property professional is, however, important to acknowledge because it signals a gap in communication which urban designers must address and fill if they are to sell their vision of publicly responsible development to the market. Koetter Kim are convinced of the potential of video for selling urban design visions and have won commissions in the US and the Caribbean on the strength of the Surrey Quays Centre work to carry out further similar studies.

In conclusion, CAD certainly has its strengths as a briefing tool, especially where it can be used to test and revise development options quickly and rigorously. The studies have also shown a potential use for CAD to form the basis for urban design-led marketing of sites via video, showing developers how they can contribute to the urban experience without cramping their style. The main strength of CAD, to make a final emphasis, is its flexibility and therefore its ability to contribute to the briefing process. Its success is not measured by any final, static design product but by its continuing usefulness right through the briefing and negotiation process. Urban designers must be able to access, use and manipulate the information stored in the computer.

Obviously, in order for this to happen, the right equipment needs to be in place and urban design staff need to be trained to use it. The most sophisticated animation, rendering and video techniques need very specialised, expensive equipment but these can be hired when needed. To take a study through to basic levels of animation and rendering, the equipment required is not particularly esoteric or unusual. That used in the two studies illustrated is:

East India Docks:

Hardware	Processors	80836 and 80486 PCs
	Graphics Adaptors	1280 × 1024 8 bit
		1024 × 768 24 bit
	Output Devices	Hewlett Packard pen plotters
		HP LaserJet printer
		Agfa film recorder
Software	Modelling	AutoCAD v.10
	Rendering	Autoshade I
		Graphics Software
		(ray tracing)
	Spreadsheet	Windows 3
		Microsoft Excel
	Presentation	Pagemaker 4

135

Surrey Quays Centre:

Hardware	Processors	Macintosh IIfx/
		Radius GDM 1950
		Hewlett Packard 9000/720
	Adaptors	Ethernet
	Output	Supplied on disk
Software	Modelling	GDS/Microstation/
		Modelshop
	Rendering	Wavefront
	Spreadsheet	Wingz/Microsoft
	Presentation	Claris/Photoshop

CAD has much potential to broaden and deepen the urban design process and to make of it a more effective bridge between society and capital. The studies illustrated here are only a beginning in realising this potential and are presented in order to stimulate interest and further investigation of the techniques involved rather than to present a definitive new approach.

My thanks for their input into this article to Roger Evans, Robert Dye and Koetter Kim and Lynne Armishaw at the LDDC.

Richard Hayward

UPSIDE DOWN AND INSIDE OUT

One of the benefits of modern global communications systems and the power of information technology is that our current attempts at doing urban design are as almost instantaneously available in Bali or Brisbane as in Bournemouth or Birmingham. Thus, the latest in thinking is available for trial across the globe and concepts of trans-global 'progress' become secondary to contextual or cultural appropriateness and appropriation.

Thankfully, a journey to the other side of the globe remains a disorienting experience, and an opportunity for reflecting on current preoccupations with a significantly different perspective. One of the reported benefits of being an academic is the opportunity for 'on the job' foreign travel. In terms of urban design, as with any discipline directly concerned with the shape of the world, the stimulation and perspective afforded by cultural shifts is invaluable.

Some years ago, S.S. Duncan took the case of housing research to focus on *The uses and abuses of comparative analysis* (1991), concluding that 'Comparative analysis must be theoretical as well as empirical.' (p. 15) and as I must agree I find myself uncomfortably capable of only offering here the crudest general hypotheses, rather than any developed theories. Yet perhaps the primary benefit of comparative reflection in as ill-defined a field as urban design is its use as a Trojan horse for presenting simple precepts that could not be countenanced coming from one's own primary sphere of activity. The observations drawn here prompted by a glimpse of practice in South Eastern Australia are inevitably, if not unashamedly, crude and partial.

Increasingly travel around Europe or to North America confirms David Harvey's view of the shrinking world (Harvey, 1989), where sadly, post-modernity really does seem to result in everywhere being just like everywhere else. My own first visit to Australia in the summer (ours) of 1992, confirmed for me that the information explosion is continuous and instantaneous. Equipped with a copy of *Urban Villages* published a month or so earlier (1992), I found this to be the latest preoccupation amongst particular groups in Brisbane. In Melbourne, I joined colleagues for a Duany Plater-Zyberk-style design *charrette*. In Byron Bay I bought a copy of a recent book I had yet to track down in the UK.

I should not have been surprised. Nor should it have taken as long to realise why Queensland houses with north facing gardens were the most popular. Nor indeed should it have been a revelation to what extent I subconsciously use the sun to navigate city streets.

To the Englishman abroad, Australia can present a confusing mix of cultural signals. Statham suggests that the founding ethnocentricity of Australia compared with Canada, South Africa or even the United States was an important factor in its early civic development (1989). Yet the present day cultural landscape mixes many unpretentious English attitudes and customs apparently from the 1950s, with a man-made and automotive landscape that is substantially American. The commercial and industrial landscape is not only obviously Japanese, but Chinese, Italian and (in Melbourne especially) Greek and Mancunian. And Sydney, well Sydney truly defies classification, although it is difficult not to think of it as a sort of super San Francisco.

Comparisons are misleading and always offensive to somebody. Yet we make comparisons. We have to make sense of what we see through what we know. We may dress much of our reaction with our hasty and little learning about the history and dynamics of the actual place, yet all the time we look to see how close or far, similar or dissimilar what we experience is to what we know.

If the issues of urban design in Brisbane were much the same as in Bristol or Birmingham, the particulars and the context were markedly different. The Department of the Environment has just commissioned a research project on intensification in urban areas: in Brisbane 'densification' or urban 'consolidation' was the issue. In Washington DC, Joel Garreau has recently published his book *Edge City* (Garreau, 1991), in Brisbane, the fringe and the doughnut effect on the city is a major concern. The problem of providing affordable housing racks minor interest groups in the northern hemisphere, in Australia also. Sense of place; safe cities; the value of mixed-use urban areas; traffic calming; the green consequences of patterns of urban development; all these and more are, unsurprising preoccupations in both hemispheres.

The context in Queensland, in particular, is markedly different to that in the UK, not only because of the sub-tropical climate, associated building tradition and the remarkable topography, but because social concerns seem to be in the ascendancy.

The south-eastern seaboard of Australia is substantially in the grip of a depression that matches that currently experienced in the rest of the 'western' world. The economic situation in Queensland is both materially and potentially better than further south. Rich and poor, expert and generalist, healthy and sick, are migrating north. Victoria and South Australia carry the burden of years of enlightened public expenditure, whilst Queensland achieves latter day liberality without the debts of past public investment. The sun, the sea, the Asiatic linkages all go to make the State a potential honeypot.

In Brisbane, State and city agencies are actively pursuing public policy initiatives to tackle not only commercial opportunities, but the everyday residential and environmental needs of the populace. Whilst the term 'affordable housing' only really crossed the Atlantic to the UK in 1988/89, in Queensland in 1992 they were struggling with the distinctive definition of 'social' rather than 'public' or 'community' housing (Edwards, 1992). At the same time, the private sector and community interest groups are inevitably moving to maximise the available development benefits for themselves.

Part of my brief whilst based at the Queensland University of Technology was to establish cross-cultural issues in housing development and urban design for public debate. My encounters with various groups and individuals were brief. But the breadth of standing of the host institution enabled me to network across public, private and community agencies in urban development and housing. John Byrne of the Queensland Department of Housing, Local Government and Planning and Paul Burns, an architect and urban designer whose practice has achieved a wide range of developments up the coast and in Brisbane, provided a design imperative for testing a version of an urban village incorporating affordable housing at higher than average densities. A number of architects, urban designers, landscape architects, developers, community enablers and academics co-operated to test and debate issues of density and quality in urban housing.

So what were the issues and the comparisons with UK approaches?

First and foremost, the issue of design intention and control regarding buildings in space. In the UK, designers tend to make housing and mixed-use urban quarters from buildings. We place buildings on the site and we create both public and private realms, at worst from the space left over and at best, positively by the placing the 'solids' of building in a way that defines and promotes potentially active urban places. In Australia, as in other parts of the 'New World,' design deals first and foremost with the sub-division of sites: the creation of a size-range of building lots.

An analysis of plot configurations in English speculative or social housing developments will show significant and unremarked variation in both area and the geometry of lots, both within development sites or between contemporary developments. Certainly, planning requirements control overall densities, but there is little consistency or explicit product orientation in terms of the area or dimensions of individual lots. Some local authorities do specify minimum rear garden dimensions, beyond the house, or less commonly, at the front, but even in this case, the restrictions tend to relate to the space left over after building.

Now in most of South-Eastern Australia, at least, there is much more of a preoccupation with the regular dimensions of lots. For example, in Brisbane,

Melbourne and Sydney, other than in the historic cores, lots tend to be in a regular range, typically from 20 by 32 or 40 metres down to 6 by 20 metres. Some of the smaller lots have resulted from the subdivision of larger lots into smaller ones over a period of time.

This is hardly a surprising revelation. In new territories, the subdivision of land into buildable lots is a common historical mechanism for bringing the hinterland into urban development. There is more than a passing resemblance to the 'sites and services' approach to the regulation of construction in the developing world. In Australia, as in much of North America, the development and construction industry has thus become oriented to providing an individual service of house building based on an evolving catalogue of dwelling types suitable for the range of lot sizes. There are, of course, two distinct profit margins: that on the serviced lot and that on the dwelling package.

The comparison of lot subdivision systems with volume housing approaches favoured particularly in England is certainly a topic that would reward more study. In passing, it is worth noting that the different approaches are quite naturally reflected in the primary drawing and mapping conventions of the two places: in the United Kingdom usually essentially figure-ground and in Australia usually subdivision. In large urban fringe developments, in particular, this leads to a preoccupation by the developer in the early stages to the creation of a definable quality of cultivated site, rather than a primary preoccupation with dwelling types.

Now just as everything else is becoming like everything elsewhere across the globe, so this differentiation is blurring and reducing. In a difficult market over the last few years, many English volume house builders have become more flexible with regard to purchaser choice in terms of the particular dwellings they can put on particular lots. Meanwhile in Australia, house builders have started to respond to 'lifestyle' changes by offering ready built smaller housing on non-standard small lots, sometimes even including family housing that is effectively terraced or row-housing rather than the cultural norm of the individual house on the lot.

In common with the UK, much of the planning guidance available to house builders is preoccupied with the relationship between dwellings and the street. In Brisbane, one form of urban consolidation exercises the mind of planners and urban designers greatly. The so called 'six-pack' of three storey walk-up rental apartments, with garaging only on the ground floor, is used to replace single family dwellings on standard lots of say, 20 metres by 40 metres. The relationship of the six apartments to the public realm is restricted to six mailboxes, a drive, maybe garage doors, but no front doors or windows. In the standard solution, the 'six-pack' is located along one boundary and due to its height and length is generally a bad neighbour which also puts most of the site under concrete. New approaches to the 'six-pack', which can increase actual occupancy densities by a factor of four, have typological similarities with the early California courtyard apartment developments (Yeates, 1992). But the pioneering exemplary guides of the State of Victoria (1992) necessarily have much to say about the placing of the dwelling on the lot, in relation to neighbours and in terms of maximising the amenity of the lot for the resident, in a way that is scarcely called for in our own volume designed residential environments.

As lot subdivision is the truly durable element in many urban and most suburban quarters in Eastern Australia, rather than the built form, a slightly different professional attitude to environmental quality is apparent. Indeed, in Queensland, the recyclable nature and form of the timber-raised Queenslander house lends a further dimension to the phrase 'up stumps' and it is possible to visit used housing lots with more than a passing resemblance to the used car and breaker's yard of the UK (Saini and Joyce, 1982).

The Queenslander house tended traditionally to have been placed on the centre line of the lot frontage (usually some way back from the front boundary). Both public agencies and private developers now urge home-buyers to consider zero lot lining, that is, placing the dwelling on one boundary, thus providing more usable space and privacy on the lot. In the case of modern narrow lots, this is accompanied by developer ranges of 'courtyard' dwelling types.

Most design professionals and much of the rest of the public in Australia are concerned by urban sprawl and in particular the costs to the environment of the consequent heavy car usage. Yet the forms and quality of denser urban development are treated with caution, particularly in Brisbane compared with Melbourne or Sydney. Tradition, topography and

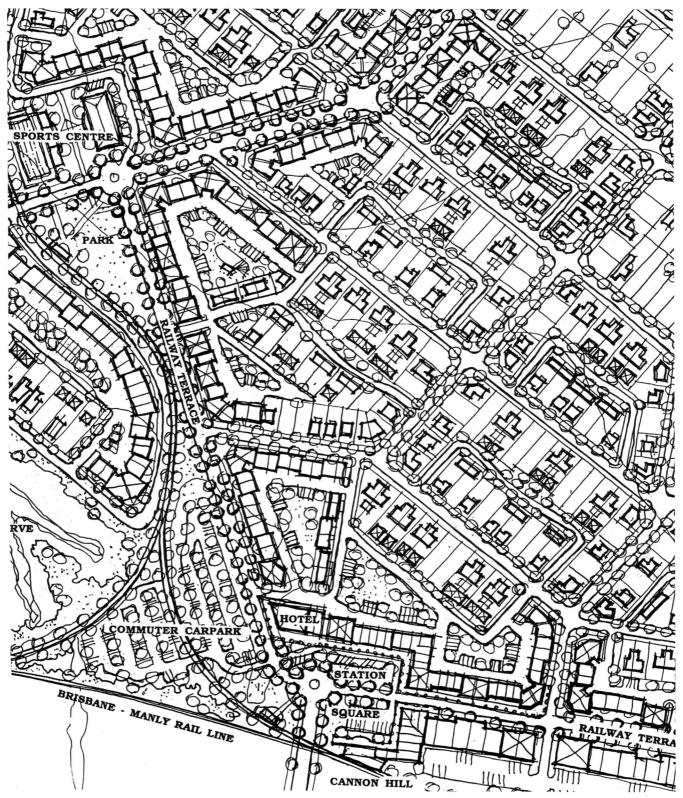

Figure 63. Part of a sketch proposal for Cannon Hill Urban Village by Paul Burns of Cummings and Burns, Queensland, in association with Richard Hayward.

climate are all marshalled in arguments as to why what has been more commonplace in the latter two cities is inappropriate for the former The home-grown 'six-pack' threatens the public and the private realm and noticeably disfigures the lush residential suburbs. (*Plate 13*) On the other hand, forms that evidently draw on the old world traditions are also suspect and often considered inappropriate with their connotations of crowded small countries with a hierarchical social structure anathema to the Australian ideal.

The workshop and public debate at the end of my visit to sunny Brisbane was of course most instructive for me. In an introduction to the day's event, I affirmed my faith in mixed-use high density urban development on the Jane Jacobs model (1961) and the need for open public dialogue and debate focused on product and cost to achieve appropriate local proposals. We divided into groups and engaged in tissue exercises (see my chapter in Section One) using local historic and developer tissues and examples from Melbourne. These were debated, with heated discussion focused on issues of density. Finally, Paul Burns, the architect, George Earl a quantity surveyor and I presented a project, largely designed by Paul, to demonstrate that an urban village could be constructed a short distance from the centre of Brisbane, using a wide range of standard lot subdivisions and terraced and apartment dwellings, for sale and rental, that could generate an adequate land value to facilitate development. (*Figure 63*)

My conclusions? Well, beyond all the issues, the experience in Brisbane confirmed for me, as had my brief involvement in the Port Melbourne Bayside Planning Forum with Paul Murrain, that design debate with professionals on tap is the only way to make humane development, and that in Australia there is a commitment to that public engagement. (*Plate 14*)

Of one thing I am sure, the informed talent and social momentum gathered in Brisbane will review global strategies and local precedents like the suburbs of Spring Hill and New Farm/Teneriffe, and make democratic better places a short public transport ride from the city centre.

BIBLIOGRAPHY

ABERCROMBIE, M. L. J. (1969) *The Anatomy of Judgement*, Penguin Books, London

ADORNO, T. (1991) The schema of mass culture. In *The Culture Industry*, (ed. J. M. Bernstein) Routledge, London

ARCHITECTS, DESIGNERS, PLANNERS, FOR SOCIAL RESPONSIBILITY (1992) Hybrid City, BBC2 Programme transmission, **November**, Open Space Series

AGGINK, H. A. and KOESTER R. J. (1989) Aleph Park and supplied computing devices: case studies in high tech. facilities. In *High Technology Workplaces*, (ed. P. Goulmain) Van Nostrand Reinhold, New York

ALDOUS, T. (1992) *Urban Villages: A Concept for Creating Mixed-use Urban Developments on a Sustainable Scale*, Urban Villages Group, England

ALEXANDER, C. (1977) *A Pattern Language*, Oxford University Press, Oxford

APPLEYARD, D. (1981) *Livable Streets*, University of California, Berkely

APPLEYARD, D. LYNCH, K. and MYER, J. R. (1964) *The View from the Road*, The M.I.T Press, Cambridge, Massachusetts

ARENDT, H. (1987) The public realm: the commons. In *The Public Face of Architecture: Civic Culture and Public Spaces* (eds N. Glazer, and M. Lilla) The Free Press, New York, pp5–12

ARNHEIM, R. (1977) *The Dynamics of Architectural Form*, University of California Press, Berkely

ASHWORTH, G. J. and VOOGD, H. (1990) *Selling the City*, Belhaven Press, London

ATTOE, W. (1979) *Architecture and Critical Imagination*, John Wiley, New York

AUDIT COMMISSION (1992) *Building in Quality: a Study of Development Control*, HMSO, London

AUTOMOBILE ASSOCIATION (1993) *Risk and Safety on the Roads: Perceptions and Attitudes*, AA Foundation for Road Safety Research, Basingstoke.

BACON, E. (1975) *Design of Cities*, Thames and Hudson, London

BANERJEE, T. and SOUTHWORTH, M., (1990) *City Sense and City Design: Writings and Projects of Kevin Lynch*, M.I.T. Press, Cambridge, Masachusetts.

BANHAM, R. (1971) *Los Angeles: The Architecture of Four Ecologies*, Allen Lane, London

BAUDRILLARD, J. (1981) *Towards a Critique of the Political Economy of the Sign*, Telos Press, St. Louis

BAUDRILLARD, J. (1983) The ecstasy of communication. In *The Anti-Aesthetic*, (ed. H. Foster) Bay Press, Washington

BAULCH, J. (1993) Towards good mixed-use districts MA Thesis, JCUD, Oxford Brookes University, Oxford

BEARDSLEY, M. (1975) *Aesthetics from Classical Greece to the Present*, University of Alabama Press, Alabama

BEER, A. (1990) *Environmental Planning for Site Development*, Spon, London.

*BENTLEY, I., ALCOCK, A., MURRAIN, P., McGLYNN, S., SMITH, G. P (1985) *Responsive Environments: A Manual for Designers*, Architectural Press, London

BERMAN, M. (1983) *All That is Solid Melts into Air: The Experience of Modernity*, Verso Press, London

BOURDIEU, P. (1977) *Outline of a Theory of Practice*, Cambridge University Press, Cambridge

BOURDIEU, P. (1984) *Distinction, a Social Critique of the Judgement of Taste*, Routledge and Kegan Paul, London

BOURNEVILLE VILLAGE TRUST (1941) *When We Build Again*, George Allen and Unwin, London

BOWLBY, S. (1990) Women and the designed environment, *Built Environment*, **Vol. 16**, 241–303

BOSTON REDEVELOPMENT AUTHORITY (1990) *Boston 2000 – A Plan for the Central Artery*, BRA

BREHENY, M. GENT, T. and LOCK, D. (1992) Alternative development patterns: new settlements. Report to Department of the Environment, London

BROLIN, B. C (1980) *Architecture in Context: Fitting New Buildings with Old*, Van Nostrand Reinhold, New York

BUCHANAN, P. (1988) Facing up to façades, *Architects' Journal*, **Vol. 188,** 21 and 28 December, 21–56

BUILDING DESIGN (1984) Richmond classic, *Building Design*, 13 January

BUTINA, G. (1991) Construction of local and regional identity. Paper presented at AESOP Conference, July, 1991 Oxford

BUTINA, G. (1992) Urban space as a negotiated product. Unpublished paper, JCUD, Oxford

CALTHORPE, P. (1989) Pedestrian pockets: new strategies for suburban growth. In *The Pedestrian Pocket Book: A New Suburban Design Strategy* (ed. P. Kelbaugh) Princeton Architectural Press, New York

CALTHORPE ASSOCIATES IN ASSOCIATION WITH MINTIER and ASSOCIATES (1990) *Transit-Oriented Development Design Guidelines*, Sacramento County Planning and Community Development Department, Sacramento

CALVINO, I. (1979) *Invisible Cities*, Picador Pan Books, London

CANADIAN URBAN INSTITUTE (1991) *Cities Without Cars*, Canadian Urban Institute, Toronto

CANIGGIA, G. and MAFFEI, G.L (1981) *Composizione Architectonica e Tipologia Edilizia*, Marsilio, Venezia

CARP, J. (1984) What — When? a practical description of the design process

CARTER, N. (1989) *Science Parks*, The Estates Gazette, London

CASTELLS, M. (1989) *The Informational City* Basil Blackwell, Oxford

CASTELLS, M (1992) The world has changed: can planning change? *Landscape and Urban Planning*, 22

CENTRE FOR RESEARCH AND CONTRACT STANDARDISATION IN CIVIL AND TRAFFIC ENGINEERING (1989) *Van Woonerf tot Erf*, Ede, Netherlands

de CERTEAU, M. (1984) *The Practice of Everyday Life* (translated S. F. Rendall) Berkeley University Press, Berkeley, California

COLLINS, G. R and C. C (1986) *Camillo Sitte: The Birth of Modern City Planning*, Rizzoli, New York

COLEMAN, A. (1985) *Utopia on Trial*, Hilary Shipman, London

COMEDIA (1991) *Out of Hours*, Comedia, London

CONZEN, M. R. G (1969) Alnwick, Northumberland: a study in town plan analysis, *IBG Publications* No. 27, Institute of British Geographers, London

CORPORATION OF LONDON (1989) *City of London Local Plan*, London

CULLEN, G. (1971) *The Concise Townscape*, Architectural Press, London

DAUNTON, M. (1984) *House and Home in the Victorian City*, Edward Arnold, London

DAVIS, R. (1993) *Death on the Streets*, Leading Edge Press, Hawes, North Yorkshire

DEBORD, G. (1972) *Society of the Spectacle*, Red and Black, Detroit

DEPARTMENT OF THE ENVIRONMENT (1989) *Planning Control in Western Europe*, HMSO, London

DEPARTMENT OF THE ENVIRONMENT (1992) *Town centres and retail development*. Draft Policy Guidance Note, HMSO, London

DEPARTMENT OF TRANSPORT (1992) *Accident Fact Sheet No 8: Pedal Cyclist Casualties Great Britain 1990: the Facts*, Directorate of Statistics, HMSO, London

DEPARTMENT OF TRANSPORT and DEPARTMENT OF THE ENVIRONMENT (1992) *Residential Roads and Footpaths, Design Bulletin 32, 2nd edn.* HMSO, London

DICK, P. K (1985) *I Hope I Shall Arrive Soon*, Victor Gollancz, London:

DUANY, A. and PLATER-ZYBERK, E. (1990) Principles of town planning for the town of Wellington. Unpublished paper for Wellington, Palm Beach County, Florida

DUFFY, F. and HENNEY, A. (1989) *The Changing City*, Bulstrode Press, London

DUNCAN, S. S (1991) The uses and abuses of comparative analysis: the case of housing research. Paper to the Housing Studies Association Conference, Oxford

DVV ROAD SAFETY DIRECTORATE (1985) *Voorbeelden van Experimentele Verkeersvoorzieningen, (BREV projecten,)* Ministerie van Verkeer en Waterstaat, Staatsuitgeverij, The Hague

EAHV (draft) (1992) Forschungsgesellschaft Für Strassen-Und Verkehrswesen, Arbeitsgruppe Strassenentwurf, Aachen

EDWARDS, S. (1992) Community housing review draft phase II. Report to Department of Housing and Local Government, Queensland

ELKIN, T. MCLAREN, D. and HILLMAN, M. (1991) *Reviving the City: Towards Sustainable Urban Development*, Friends of the Earth, London

ENGLISH ESTATES et al, (1986) *Industrial and Commercial Estates: Planning and Site Development*, Thomas Telford, London

ENGWICHT, D. (1992) *Towards an Eco-City: Calming the Traffic*, Envirobook, Sydney

ESSEX COUNTY COUNCIL (1973) *A Design Guide for Residential Areas*, Anchor Press, London

EWEN, S. (1988) *All Consuming Images*, Basic Books, New York

EWEN, S. (1990) Marketing dreams. In *Consumption, Identity and Style: Marketing Meanings and the Packaging of Pleasure* (ed. A. Tomlinson) Routledge, London

FEAGIN, J. R and PARKER, R. (1990) *Building American Cities: The Urban Real Estate Game*, Prentice Hall, New Jersey

FINANCIAL TIMES (1990) *Business Parks: Survey*, May 11, 1990

FIRTH, R. (1975) *Symbols: Private and Public*, George Allen and Unwin Ltd, London

FISHMAN, R. (1990) *America's New City*, The Wilson Quarterly Review

FORTY, A. (1990) The lure of the picturesque. *Architecture Today*, **No.** 11 September, 44–47

GANE, N. (1991) *Baudrillard's Bestiary*, Routledge, London

GARDINER, S. (1988) Confusion upon Thames. *The Observer*, 5 June

GARREAU, J. (1991) *Edge City: Life on the New Frontier*, Doubleday, New York

GEMEENTE MAASTRICHT (1986) *Verkeersveiligheid in Maastricht, 1983–1984*, Netherlands

GEMEENTE MAASTRICHT (1990) *Verkeersveiligheid in Maastricht, 1987–1988*, Netherlands

GERRIE, J. (1988) Bridging the gap: an exploration of communication methods in user participation. MA Thesis, JCUD, Oxford Polytechnic, Oxford

GIEDION, S. (1954) *Space, Time and Architecture*, Oxford University Press, Oxford

GIROUARD, M. (1985) *Cities and People*, Yale University Press, London

GLANCY, J. (1992) Gor blimey guv, all it needs is muffin men and sweeps. *The Independent*, 14 October

GOODMAN, R. (1972) *After the Planners*, Pelican, London

GOODEY, B. (1979) Going to town in the 1980s: towards a more human experience of commercial space. *Built Environment*, 5 (1), 27–36

GOODEY, B. (1989) A cidade multi-imagem, multi-centro, *Espaco Imperfeito: Area Metropolitana do Porto*, Porto: Forum Portucalense, 123–31

GOODEY, B. (1992) In league with Smigielskiville. *Town and Country Planning*, **June**

GOODEY, B. (1992) Dix paysages européens dominants. *Paysage et Aménagement*, **No.** 21 8–13

GOODEY, B. (1993) The heart of the matter: Trafalgar Square, New Year's Eve. *Town and Country Planning*, **Jan/Feb**, 24–25

GOULMAIN, P. (ed) 1989) *High Technology Workplaces*, Van Nostrand Reinhold, New York

GREATER LONDON COUNCIL (1978) *An Introduction to Housing Layout: A GLC Study*, Architectural Press, London

HANDY, S. (1993) Regional versus local accessibility: neo-traditional development and its implications for non-work travel. *Built Environment*, **Vol. 18, No. 4**, 253

HARRIS, A. (1991) Telecommuting: a growing transport alternative for office commuters. In conference proceedings *Technological and Societal Alternatives in Transportation 1991* Report sponsored by the IEEE Society on Social Implications of Technology

HARVEY, D. (1988) *Social Justice and the City*, Blackwell, Oxford

HARVEY, D. (1989) *The Condition of Postmodernity*, Blackwell, Oxford

HAYWARD, R. (1987) The use of housing tissues in urban design. In *Urban Design Quarterly*, **No. 25**, December

HAYWARD, R. (1992) The architectural design studio. In *Developing Professional Education*, (eds H. Bines and D. Watson) The Society for Research into Higher Education and Open University Press.

HENSON, R. and WHELAN, N. (1992) Layout and design factors affecting cycle safety at T-junctions. *Traffic Engineering and Control*, **October,** 548–551

HENNEBERRY, M. (1987) *British Science Parks and High Technology Developments: Progress and Change, 1983–86*, Sheffield City Polytechnic, Sheffield

HERBERT, S. (1992) This is 'Mega-Mall Land' and they don't want you to go anywhere else. *The Daily Telegraph*

HILLIER, B. and HANSON, J. (1984) *The Social Logic of Space*. Cambridge University Press, Cambridge

HILLIER, B. (1988) Against enclosure. In *Re-humanising Housing* (eds Teymur, Markus, and Woolley) Butterworths

HILLIER, B. (1992) Look Back to London *Architects' Journal*, **15 April,** 42–46

HILLIER, et al (1993) Natural movement: or, configuration and attraction in urban pedestrian movement. *Environment and Planning B: Planning and Design*, **Vol. 20** (1), 29–66

HILLIER, B. and O'SULLIVAN, P. (1992) *Architecture and climate change* Conference proceedings C59 of the Solar Energy Society, Kings College London

HILLMAN, J. (1990) *Planning for Beauty: The Case for Design Guidelines*, HMSO, London

HOLDEN, R. (1987) Development economics, office/industrial – two business parks. *Architects' Journal*, **27 May,** 53–59

HOLDEN, R. (1989) Buildings update: business parks. *Architects' Journal*, **22 February,** 79–83

HOLLAND, G (1989) A review of the present. *Urban Design Quarterly*, 31

HOLLIS, M (1985) *Invitation to Philosophy*, Basil Blackwell, Oxford

HOLTZCLAW, J. (1991) Explaining urban density and transit impacts on auto. use. Report to State of California Energy Resources Conservation and Development Commission. In *Towards Sustainable Communities*, (ed. M. Roseland, 1992), National Round Table on the Environment and the Economy, Ottowa, Ontario

HOUGH, M. (1984) *City Form and Natural Process*, Croom Helm, London

HRH THE PRINCE OF WALES (1988) A Vision of Britain, BBC2 'Omnibus' programme transmission, 28 Oct

HRH THE PRINCE OF WALES (1989) *A Vision of Britain: A Personal View of Architecture*, Doubleday, London

HUME, D. (1974) *Essays Moral, Political and Literary*, Oxford University Press, Oxford

HURTADO, F., DANIEL, M., KOHLSDORF, M. E. and REYES, P. (1988) Uma appreensao do espaco de Brasilia a partir de tres escales. Paper to Third Brazilian Urban Design Seminar, Brasilia, September 1988

JACOBS, J. (1961) *The Death and Life of Great American Cities*, Random House, New York

JAMESON, F. (1983) Postmodernism and consumer culture. In *The Anti-Aesthetic* (ed. H. Foster) Bay Press, Washington

JAMESON, F. (1991) *Postmodernism or The Cultural Logic of Late Capitalism*, Verso, London

JANSEN-VERBEKE, M. (1992) Managing and monitoring the tourism carrying capacity in a historical city: the planning issues. Unpublished paper, Urban and Regional Planning Department, Catholic University, Nijmegen

JARVIS, R. K (1980) Urban environments as visual art or as social settings. *Town Planning Review*, **Vol. 51** No. 1, 50–66

JENNINGS GROUP LTD (1992) Report of *The Cranbourne Lyndhurst Town Planning Charrette*, Victoria, Australia

JONES, N. (1989) Business parks: making of a millenium. *Building Design Supplement*, **July**, 28–36

JOSHI, M. and SMITH, G. P (1992) Cyclists under threat: a survey of Oxford cyclists' perceptions of risk. *Health Education Journal*, **Vol. 51/4**

KARSKI, A (1990) Urban tourism – a key to urban regeneration? *The Planner*, **6 April**, 15–17

KEEBLE, L. (1971) *Town Planning at the Crossroads*, Estates Gazette, London

KENDALL, S. (1984) Teaching with tissues: observations and reflections. *Open House International.*

KING, A. (1988) *UK 2000 – An Overview of Business Parks*, Applied Property Research, London

KING, A. (1989) Business parks: vital statistics. *Building Design Supplement*, **July**, 36–37

KOOLHAAS, R. (1978) *Delirious New York*, Thames and Hudson, London

KROPF, K. (1985) Urban morphology considered. MA Thesis, JCUD, Oxford Polytechnic, Oxford

KROPF, K. (1993) An enquiry into the definition of built form in urban morphology. PhD Thesis, University of Birmingham, Birmingham

LEFEBVRE, H. (1991) *The Production of Space*, translated, D. Nicholson-Smith, Blackwell, Oxford

LUCAN, J. ed. (1991) *OMA-Rem Koolhaas*, Princeton Architectural Press

LYNCH, K. (1960) *The Image of the City*, Technological Press/Harvard University Press, Cambridge, Massachusetts

LYNCH, K. (1976) *Managing the Sense of a Region*, MIT Press, Cambridge, Mass

LE CORBUSIER (1967) *The Radiant City*, Faber and Faber, London

MCMORRAN, J. (1973) *Municipal Public Works and Planning in Birmingham*, City of Birmingham

MAIRIE D'ASNIÈRES SUR OISE, SAMUELS, I., KROPF, K. et leurs COLLABORATEURS (1992) *Plan d'Occupation des Sols*, Unpublished draft

MARCUS, C. C. (1990) *People Places: Design Guidelines for Open Space*, Van Nostrand Reinhold, New York

MARCUS, C. C. and SARKISSAN, W. (1986) *Housing as if People Mattered: Site Design Guidelines for Medium Density Family Housing*, University of California Press, Berkely

MARMOT, A. and WORTHINGTON, J. (1987) Great fire to big bang: private and public designs in the City of London. *Built Environment*, **Vol. 12, No. 4**

MARSH, P. and COLLETT, P. (1986) *Driving Passion: The Psychology of the Car*, Jonathan Cape, London

MARX, K. (1957) *Capital: A Critique of Political Economy*, Dent, London

MARX, K. and ENGELS, F. (1985) *The Communist Manifesto*, Penguin, London

MINISTERIE VAN VERKEER EN WATERSTAAT (1984) Handboek, 30 km/h Maatregelen, The Hague.

MONCK, C. S. P *et al.* (1988) *Science Parks and the Growth of High Technology Firms*, Croom Helm, London

MOUDON, A. V. M (1989) A catholic approach to organizing what urban designers should know. Paper to Built Form and Culture Research Conference, 'Intercultural Processes', Arizona State University, Tempe, Nov. 1989

MOULDEN, S. A (1992) A transactional approach to the evaluation of mall and street shopping developments. M.Sc Thesis, Department of Environmental Psychology, University of Surrey, Guildford

MUKAROVSKY, J. (1979) *Aesthetic Function, Norm and Value as Social Facts*, Ann Arbor, Michigan

MUMFORD, L. (1961) *The City in History*, Harcourt Brace, New York

NEUTELINGS, W. J. (1991) *Patchwork Metropolis*, 910 Publishers, Rotterdam

NEWMAN, P. and KENWORTHY, G. (1951) *Towards a Sustainable Canberra*, Murdoch University, Perth, W. Australia

OLIVER, P. DAVIS, I. and BENTLEY, I. (1981) *Dunroamin; The Suburban Semi and its Enemies*, Barrie and Jenkins London.

OWEN, S. (1991) *Planning Settlements Naturally*, Packard, Chichester

OWEN, S. (1985) Energy demand; links to land use and forward planning. *Built Environment* **Vol. 11 No 1**

PAGE, S. (1992) Tourism planning: managing tourism in a small historic city. *Town and Country Planning*, **July/August**, 208–11

PARKIN, I. MIDDLETON, P. and BESWICK V. (1989) Managing the town and city for visitors and local people. In *Heritage Interpretation Vol. 2 The Visitor Experience*, (ed. D. Uzzell), Bellhaven, London

PATRICK, J. (1991) Renewing the merchant city. *Urban Design Quarterly*, **January** 16–18

PAWLEY, M. (1989) The fall of Legoland. *The Guardian*, 3 April

PETERSON, R. A. (1990) Designing cities without designing buildings? *Urban Design Quarterly* **April** 6–11

PETHERICK, A. and .FRASER, R (1990) *Living Over The Shop*, University of York, York

POLANYI, M. (1958) *Personal Knowledge*, Routledge and Kegan Paul, London

POPPER, K. R (1972) *Objective Knowledge: An Evolutionary Approach*, Oxford University Press, Oxford

PORPHYRIOS, D. (1982) *The Sources of Modern Eclecticism*, Academy Editions, London

POWER, N. (1965) *The Forgotten People*, Arthur James, Evesham

POYNOR, R. (1989) *Nigel Coates: The City in Motion*, Fourth Estate, London

PRAK, N. L. (1984) *Architects: The Noted and the Ignored*, John Wiley and Son, Chichester

PUNTER, J. V. (1984) *A History of Aesthetic Control*, University of Reading

PUNTER, J. V. (1990) The ten commandments of architecture and urban design. *The Planner*, **5 October** 10–14

PUNTER, J. V. (1993) Aesthetics in planning. In *Values in Planning* (ed. H. Thomas) Avebury (forthcoming), London

RABAN, J. (1975) *Soft City*, Fontana/Collins, London

RAVETZ, A. (1980) *Remaking Cities: Contradictions of the Recent Urban Environment*, Croom Helm, London

RAVETZ, A. (1986) *The Government of Space*, Faber and Faber, London

REEVE, A. R (1992) Postmodernism is not a style, MA Thesis, JCUD, Oxford Brookes University, Oxford

RELPH, E. (1987) *The Modern Urban Landscape*, Croom Helm, London

REY, I. (1993) Asnières sur Oise: une nouvelle génération de POS. *Le Moniteur des Villes*, No. 21, 22–24.

RICHARDSON, N. (1991) Sustainable development and land use planning. Paper to Symposium on *Implementing Sustainable Development in Municipalities*, Hockley Valley, Ontario

RISBERO, B. (1992) *Fantastic Form: Architecture and Planning Today*, Herbert Press, London

ROGERS, B. (1992) When a town is murdered, what hope for its people? *The Daily Telegraph*, 11 May

ROSEHAUGH STANHOPE DEVELOPMENTS (1991) Broadgate: A Working Guide, Rosehaugh Stanhope Promotional Literature, Sound Recording, London

ROSELAND, M. (1992) *Towards Sustainable Communities*, National Round Table on the Environment and the Economy, Ottawa, Ontario

ROSENCRANTZ, V. (1992) Urban designs towards a sustainable public transport system. Conference paper *New Communities for the Urban Fringe*. Melbourne, Australia

ROSSI, A. (1982) *The Architecture of the City*, MIT Press, Boston

ROWE, P. (1991) *Making A Middle Landscape*, MIT Press, Cambridge, Massachusetts

ROYAL TOWN PLANNING INSTITUTE (1991) *Planning in Europe: An Introduction to France*, Didasko Ltd, London

RUBIN, B. (1979) Aesthetic ideology and urban design. *Annals of the Association of American Geographers*, **Vol. 69** September No. 3, 339–361

SAINI, B. and JOYCE, R. (1982) *The Australian House: Homes of the Tropical North*, Weldon, Sydney

SAMUELS, I. (1985) Urban morphology in design. Research Note 19, JCUD, Oxford Polytechnic, Oxford

SAMUELS, I. (1990) Architectural practice and urban morphology. In *The Built Form of Western Cities*, (ed. T. R. Slater), Leicester University Press, Leicester

SCHMIDT, E. (1991) Boston 2000: building Boston for the 21st century, unpublished paper

SCHUSTER, J., DAVIDSON, M., SIMMONDS, R., and FRENCHMAN, D (1990) *Housing Design and Regional Character: A Premiere For New England Towns*, Department of Urban Studies and Planning, MIT

SCRUTON, R. (1979) *The Aesthetics of Architecture*, Methuen, London

SCRUTON, R. (1988) A real classic. *Sunday Telegraph*, 16 May

SENNETT, R. (1990) *The Conscience of the Eye: The Design and Social Life of Cities*, Faber and Faber, London

SITTE, C. (1965) *City Planning According to Artistic Principles*, Random House, New York

SMITH, G. P. (1987) Sharing streets. MA Thesis, JCUD, Oxford Polytechnic, Oxford

SMITH, P. F. (1987) *Architecture and the Principles of Harmony*, RIBA Publications, London

SOJA, E. (1989) *Postmodern Geographies – The Reassertion of Space in Critical Social Theory*, Verso, London

SORKIN, M. (ed) (1992) *Variations on a Theme Park*, Noonday Press, New York

SPINK, F. H. (ed) (1975) *Industrial Development Handbook*, Urban Land Institute, Washington DC

SPRING, M. (1988) Stretching city limits. *Building*, 14 **October**

STATHAM, P. (ed) (1989) *The Origins of Australia's Capital Cities*, Cambridge University Press, Cambridge

SUMMERSON, J. (1949) *Heavenly Mansions and Other Essays on Architecture*, (chapter VIII Architecture, painting and Le Corbusier), Cresset Press, London

THOMAS, M. J. (1990) The planning project. Unpublished paper, Department of Urban Planning, Oxford Brookes University, Oxford

THORNE, S. (1993) Towards the definition and achievement of good mixed-use town. Unpublished paper, JCUD, Oxford Brookes University, Oxford

TILGHMAN, B. R. (1987) *But is it Art?*, Blackwell, Oxford

TIBBALDS, F. (1992) *Making People-Friendly Towns*, Longman, London

TOMLINSON, A. (1990) Home fixtures: doing-it-yourself in a privatised world. In *Consumption, Identity and Style, Marketing Meanings and the Packaging of Pleasure* (ed. A. Tomlinson) Routledge, London

TOUCHE ROSS MANAGEMENT CONSULTANTS and GOODEY, B. (1992) Discover Islington: interpretation, information and visitor management strategy. Consultancy proposals, Touche Ross, London

TRAFFIC DEPARTMENT ANWB AND ROAD SAFETY DIRECTORATE DVV (1980) *'Woonerf, a new approach to environmental management in residential areas and the related traffic legislation'*, 2nd edn. The Hague, Netherlands

TUGNUTT, A. and ROBERTSON, M. (1987) *Making Townscape, A Contextual Approach to Building in an Urban Setting*, Mitchell, London

UNWIN, R. (1909) *Town Planning in Practice, an introduction to the Art of Designing Cities and Suburbs*, Unwin, London

US DEPARTMENT OF TRANSPORTATION (1991) *Intermodal Surface Transportation Efficiency Act of 1991*, Washington

VELDHUISEN, K. J *et al.* (1984) Conjoint measurement applies to the judgement and design of dwellings. *Open House International*, **Vol 9, No 4**

VENTURI, R., SCOTT-BROWN, D. and ZENOUR, S. (1972) *Learning From Las Vegas*, MIT Press, Cambridge, Massachusetts

VAIZEY, M. (1987) Birthday 1: all the fun of the fair. *The Sunday Times*, 22 February

VICTORIA STATE GOVERNMENT (1992) *Victoria Code for Residential Development*, Department of Planning and Housing, Melbourne, Australia

VIGHETTI, J. B (1986) The development of old town centres. *Conservation Policies and Urban Management in Small and Medium-Sized Towns*, Council of Europe — Urban Renaissance in Europe Study Series 32, Strasbourg

WARD, S. (1992) Dissatisfied city dwellers dream of rural 'good life'. *The Independent*, Nov. 2 p. 6

WEBER, M. (1958) *The City* (trans D. Martindale) Collier Macmillan, London

WEBBER, M. M. (1963) The urban place and the non-place urban realm. In *Explanations into Urban Structure* (ed. M.M. Webber) University of Pennsylvannia Press, Philadelphia

WHITELEGG, J. (1990) Traffic calming: a 'green' smokescreen. Paper to the *London Borough of Ealing Conference in Traffic Calming — Ways Forward*, January 1990

WHITE MOUNTAIN SURVEY COMPANY INC (1991) *The City of Portsmouth Traffic/Trip Generation Study*, Portsmouth, New Hampshire, USA

WILFORD, M. (1984) Off to the races or going to the dogs? *Architectural Design*, Special issue **Urbanism**, 8–15

WILLIAMS, P. W and GILL, A (1991) *Carrying Capacity Management in Tourism Settings: A Tourism Growth Management Process*, Centre for Tourism Policy and Research, Simon Fraser University, Burnaby BC

WILLIAMS, R. (1976) *Keywords*, Fontana/Croom Helm, London

WILLIAMSON, R. (1989) A discipline for change in the City of London and environs, MA Thesis, JCUD, Oxford Polytechnic, Oxford

WITTGENSTEIN, L. (1953) *Philosophical Investigations*, Basil Blackwell, Oxford

WITTKOWER, R. (1988) *Architectural Principles in the Age of Humanism*, Academy Editions, London

WOOD, J. (1991) Urban design and commercial office development. MA Thesis, JCUD, *Oxford Polytechnic*, Oxford

WORPOLE, K. (1987) Part-time places. *The Guardian*, Sept. 16 p. 15

WORTHINGTON, J. (1989) Accommodating the Knowledge-based Industries. In *High Technology Workplaces*, (ed. P. Goulmain) Van Nostrand Reinhold, New York

YEATES, M. (1992) New era for the Brisbane six-pack. *Development Now*, **No. 7**, June, Canberra.

YOUNG, M. and WILLMOTT, P. (1957) *Family and Kinship in East London*, Routledge and Kegan Paul, London

ZUKIN, S. (1988) *Loft Living: Culture and Capital in Urban Change*, Radius, London

INDEX